SELF AND OTHERS
Object Relations Theory in Practice

COMMENTARY

"Winston Churchill once said, 'The United States and Great Britain are two great democracies divided by a comon language.' This 'Tower of Babel' motif is apparent today in the United States in the debate between ego psychology and self psychology and between the British school of object relations and the American version of object relations, that of ego psychology's representational world. Dr. Hamilton has taken upon himself the task of integrating these disparate lines of thinking and of reconciling them with current developmental concepts. He moves gracefully and accurately through Freud, Klein, Erikson, Hartmann, Bion, Fairbairn, Winnicott, Kohut, Tolpin, Kernberg, and particularly Mahler. He employs these and many other key contributors in order to develop the thesis of the overarching importance that object relations, including Kohut's selfobject functions, Kernberg's affective self-object units, Klein's internal objects, and Jacobson's object representations, has for the development of the self.

"The fact that his formative training took place at the Menninger Foundation gives an even deeper perspective to this book. It was there that ego psychologists from the United States met classical analysts from central Europe, Kleinian analysts from South America, and Middle School analysts from Great Britain. It was also there that analytic ideas were seriously and methodically studied in psychotics, borderlines, and narcissistic disorders. It was here also that analytic group psychology, including the Tavistock method of Bion's, was put into operation. With all this as his backdrop, Dr. Hamilton takes us on an object relations guided tour through psychosis, borderline conditions, narcissistic personality disorders, neuroses, group phenomena, and mythology, integrating each step of the journey with developmental signposts.

"This book best approximates what every psychiatric resident, clinical psychologist, psychiatric social worker, and analytic institute candidate would have wished for. It is an extraordinary handbook of the new developmental psychologies of psychoanalysis."

—James S. Grotstein, M.D.

"Dr. Hamilton has provided us with a text that is at once comprehensive, sophisticated, clinically relevant, and perfectly understandable to the budding professional. The author breathes life into the theory with his liberal use of clearly written clinical vignettes and literary references. Moreover, Hamilton is blessed with a touch of the poet, which makes his prose a supreme pleasure to read. This is a superb achievement that deserves a place on the shelves of psychiatric residents and other trainees in the mental health disciplines."

—Glen O. Gabbad, M.D.

SELF AND OTHERS
Object Relations Theory in Practice

N. Gregory Hamilton, M.D.

Jason Aronson Inc.
Northvale, New Jersey
London

The author gratefully acknowledges permission to reprint the following material:

Bulletin of the Menninger Clinic, Topeka, Kansas. Case description based on material in *Bulletin of the Menninger Clinic* 50:323–340.

Doubleday & Company, Inc., New York, New York, and A. P. Watt, Ltd., London, England. Quote from W. Somerset Maugham's *The Razor's Edge,* 1944.

Indiana University Press, Bloomington, Indiana. Quote from Rolfe Humphrie's translation of Ovid's *Metamorphoses,* 1955.

Los Angeles Times–Washington Post News Service, Washington, D.C. Quote from Saundra Saperstein and Barbara Vobejda's story as it appeared in *The Oregonian,* May 22, 1986.

Macmillan Publishing Company, New York, New York. Quote from W. B. Yeats' "Among School Children," 1927.

NAL, New York, New York. Quote from R. B. Blakney's translation of Lao Tzu's *The Way of Life: Tao Te Ching,* 1955.

Random House, Inc., New York, New York. Quotes from William Faulkner's "Nobel Prize Speech," in *The Faulkner Reader,* 1954, and from E. L. Doctorow's "Willi," in *Lives of the Poets,* 1984.

New Printing 1992

10 9 8 7 6 5 4 3

Library of Congress Cataloging-in-Publication Data

Hamilton, N. Gregory
  Self and others.

  Bibliography: p.
  Includes index.
  1. Self. 2. Object relations (Psychoanalysis)
3. Psychology, Pathological. 4. Psychotherapy.
I. Title. II. Title: Object relations theory in
practice. [DNLM: 1. Ego. 2. Object Attachment.
3. Psychoanalytic Theory. WM 460.5.02 H221s]
RC455.4.S42H34 1987   154.2'2   87-19479
ISBN 0-87668-961-6 (hardcover)
ISBN 0-87668-544-0 (paperback)

Manufactured in the United States of America. Jason Aronson Inc. offers books and cassettes. For information and catalog write to Jason Aronson Inc., 230 Livingston Street, Northvale, New Jersey 07647.

FOR MY SONS

SAM, KURT, MIKE, AND ROB

CONTENTS

PART V
BROADER CONTEXTS

Preface and Acknowledgments

At its inception, this book was intended to be a translation of object relations theory into understandable English, one that does not water down concepts or sacrifice richness of thought. All students of self–other relationships, graduate analysts as well as those just beginning their mental health careers, have decried the difficulty of object relations literature. It was time for a new version.

Like most intellectual movements, object relations theory began as a series of arguments against viewpoints held by particular colleagues, or as an attempt to insinuate new ideas into the old framework of a then dominant group. These discussions had to use established technical words, sometimes with new meanings or even with shifting meanings. Therefore, the original language was cumbersome and confusing, though appropriate to the purpose and audience.

Recently, there has been such a widening interest in and acceptance of object relations ideas that increasing clarity is both possible and needed. The defensiveness of awkward wording is no longer in order. Jargon requiring knowledge of once prominent debates has become more hindrance than help. Yet I was hesitant to discard the original terminology entirely. I did not want this book to become a popularization. I hoped it could serve as both a translation for the contemporary therapist and a key to entering into and understanding existing literature. Such an approach required consolidation of ideas from numerous authors, comparison of viewpoints, and introduction of my own version of object relations. To make it understandable, yet compatible with earlier works, I shifted from abstraction to metaphor to clinical example to everyday life and back to abstraction—that is, back to the original theoretical terms. The book thus became a synthesis and transformation of ideas and observations, more than a translation.

Initial readers and classroom instructors have been thoughtful in expressing their appreciation of this approach. They have commented that it is understandable and has sufficient complexity. Consequently, many have requested that this printing take place without revision, which is gratifying indeed.

This is a fruitful and growing field, however. In one area, I have changed my position. More current infant research has demonstrated that Mahler's delineation of autism is untenable. Children can distinguish human from nonhuman stimuli from birth. They can even show preference for the specific individuals who care for them. They do seem to be object related from the very beginning, at least much of the time, as the early theorists Klein and Fairbairn suspected. And the timing of infant development is being revised even now. As for the rest of *Self and Others: Object Relations Theory in Practice*, I believe the ideas remain both current and useful.

I am grateful to Dr. Karl Menninger, who encouraged his students to observe their patients closely and write about them as clearly as they could, and to Dr. Donald Rinsley, who insisted that his students observe themselves as closely as they did their patients. Both these fine men died within the past year. Their many students continue to value and benefit from the guidance they gave. We carry their memories and influence within us.

I appreciate the help of my teachers, only a few of whom I can mention here: Drs. Herbert Woodcock, William Sack, Diane Schetky, Ann Applebaum, Samuel Bradshaw, Normund Wong, Diego Rodriguez, Jack Ross, Meredith Titus, Robert Obourn, Stuart Averill, Tetsuro Takahashi, Richard Roskos, Peter Novotny, and Jerome Katz. Ms. Jan Larson and Dr. Mary Cerney helped in my attempts to understand patients with psychoses. Members of the Training Committee of the Topeka Institute for Psychoanalysis, particularly Drs. Peter Hartocollis and Ramon Ganzarain, afforded me a valuable opportunity to learn and grow. Drs. Walter Menninger, Roy Menninger, Roland Atkinson, James Shore, and Joseph Bloom provided administrative support as I undertook this project.

Ms. Catherine Ponzoha read the manuscript on her own time and with her usual goodwill. She made numerous useful suggestions, both tactfully and incisively, always in the context of encouragement and support; I cannot thank her enough. My father, Dr. Norman K. Hamilton, helped with the first four chapters, as did Dr. Robert Frick. Ms. Joan Langs edited the entire manuscript, suggesting when warranted, challenging when necessary.

My students provided case examples, as well as useful criticisms and questions. They were patient as I discovered these ideas with them.

My patients are already aware that I have learned and benefited from my work with them. Some of them may wonder if they will recognize aspects of themselves in the case material. I regret that I could not write about each of them personally, because they are each important as individuals with particular circumstances and in their entirety, but respect for their privacy forbade my doing so. I was obliged to disguise the particulars, combine case material, and divide examples in such a way as to make recognition by family and friends impossible and recognition by the patients themselves uncertain. I extend my deepest gratitude to my patients for the privilege of knowing them, working with them, and learning from them.

PART I
SELF, OBJECT, AND EGO

O chestnut-tree, great-rooted blossomer,
Are you the leaf, the blossom or the bole?
O body swayed to music, O brightening glance,
How can we know the dancer from the dance?

—William Butler Yeats, "Among School Children"

INTRODUCTION

In addition to our loves, friendships, and rivalries, we have intricate relationships within us. They are not static images, but rather, powerful influences on how we feel about ourselves and relate to others. The people around us also affect us within ourselves. The exploration of these internal and external relationships has led to a growing body of knowledge called object relations theory.

Developmentally, we begin in an undifferentiated state, unable to separate ourselves from our environment. We gradually come to know who we are in relation to those who care for us, our parents. We cannot at first conceive of ourselves as separate from these people upon whom we depend for our very existence. Afraid of our aloneness and smallness, we need to gain courage by taking in love and nurturance from our caretakers. To protect this self-parent relationship, we begin to attribute difficulties to things outside of it. Only after we receive the concern which we need can we grow strong and confident enough to accept our weaknesses and longings as our own and care about others.

This process continues in early life and throughout adulthood. We take in aspects of our relationships and make these a part of ourselves. We also attribute aspects of ourselves and our accumulated internal relationships to those around us. We continue this process when we are mentally healthy.

When people are mentally ill, this internalizing and externalizing becomes stymied or stuck in a repetitive or extreme pattern. Some reenact acquired internal relationships with everyone they meet, regardless of the inclinations of the other person. Others thoroughly isolate themselves and cannot relate to or care about anyone; they become imprisoned in their internal world. Many individuals are so vulnerable to influence that they acquire the characteristics of whomever they meet, chameleon-like. They are unable to establish a stable identity or self.

Object relations theory is the study of these internal and external relationships in healthy children and adults and in patients. Over the past 30 years students of object relations have breathed new life into psychoanalysis. The concepts of this theory are compelling in their immediacy and usefulness and have permeated and influenced not only psychoanalysis, but also psychotherapy, group therapy, family therapy, and hospital administration.

There are natural rivalries among mental health clinicians, as there are in any field. These rivalries foster a tendency to splinter off object relations theory by calling it a new school or a deviant theory. Similarly, ego psychology was once considered deviant, and self psychology is often currently described as outside the mainstream. Some clinicians have claimed that object relations theory is not new, but is merely a rearrangement and elaboration of one part of old theories.

Knowledge cannot be owned, controlled, relegated to splinter groups, or kept neatly within the bounds of any school or discipline. Like other bodies of knowledge, object relations theory is a set of ideas to be considered. For the present, the intellectual ferment in the exploration of interpersonal and intrapsychic functioning centers on concepts of self and object. It is with these basic concepts, self and object, that the study of object relations begins. In Part I, I also discuss the ego, which integrates and differentiates our internal and external self- and object-experiences.

CHAPTER 1

THE OBJECT

Object means a loved or hated person, place, thing, or fantasy. Some people find the word object dehumanizing when used for persons, distasteful or inaccurate. Yet, it has persisted in widespread use.

Freud (1905a) introduced the term. In his "Three Essays on the Theory of Sexuality," he studied the perversions. He discovered how people can relate to an object, a thing such as a shoe or stocking, as if it were a sexual partner or loved one. It became convenient and accurate, then, to use the word object to denote something invested with emotion, whether it was another person, an inanimate thing, an idea, or a fantasy.

When people say they love their country and are loyal to their country, they have a feeling in relation to a thing, their country. Just what that thing is, however, is variable. A country can be denoted by geographic boundaries. It can be an abstraction as defined by a set of documents. It can be a collection of people who have citizenship. It can be a fantasy referring to a complicated set of loyalty and identity issues. Any of these concepts of one's country can be an object, because a country can be important enough for people to love or hate. People work, fight, and sometimes die for their country. They disparage, flee, and sometimes rebel against their country. Clearly, people have strong feelings about their country, though a country is not a person, not a mother, father, child, husband, wife, lover, or friend. Nevertheless, a country can be an object in object relations terms.

People can love houses, cars, cats, dogs, mountains, valleys, trees, and rivers. They can love a painting, book, poem, God, or an image. Similarly, they can hate all these things, related things, parts of these things, or entirely different things. Although the first love object is the mother, still, the less personal term, object—to denote a thing invested with emotional energy, with love and with hate—remains useful. The word other can sometimes be used interchangeably with object.

Klein (Segal 1964) was one of the earliest and most controversial object relations theorists. She demonstrated that studying the relationship between internal fantasies, called *self*, and internal fantasies, called *objects*, could help us understand many previously confusing mental states in both healthy and ill people. These fantasies could be either conscious or unconscious.

There are internal objects and external objects. An internal object is a mental representation—an image, idea, fantasy, feeling, or memory relevant to another person. An external object, in contrast, is an actual person or thing. One of the most confusing aspects of object relations literature is that many authors fail to clarify whether they are referring to an internal or external object; they may even change usage in midsentence.

This subject of internal versus external is more complex than it first appears. It takes us into epistemology and the nature of reality—subjects of debate for thousands of years. How do we know what we know? Is there really a world out there? What does the world out there have to do with what we perceive? Rather than venture further into such abstractions here, we will simply acknowledge that the failure to distinguish internal from external objects obscures much of object relations literature. I will return to this subject of internal and external worlds in later chapters.

It is no coincidence that the psychological term object is equivalent to the word object in its grammatical sense. Prototypical sentences have the structure of subject, verb, and object. Object relations theory has this same structure. There is a subject—the self; there is a verb—to love or to hate; and there is an object of that love or hate. This simplified grammatical construction particularly helps in studying psychological states in which there is no clear distinction between subject and object. Such psychological states precede the development of language and the grammatical ordering of experience in children; they are preverbal. There will be more to say about self–object confusions throughout this book.

An object is a person, place, thing, idea, fantasy, or memory invested with emotional energy (love or hate or more modulated combinations of love and hate). An external object is a person, place, or thing invested with emotional energy. An internal object is an idea, fantasy, or memory pertaining to a person, place, or thing.

CHAPTER 2
THE SELF

Psychoanalytic literature abounds with discussion of the self. Several journals have devoted entire issues to this topic. There is even a branch of object relations theory called self psychology (Kohut 1971, 1977).

The word self historically has meant wind, breath, shade, shadow, soul, mind, universal self, transcendental oneness, one, the unmoved mover, spiritual substance, the seat of good and evil, a supraordinate agency, and so forth. More mundanely, it has meant body, a bundle of perceptions in constant flux, a person and all that pertains to a person. A word with such a history is bound to carry with it issues of spiritualism versus physicalism and mind–body duality versus mind–body unity.

One's very self—the thing in the world which is closest to a person—defies definition. Theoretically and developmentally the concept of self lags behind that of object. A baby learns to discriminate its mother from strangers before developing a firm awareness of self as distinct from mother. The mother–other distinction precedes the self–mother distinction. In other words, the ability to see objects as different from one another precedes the ability to appreciate self as a separate entity.

Nevertheless, there have been advances in understanding the concept of self. Many authors conceptualize the self as a mental representation—that is, an idea, feeling, or fantasy. Like object, this representation refers to a loved or hated person or thing. Unlike the object, this idea, feeling, or fantasy pertains to one's own person in a fundamental, biologic way. As Freud (1923, p. 26) put it, "The self is first and foremost a bodily self."[1]

Although self-representations are private, they can be described, as can other private experiences, such as emotions.

A 2-year-old boy and his father walked back from the park one summer evening. They commented on their shadows stretched out before them on the sidewalk.

"That's my shadow," the boy said, "and that's my Daddy's shadow."

"Yes," his father answered, "there they are."

Shortly, he lifted his son to his shoulders. The boy laughed at the change in their shadows.

"What's that on top of my shadow?" his father demanded.

"That's me," the boy said, giggling.

Over and over he said, "That's me." Previously, he had said it was his shadow. Now he said only, "That's me." His shadow had become a self-image.

"That's me" is what is meant by the self in object relations theory. Because the "that's me" experience is so variable, I shall give several more examples.

B.G., a 30-year-old man, began psychotherapy because rapid changes in his ideas, plans, and religion had made life confusing and difficult. He entered a career only to end it. He joined a religious cult and began to think he was a saint. Soon he believed he was a devil. Then, he felt he was an objective scientist watching the play of biologic forces from afar.

Over months of psychotherapy, his severe self-confusion lessened. One day a year later, he entered the office relaxed and interested. "I had a strange dream last night," he said. "I dreamed I was in a theater line waiting with some others. There

---

[1]This statement is often translated, "The ego is first and foremost a bodily ego" (Freud 1923, p. 26). However, Freud used the word "*Ich*," which means "I." In the *Standard Edition* Strachey (Freud 1923, p. 7) usually translated "*Ich*" as "ego," though it certainly means self in this case. Ego has come to have other, more specific meanings, which will be discussed in Chapter 4.

were people from all walks of life and all ages and both sexes in line. As if by magic, a door appeared and who should walk in but me."

"What were you like?" the therapist asked.

"I was just the same as I was in line, as I am, I mean. I walked right up to me. As I got closer to me, I had a pleasant feeling of recognition."

"What happened then?"

"I walked right into me and disappeared, and we were one."

As the patient discussed his thoughts about this dream, his therapist was reminded of watching an infant exploring his image in a mirror. At 7 to 10 months of age, B.G., like other children that age, may have approached a mirror closer and closer until his image disappeared. This only happens with the self-image, not with the object-image. B.G. was beginning to rework his early self-experiences. At a fundamental level, he was beginning to experience who he was. These images are the self.

An insurance executive sought respite from administrative details by visiting a friend. She greeted him in the foyer of her fifth-floor studio. When she opened the door, a wide, well-lighted work space spread out before him. "Come in," she said. She gestured to the walls with a sweep of her hand, "Look around."

Huge, bold canvases covered the walls. Black shapes alternated with whites and grays, dynamic, yet integrated. All the paintings were variations of black.

"All black," he said.

"I guess I've been depressed," she said. "But that's me. That's all I have to work with, so I'm working with it." Her twinkling eyes and smiling face revealed that she was not now depressed, though she was telling him she had been or could be depressed. She was telling him something about her self.

The paintings were not self or self-images in the psychoanalytic sense. They were canvas and paint. Neither were her words her self. But her paintings and comments communicated something about her internal self-representations. These internal images are what is meant by self. In this case, she was referring to her depressed self, though she did not currently feel depressed.

Self-images are not necessarily visual. They are also kinesthetic— having to do with deep muscle sensation.

At the community swimming pool, a young man poised thirty feet above the surface. He leaped, tucked to pike position, spun one-and-a-half turns as he dropped, opened his pike, and slipped into the water. The water barely rippled around his ankles.

This diver relied on a finely tuned self-awareness of which he had no consciousness. He could not have consciously kept track of each balanced movement as he hurtled down through the air. He remained in control, because as he whirled he kinesthetically sensed exactly where he was in time and space. This sense is self.

Twenty years ago, near the Spanish Steps in Rome, I met a man from Virginia. He had no money, but he did have a guitar. When he played the blues and sang the popular, forlorn songs, a crowd gathered around him. Sad, hopeless complaints were transformed by the melody and rhythm. This man's music changed the words from whining self-pity to expressions of endurance and hope and joy in the folly of our humanness.

The sounds were not his self, but they indicated something about his self. His sense of mood, of sadness mixed with hopefulness, of rhythm linked with melody, mirrored his internal sense of himself, at least one aspect of himself.

His fingers picked the strings, too rapidly to be noticed individually. Yet, he sensed exactly where each finger was and would be and what sound and tone and rhythm was associated with each movement and what words and meaning and mood pulled it all together. His song reflected an internal integration of at least some aspects of his self.

Self refers to conscious and unconscious mental representations that pertain to one's own person. In this book, whereas object sometimes means an external person, place, or thing and sometimes an internal image, self always refers to an internal image. According to this usage, someone viewed by an outside observer is not a self, but a person. The self is private.

CHAPTER 3

SELF-OBJECT

Object relations are the interactions of the self and internal or external objects. Studies of fantasies have led to the conclusion that self- and object-representations do not exist independently but, rather, in relationships called object relations units. These units consist of a self-representation and an internal object-representation connected by a drive or affect such as love or hate, hunger or satiation (Kernberg 1976, Rinsley 1978).

Psychotherapists have learned a great deal about these units from borderline patients who have prominent all-good and all-bad object relations. The polarization of their self- and object-representations and affects makes them more obvious.

S.W. was a 32-year-old woman who entered all-good and all-bad self-object states. She began one session by complaining that her psychiatrist had forgotten to renew her antidepressant medication. He actually had refilled it, and she had overlooked that fact. He waited to clarify the misunderstanding. She went on to describe how she had had a difficult time over the weekend. She had told her husband she wanted him to look after the children on Saturday while she visited a friend. He replied that

13

she had gone to her dance class every evening the previous week while he stayed with the children. He would like to have some "family time" with her and the children.

She went on, "He said he wouldn't stand for me taking off every time he was with the kids. He was going to put a stop to that kind of behavior. That made me so mad. He was going to put a stop to who? Who is he to tell me what to do? And I told him so, too!"

"Sounds like you had an argument," the psychiatrist said.

"Not really an argument. I unloaded on him. He didn't say more. I got it off my chest. But when I woke up in the morning, I was still mad. I was mean, bad mean. I looked over at him asleep. I wanted to . . . to strangle him. I wanted to hit him with my fist as hard as I could in the face while he was asleep. I was mean. And with the kids, after I got up, I was cross with them. I scolded them. They hadn't done anything to deserve it, but I kept after them. The whole weekend was a waste."

The patient went on to talk about how let down she felt by her psychiatrist because he had not reminded her that she had a refill available on her antidepressant. She described how Easter Sunday had been depressing. She had visited the cemetery to look at her mother's and father's graves. The caretakers had neglected the graves. She was angry about that.

S.W. was in an all-bad self-other state. The self was bad, mean, depressed. Her objects, as represented by the psychiatrist, husband, parents, and cemetery caretakers, were forgetful, ungratifying, absent, dead, and neglectful. The affect connecting self and object was anger. The bad self, bad object, and angry affect comprise an all-bad object relations unit.

The same patient described an all-good object relations unit later in the hour.

The therapist asked S.W. what Easter had been like when she was a child. "It was great," she said, smiling brightly. "I got a new Easter dress and pretty new shoes. My mother always gave me something very special for Easter—a chocolate bunny. I got a chocolate bunny every Easter." Her tone of voice and facial expression were filled with warmth and tenderness. "I loved those chocolate bunnies. My father made a big breakfast. The whole family put on their Easter clothes. I looked so pretty in my new dress and shoes—and gloves, too; we got gloves, too. We'd go to church. Afterward, my mother would make Easter dinner. It was great."

S.W. was now in an all-good, self-object state. The good self was represented by the pretty little girl in her new Easter clothes. The good objects were represented by mother and father feeding the family and by the chocolate bunny. The affect was love. The good self, good object, and loving affect comprise an all-good object relations unit.

Developmentally, the earliest object relations unit is a symbiotic self-object in which the distinction between self and object is not clear. In the psychological sense symbiosis means a state of experiencing the self as inextricably intermingled with the object. When the word unit is used for symbiosis, it is misleading because it implies something discrete. This problem is encountered in all attempts to describe preverbal experiences with words. Words refer to differentiated experiences, whereas symbiosis is undifferentiated.

Symbiosis is the most undifferentiated self-object. It is traditionally associated with pleasant feelings, such as love, warmth, satiation, or even ecstasy, though it can also refer to unpleasant experiences. All mental life begins with symbiosis. It is the matrix out of which our very selves emerge. It is the emotional sea, the oneness to which we long to return. Although symbiotic longings are normal, psychotherapists have learned most about them from patients.

D.F. was a 26-year-old man with a five-year history of psychotic illness. He told his therapist that he was "enlightened" by a wonderful being named Light. Light had come to him as a presence one day. "He descended on me and told me all the mysteries. Do you know that if I peel off my skin, I am pure, white light? I can unpeel my skin like someone else takes off a jacket. Light and I are the same thing. When I felt this truth, everything was peaceful and warm and beautiful. All my worries were gone. Things were quiet and all right."

"Is that why you forget to come to appointments, because you are with Light and everything is all right?" his therapist asked.

"Yes, that too, but mostly, there is no time."

"You forget the appointment?

"There is no appointment," the patient said. "You see, everything is relative to the speed of light. When you are light and when you are with light and everything is light, there is no time. That is one of the secrets. It's all one thing. There's no place either. That's why I can go into light and be in a different universe when I come out. It's all the same.

D.F. was describing a symbiotic experience. He and Light were the same thing, not limited by boundaries, peaceful, and unified. Stable concepts of time, space, and reality dissolve during symbiosis. Neither are space and proportion a given. Later in the treatment he began to feel himself to be at one with his therapist. He gave up his delusion of Light to become immersed in the treatment. He would sit silently with his doctor, certain he did not need to speak because the doctor knew his thoughts. This stage was a long time in developing. It was even longer before D.F. could begin to differentiate and move toward becoming his own person.

Symbiotic or fusion experiences are also called mergers. Federn (1952) called them blurring of ego boundaries. By whatever name, these states involve indistinct senses of self and object combined with a strong feeling to form the symbiotic object relations unit.

Symbiotic experiences are not peculiar to people suffering from psychoses. Everyone loosens his or her boundaries at times.

Artists, poets, and mystics have best described normal merger. In his poem "Ode on Intimations of Immortality from Recollections of Early Childhood," Wordsworth described a symbiotic experience when he said:

There was a time when meadow, grove, and stream,
The earth, and every common sight
To me did seem
Apparell'd in celestial light,
The glory and the freshness of a dream.

E. L. Doctorow (1984) provided another description of symbiosis in the following passage from "Willi." This story begins with the description of a small boy who wanders into a field. Delighted with the warmth of the sun and the brilliant conviction in the colors, the boy describes: "I fell at once into a trance and yet remained incredibly aware, so that whenever I opened my eyes to look, I did not merely see but felt its existence." Such states come naturally to children (p. 7).

Doctorow depicted a state we have all experienced, a state in which the distinction between the self and the not-self becomes irrelevant. He skillfully described this blurring of self–other boundaries by attributing Willi's thoughts and feelings to the environment and equally by attributing characteristics of the environment to Willi. The "exhalations of the field" (p. 27) envelop Willi. Colors have conviction. Visualized objects are felt as his existence. There is a merging of self and other in a welter of undifferentiated experience. Freud (1930) called this the oceanic feeling.

Doctorow went on to describe how journeys of a lifetime passed before the boy's eyes and how the scale of the universe was not pertinent.

Here again, time and space mingle; they fluidly expand and contract. During merger experiences, large and small, fast and slow become unities. There is no duality, because there is no subject–object distinction, upon which all order in the internal world depends.

Everyone experiences the warmth, or even the ecstasy of fusion from time to time:

Two lovers hold hands as they stroll by the river. In the twilight of the first warm spring evening, they do not clearly distinguish themselves from one another. They are a couple.

A gray and twisted man leans on his cane before Renoir's *Rowers' Lunch*. Alone, in the cool, white halls of Chicago's Art Institute, he gazes unselfconsciously. As he views the painting, alone, he enjoys the pleasure of youth and companionship and quiet flirtation. The flush of wine, the warm shade, and the repose after exercise are his— all this, as if he were there, in the scene of nineteenth-century France, which no longer exists, as depicted by an artist long dead.

Anyone who has been injured and given a narcotic understands the warmth and peace within oneself and the environment, the slowness of time and irrelevance of space, which we feel during narcotic intoxication.

People who meditate enter such states. The devout of any religion feel at one with their God.

A pregnant woman who pauses with her shopping cart contemplates the first flutter of new life within her. Amid the supermarket bustle, the rows of brightly colored cans, she smiles a quiet smile, betraying her symbiotic experience with her new fetus.

The loss of sense of self, of time and space, of distinction from one's lover, of existence itself, during orgasm is perhaps the most powerful fusion experience available to adults.

Less physiologically compelling than orgasm, but equally intimate, is the warmth and pleasure of feeling empathically understood. The conviction that another person knows what we feel and listens compassionately to us and understands entails a blurring of self–other boundaries. Conversely, understanding another person empathically also involves a blurring of self–other boundaries. Although empathy can, in retrospect, be dissected and translated into everyday observations (Hamilton 1981), we cannot empathize while maintaining clear self–other boundaries. By definition, empathy requires the absence of such objectivity.

If symbiosis is a psychological state during which self and other are fused in a warm, satiated, loving, or ecstatic feeling state, what would happen if we went to the opposite extreme? What would happen if we isolated a person from his environment in an attempt to find out just what a person is, in and of himself? Would isolation of a person from external objects change his internal self- and object-experience?

Following World War II, scientists took an interest in the effects of the isolation used in brainwashing during the war. They performed thousands of experiments over a period of 30 years (Solomon and Kleeman 1975). This work led to the development of elaborate sensory deprivation chambers. Volunteers were submerged in tepid water inside insulated walls. A hood placed over their heads allowed them to breathe. Thick concrete and cork walls screened out all sounds. Skimmers at the water surface even dampened whatever wave action the subjects might generate themselves.

Isolated from the outside world, these volunteers underwent profound psychological changes. They lost their ability to organize their thoughts and concentrate. Vivid imagery and bodily illusions came to mind. Some hallucinated. Most became susceptible to suggestion. Their sense of identity dissolved. Time and space would not hold steady.

In object relations terms, bodily illusions are a change in the sense of self. Hallucinations are the confusion of self and other. In hallucinations, thoughts or fantasies, which are internal, are experienced as perceptions of external events. Internal and external, self and object, are confused in hallucinations. The suggestibility experienced in sensory deprivation and used in brainwashing also results from boundary confusion. It results from thinking that someone else's thoughts and opinions are one's own. Time and space become irrelevant, just as they do during the self–other confusion of symbiosis.

Surprisingly, then, attempts to isolate a person from external objects result not in a pure sense of self uninfluenced by the surroundings, but the opposite, a state similar to symbiosis, in which one person feels so close to another person or thing that he cannot distinguish himself from anything else. If there is no external object with which to compare one's self, there is no self and no stable sense of reality. As these experiments suggest, our very selves will disintegrate without external as well as internal objects, for the self is nothing except half of the self–object duality.

Many people are "rugged individualists," who like to feel certain of knowing who they are and what they stand for. Thus, they do not rest easy with the idea that their private selves are dependent upon their relation to the external environment, particularly their relationship to other people. Yet even astronauts, chosen for their fortitude, sense of purpose, and intelligence, must accept this fact. In the isolation of space, they must depend on routines, tasks, and orders from earthbound command centers to keep their orientation, to resist the pull of merger, fragmentation, and loss of self. Underwater divers must take similar precautions.

If we can all lose our sense of self as separate from the environment, what distinguishes us from those suffering from psychoses? Psychosis is characterized by self–object confusion, and everyone can develop such confusion; but not everyone is psychotic. Many clinicians think the difference is that those who are not psychotic can turn their boundary blurring on and off, as necessary, and those who are psychotic cannot. Rinsley (1982), who studied the object relations of borderline disorders, explained psychosis versus nonpsychosis this way:

As a group of psychiatry residents gathered around him, he told the story of a 12-year-old boy named Josh, who lived in Topeka State Hospital. He thought he had a radio inside his head. From outer space the radio received messages of war and invasions and spaceship battles.

The professor confided to his students, whispering behind his hand, "You know what I told him?"

He winked.

"I told him, 'I'll tell you a secret, if you promise not to talk about it outside this room.' "

Dr. Rinsley paused.

Then he went on, "Josh agreed and asked me what my secret was. So I told him, with appropriate conspiratorial inflections, 'I have a radio in my head, too.' 'You do?' Josh said."

The professor nodded and looked around at the residents to see how they were receiving him.

" 'Yes, I do,' I whispered. And do you know what he said to me? He said, 'Then why aren't you crazy like I am?' "

The professor sat up straight and grinned at his residents. He put his hand to his ear, as if turning a radio knob. " 'Because,' I said, 'I can turn it off.' " He clicked his ear and sat back.

At first, it seemed that the professor was making fun of this tormented child. But then he repeated with compassion and warmth and understanding in his voice, " 'Because I can turn it off, Josh. And you can't turn yours off yet. Do you want me to show you how to turn it off?' "

I do not know whether Dr. Rinsley ever taught Josh how to turn off that radio he was hearing, but I do know he was a talented and compassionate psychotherapist who helped many patients confused about self and other. I also know that he did not wish to imply that he had hallucinated radio transmissions, but that he vividly and empathically identified with this child's experience and could turn this identification on and off at will. He reminded his students, over and over, that everyone can understand psychosis.[1]

Because people can and do relinquish the self–other distinction from time to time, many object relations theorists assert that everyone harbors within them a psychotic self as well as a nonpsychotic self. This idea has led to uneasiness, criticism, and sometimes excessive theoretical efforts to distinguish psychotic from nonpsychotic personality structures. It seems preferable to sit still with the uneasiness, neither affirming nor denying, looking only at the evidence.

An object relations unit is a self-representation and an internal object connected by a drive or affect. When the distinction between self and object in an object relations unit is unclear, it is called a self-object. Symbiosis is the first and most thoroughly undifferentiated self-object out of which other object relations evolve. Symbiosis is conventionally described as being associated with pleasant affect, such as love or ecstasy, though other fusion states may be confusing or frightening.

---

[1]Upon reading this account, Rinsley (1987) mentioned that after many months of inpatient treatment, Josh was able to turn off the "radio"—he eventually recovered and is doing well as a family man and in his own business.

CHAPTER 4

THE EGO

The ego cannot be experienced subjectively. The ego perceives, integrates, thinks, and acts. It is central to our personalities, yet unknowable. Its functions can be measured and observed from outside, but it can never be known firsthand. During introspection, the ego remains the observer within the observed.

When we contemplate the subjective experience of ego, we are conjuring up a self-representation or self-image, which we take to be equivalent to the ego, but it is not the ego. Some people like to identify with an aspect of their ego functioning—rational thinking, for instance. This identity, however, is not ego; it is a self-representation. Ego can never be known subjectively, because it is not a person, place, thing, idea, or fantasy. The ego is an abstraction denoting a set of functions.

Much object relations literature is confusing partially because the word ego is used in so many ways without informing the reader when the meaning has been changed. In many publications, ego can mean self, organization, and organizer, interchangeably. Here, it refers only to the organizer, not to the organization of the personality, nor to the self. It is one aspect of the broader concepts of ego. There has been a move in recent years toward such specificity (McIntosh

1986). Because the term ego is central to object relations literature, it may be useful to discuss the history of this concept.

Freud defined *Ich*, or ego, in various ways as his work evolved, but at no time was his definition very clear.[1] In his most highly developed version, *The Ego and the Id* (1923), Freud described three major structures of the personality—ego, id, and superego. The ego had several attributes and functions, but two were basic: (1) the ego was equivalent to the self; and (2) it was a coherent organization-organizer. Freud condensed these separate but overlapping ideas into a single concept, the ego.

As self, the ego represented conscious and unconscious awareness of various aspects of one's own being, primarily body image and the subjective sense of self. This concept of self is similar to the one proposed in Chapter 2.

As system, the ego had a synthetic and organizing function. It balanced, integrated, and stabilized perceptions, impulses, emotions, and the demands of conscience. The impulses were called id; and the demands of conscience were called superego. Thus, the ego balanced id and superego. Freud did not clearly make the distinction between ego as self and ego as organizer and system. Rather, he described the ego in both ways interchangeably.

It was Hartmann (1952, 1959), an ego psychologist, who differentiated more clearly between ego as self and ego as organizer or system. He described the system ego as the agent of centralized functional control (1959). He emphasized the functions of differentiation, synthesis, integration, and balancing in the realms of perception, cognition, impulse control, and motor function. Hartmann (1952) predicted that these integrative ego functions would eventually provide the link between psychology and biology, mind and body.

Hartmann clarified the concept of the ego as system and organizer, though he did not distinguish between the concepts of organizer and organization. He probably did not do so because there is always a relationship between structure and function. Unlike Hartmann's conceptualization, in this work, ego refers only to the ego as agent—an organizer, balancer, and central regulator. It does not refer to a structure or organization, but to "the process of organization per se" (Blanck and Blanck 1979, p. 9). To make this distinction clear, the phrase integrative ego functions will sometimes be used in place of the word ego.

---

[1] I am indebted to Dr. Robert B. Frick for discussing these issues with me in detail.

Jacobson (1964) carried Hartmann's thinking further when she described the formation of self-representations in *The Self and the Object World*. She delineated the progressive differentiation and integration of multiple, primitive self- and object-representations to form a stable identity. The ego was the agent of this process.

Although it is not necessary to delineate all the theoretical problems concerning the ego, it may be useful to indicate some areas of controversy in the object relations literature. Klein (Segal 1964) used ego as synonymous with self. Fairbairn (1954) changed the ego concept radically, defining three egos: central ego, libidinal ego, and antilibidinal ego; these are the key elements of his object relations theory. Unlike Fairbairn, Federn (1952) largely adhered to Freud's description of the ego as the organized and organizing self, but added further elaborations, such as ego boundary. In this book, Federn's useful concept will not be referred to as ego boundary, but as the self–other or self–object boundary. His concepts of ego feelings and the subjective awareness of one's ego (Rinsley 1982) refer to what will here be termed self-awareness.

Kohut (1971) developed a self psychology excluding the ego as a useful element. His idea of transmuting internalizations is similar to integrative ego functions. Kernberg (1976) at first seemed to differentiate between ego and self. More recently, he has argued that Freud's ambiguity concerning ego as self and as system reflects the actual state of things (Kernberg 1982).

Because of this welter of definitions, readers of object relations literature often find it useful to consider in each instance, even within the same work, whether ego means self, organization–structure, or organizer. As examples of the distinction between self and ego, I will present cases of severe psychiatric disorder with separate disturbances of self and integrative ego function.

E.J.[2] was a 17-year-old girl whose referring physician reported that she had had visual hallucinations, paranoid ideas, inappropriate affect, and difficulty completing school work for a year. A more detailed history revealed that her symptoms had begun the day before she was to go on an extended tour with her high school dance team. She went to a neighbor's home where they smoked marijuana in his bedroom. She suddenly hallucinated

---

[2]Aspects of this example were originally described in the *Bulletin of the Menninger Clinic* (Hamilton and Allsbrook 1986).

fire emanating from her eyes and heard a stuffed animal warning her that people might try to kill her. Her hallucinations immediately ceased when she was hospitalized and given neuroleptic medication. Over the next year, she intermittently took the neuroleptic medication that was prescribed, and she continued to use marijuana regularly.

On examination she was found to be an attractive, dark-haired girl who dressed in cover-girl fashion. She alternately pouted coquettishly and smiled with a giggle as she talked. She was alert and oriented and denied recent or current hallucinations of any type. Concentration, memory, and general intelligence were above average. Her ability to abstract was intact. When presented with material above her educational level, she responded in a dramatic and embellished fashion. Her subtests on Wechsler intelligence tests were uniformly moderately above average.

Her mood was difficult to assess because she smiled and acted superficially happy, while admitting that she was hiding her depression. When further questioned about her unhappiness, she demonstrated it by weeping in an unconvincing fashion, which hid any genuine expression of emotion.

E.J. had displayed self-fragmentation. She had experienced a fantasy of fire as a perception of something external, actually coming out of her eyes. She also perceived the warning that people might harm her as a message from a stuffed animal. Aspects of self were attributed to the environment.

This self–other confusion took place while she was faced with separation from home, in an intimate setting with a boy, and intoxicated by marijuana. Her strong feelings and the intoxicant impaired her otherwise healthy integrative ego functions. The combination of neuroleptic medication, marijuana, and internal conflicts about graduating from high school and entering adult life contributed to her ongoing self–other confusion over the next year.

Her symptoms resolved entirely when she was placed in a calm and healthy living situation where marijuana was not available and neuroleptic medications were discontinued. In these circumstances, her constitutionally intact integrative ego functions allowed her to sort out her difficulties in psychotherapy. Self–other confusion had not recurred by the three-year follow-up.

F.Y. provided another example of time-limited self–other confusion in a patient whose integrative ego functions were usually intact.

This 34-year-old woman told her psychiatrist in a first interview that she was afraid she was going crazy. Her mother had recently died, her marriage was tenuous, and she felt pressured by having to work under critical supervision. She was beginning to have uncontrollable crying spells and difficulty sleeping.

Ten years previously she had had a similar difficulty which did develop into a time-limited psychosis. She was about to leave the country as a Peace Corps volunteer. She had broken up with her boyfriend, and her best female friend was ill. She developed crying episodes, sleep problems, and suspicions that she was being sent out of the country for malignant purposes. She hallucinated voices telling her to kill herself. She was hospitalized briefly and treated with antidepressant and neuroleptic medications for a few months. She recovered fully, worked on an assembly line, married, and had two children.

She now feared she would have another psychotic episode. The psychiatrist questioned her further about this possibility. "I get disorganized," she said. "It's my purse. I can tell because of my purse. Everything is out of order. I dump everything out and try to get it organized, but it seems like the more I try to put things back together, the more they get mixed up."

The psychiatrist wanted to see how she would deal with these anxieties in an unstructured situation. He remained quiet despite the patient's obvious anxiety.

She went on, "A woman's purse is a part of her. I mean it really is her. I don't know if you understand. It's not like a man's wallet. Men have wallets, and they may care about them; but a woman's purse is actually her." She stopped for a moment, shaking her head. She looked confused. "My purse is messing me up. I mean . . ."

The patient looked frightened. The psychiatrist decided to intervene. "It sounds like your purse is important to you, a symbol for yourself. When you are upset and feel disorganized, you feel like your purse is disorganized. So you try to organize your purse, but it is your thoughts that are getting mixed up."

"That's right," the patient said sitting back in her chair. She was obviously relieved.

"You have had several losses recently. Your mother died, and now you are afraid you might lose your marriage, your job, and even your sanity. It sounds like you need someone to talk with so you can sort things out."

"Yes, I would like that," she said. She regained her composure and remained lucid in that and subsequent interviews.

F.Y. had brief episodes when she became confused about self and other in an extreme way. She had heard voices telling her to kill herself during her first psychotic depression; she had experienced her own suicidal thoughts as coming from outside her. She recovered fully from this episode until she had several serious losses once again. The distinction between her purse as a metaphor for self and her purse as a volitional being became hazy. She said, "My purse is messing me up." Her usually intact integrative ego functioning had lapsed under pressure from recent losses so she could not compare and contrast sufficiently to keep straight what was inside her and what was outside her. Perhaps the loss of her mother had again aroused longings for closeness of such intensity that she had suspended her self–other distinction. Her ability to recover her balance as soon as the psychiatrist made meaningful contact with her suggests that good ego functions were potentially available to her. Her problems were mainly in the area of self and object relationships.

Some patients, in contrast to F.Y., show evidence of psychopathology that is more clearly in the realm of integrative ego functions.

K.A. was a 19-year-old man who had been adopted at birth. Even as a newborn, he was distinctly motorically overactive and hyperresponsive to stimuli. He had difficulty sitting still and was diagnosed as having a mild learning disability in elementary school. Spelling and arithmetic were particularly hard for him.

K.A.'s foster parents were tolerant and well-modulated people. Being active in sports themselves, they kept their son busy with activities. He garnered considerable self-esteem from his skills in baseball and hockey. His parents believed in positive reinforcement and praised him for his athletics, while overlooking his social and academic deficiencies.

As a teenager, K.A. lacked social abilities and the cognitive capacity to compare, contrast, and abstract. These problem areas caused him no end of trouble in high school. Socially, he was immature and impulsive. He fell in and out of love daily and grandiosely overestimated his athletic prowess. The other boys delighted in showing him that he was not the star he thought he was. Soon, he began to associate with other youths who were outcasts. He turned to marijuana, alcohol, and hallucinogens. At age 17, he developed the delusion that he had special knowledge of a murderous plot. His refusal to take medication hampered his outpatient treatment, until at age 19, he attacked his parents and was referred for long-term hospitalization.

Upon admission to the hospital, K.A. grinned and walked high on the tips of his toes, greeting everyone he encountered. He wore brightly colored suspenders and pressed jeans that were too short for his spindly legs. He was taking antipsychotic medication at that time and had no hallucinations. He had a fixed paranoid belief system. His concentration and ability to abstract were poor. He could not integrate complex stimuli and jumped from thought to thought. His mood shifted from moment to moment. Moreover, he had nighttime panic attacks following physical activity. Occasionally, he flew into rages and attacked the nurses.

Psychologic and neuropsychologic testing demonstrated mild diffuse cerebral dysfunction. Neurometric testing (a computerized electroencephalogram), carried out while K.A. was off medication, showed a generalized cortical deficit.

These impairments in integrative ego functions led to problems in his hospital routine. For example, on the volleyball court, each player is responsible for a vaguely defined area that changes with the serve. He was incapable of keeping track of such boundary changes and would rush about the court in widening circles, becoming increasingly anxious. After volleyball, he would pace the ward, painfully grimacing and complaining of overwhelming anxiety. When he was changed to an all-male basketball team, he no longer became overexcited and confused, as long as they played man-to-man. When the team played a zone defense, he could not stay within the ill-defined zones and would run from place to place, interfering with others' responsibilities and neglecting his own zone. This failure to discriminate is but one aspect of impaired integrative ego function.

K.A. had difficulty with his primary nurse. This 40-year-old woman approached her patient in a professional and caring fashion. Her attractive physical appearance, combined with her capacity for concern, confused and overstimulated the patient. If she was left alone on one end of the ward with him, he would burst into physical violence. Once, he threw a potted plant against the wall near her head. Another time he struck her face with his fist. Afterwards, he wept bitterly, explaining that he had hit her because, as he put it, "She is my favorite nurse, and she's so sexy I can't stand it." He could not differentiate between his sexual and aggressive feelings. Neither could he modulate and integrate his emotions and behavior. He erupted into chaotic activity because of this failure in integrative ego functions.

K.A. eventually improved when ward personnel adjusted the stimulation around him and provided him with insight into his illness and his strengths and weaknesses. They physically contained his violence. After months of calm, deliberate treatment, he could work on the grounds, but he continued to need frequent reminders to persist with tasks. Five years later, he called to thank his helpers for their assistance and to inform them he was stable, but required moderate doses of neuroleptic medication and a structured living situation. He had recently tried to leave a halfway house to live on his own in an apartment, but had become disorganized and again displayed chaotic behavior until he returned to sheltered living. He realized he might always need a structured environment because he could not sufficiently organize his experience.

K.A. had impaired integrative ego functions and, therefore, self–object pathology. His delusion about murderous plots was a confusion of internal fantasies with an accurate assessment of everyday external events. Because the ego organizes self-image and object-image, ego deficits nearly always lead to self pathology. This interrelationship between ego and self has contributed to the blurring of the two concepts in much psychoanalytic literature.

Separating the concepts of self and ego provides clarity but also detracts from the richness of certain usages. For instance, observing ego has come to mean the ego as subject reflecting on itself as object. Descriptions of the observing ego used in this reflexive sense denote a contemplative state of mind that one can almost feel. Clearly separating self and ego as concepts does not allow for the reflexive meaning of observing ego. The ego is always the subject and does not observe itself; it observes self-image and object-image and their associated feelings. Observing the self becomes just another ego function, like acting, thinking, feeling, integrating, and organizing. While sacrificing some richness of meaning, the clarity achieved by separating the concepts of ego and self allows more comprehensible discussion of increasingly complex and ambiguous states of mind, thereby providing a richness of its own.

The ego is an abstraction denoting the mental functions of differentiation, integration, balancing, and organizing in the realms of perception, memory, cognition, emotions, actions, and the demands of conscience. The ego compares, contrasts, and decides. It is the perceiver within the perceiver, which we can never know. People sometimes identify with their ego functions, as if the ego were the self or the person; but we are much more complex than our egos. The ego is a passionless thing, useful, but emotionally meaningless in itself. It is an abstraction denoting a set of mental processes.

PART II

DEVELOPING
OBJECT RELATIONS

Out of the cradle endlessly rocking
Out of the mocking-bird's throat, the musical shuttle,
Out of the ninth month mid-night . . .

—Walt Whitman, "Out of the Cradle Endlessly Rocking"

INTRODUCTION

The sense of who we are in relation to others begins in infancy and evolves in a to-and-fro fashion. Through differentiation and integration, we form self- and object-images. Two sources of information have converged to indicate how this process takes place—observations of patients growing and changing in psychotherapy and observations of infants in relation to their mothers.

The most influential developmental studies in American object relations literature have been those of Mahler and her colleagues (Mahler et al. 1975). Other investigations, such as those of Spitz (1965) and Bowlby (1969, 1973), also demonstrate the importance of early mother–infant relationships in establishing a sense of self and other, though they emphasize slightly different aspects of the same process. Piaget's (1936, 1937) detailed descriptions of cognitive development are compatible with the findings of Spitz (Cobliner 1965) and Mahler (Fraiberg 1969, Lester 1983).

The seminal psychoanalytic observations have been brought together by Kernberg (1976, 1980). He relied on previous work by Hartmann (1964), Jacobson (1964), and Klein (Segal 1964), among others. The mental processes he observed in patients with borderline personality disorders have striking parallels to the behavior of children in certain phases of development. These two lines of investigation, represented by the work of Mahler and Kernberg, have come together to form modern object relations theory.

This emphasis upon the work of Mahler and Kernberg is, of course, a vast oversimplification. In Chapter 19, I will discuss some of the other contributions. The ego psychologists, interpersonal psychiatrists, and self psychologists, not to mention the myriad individual therapists who have not written down their findings but have discussed them informally with colleagues, have all played their part. For clarity of conceptualization, however, the focus for now will be on these two prominent investigators.

Various mental dynamics seen in patients undergoing psychoanalysis or psychotherapy will be described in Chapter 6. Taken together with the developmental observations described in Chapter 5, these concepts form the heart of object relations theory.

CHAPTER 5

SEPARATION AND INDIVIDUATION

After studying severely disturbed infants, Mahler and her colleagues undertook a ten-year observation of 38 normal children and their 22 mothers. These children entered the study in their first few months of life. Psychoanalytically informed investigators observed them, both alone and interacting with their mothers, through their third year. This series of detailed and empathic observations were used to delineate what they called the psychological birth of the human infant (Mahler et al. 1975).

The phases and subphases of this growth process include:

Autism, 0–2 months
Symbiosis, 2–6 months
Separation–Individuation, 6–24 months
    Hatching Subphase, 6–10 months
    Practicing Subphase, 10–16 months
    Rapprochement Subphase, 16–24 months
Developing Object Constancy, 24–36 + months

AUTISM (0 TO 2 MONTHS)

Some object relations theorists (Fairbairn 1943, Isaacs 1943, Klein 1959) have suggested that people relate to objects from birth or even in intrauterine life; but Mahler, like most American theorists, proposed an autistic phase preceding the capacity for relationships. In this phase, the infant forms a more or less closed psychological system and is cloaked in the reverie of a sleeplike state. The newborn's psychological withdrawal approximates the insulation of intrauterine life. Such an oblivion provides an intermediate zone between intrauterine and extrauterine life.

Spitz (1965), best known for his work *The First Year of Life*, similarly concluded that newborn infants do not yet have the neurophysiologic sophistication to differentiate between self and object. An infant must be able to distinguish internal from external in order to sustain an object relationship. It also must be able to organize perceptions into consistent internal images, a capacity which it apparently does not have. On the basis of these factors, Spitz argued that babies begin life in an objectless stage. Their eventual ability to enter a relationship awaits the maturation of neurophysiologic capacities, as well as the accumulation of experiences, such as feeding, holding, and cuddling.

Newborns respond to a touch on their cheek by turning in that direction and moving back and forth, beginning to suck—the *rooting reflex*. They may root toward the touch of a finger, or even a block, with the same vigor as toward the mother's breast. They show no special interest in their mothers, or anyone else, as yet. Findings like these led both Mahler and Spitz to concur that newborns have only reflexes—such as grasping, rooting, and startle reflexes—that channel their interaction with the environment. This rudimentary reactivity to the environment evolves into a relationship.

Infants younger than 1 month old spend much of their day in half-sleep and half-waking states. They seem to form a monadic system. Freud (1914a) called such a phase *primary narcissism;* during it, all emotional energy remains within or attached to the baby's own body. Emotional energy is not yet directed outward to external objects or inward to self- and object-representation. In Freud's terminology, the infant cathexts his own body, or in more everyday parlance, he invests emotional energy in himself. Since Freud considered erotic energies to be primary, before he developed the dual-drive theory of sex and aggression, he also called this phase autoerotic.

Much debate surrounds Freud's comments on primary narcissism, because it mixes the concepts of self and person. How can an infant invest emotional energy in its own body if it has no experience of a bodily self as an entity? The newborn seems to have no discrete self with emotional energy to invest in another aspect of the self. From an external viewpoint, however, the infant as a whole person seems to direct most of its emotional energy inward. These concepts of Freud's remain problematic because of a terminological unclarity.

Fairbairn (1941) stated that during the first few weeks of life the infant retains its mental state as it existed before birth. It resides in such total merger with its mother that it does not allow "entertaining any thought of differentation from the maternal body, which constitutes its whole environment and the whole world of its experience" (Fairbairn 1943, p. 275). The issue for Fairbairn was not so much one of cathexis, or where the drives are directed, but of how the infant experiences itself as a part of its mother. Unlike Fairbairn, I agree with Mahler and Spitz that the newborn probably does not as yet entertain any coherent thoughts at all. The merger Fairbairn described begins later, during symbiosis.

There is evidence that infants respond to light, color (Oster 1975), movement (Bower 1965), and sound (Wertheheimer 1961), as well as to taste (Jensen 1932), smell (Engen and Lipsitt 1965), and touch (Lipsitt and Levy 1959). Infants appear unable, however, to distinguish between human and nonhuman stimuli. Additionally, they respond to their own bodies, just as they do their blankets, their cribs, or their mothers. They seem to live in a world of light and color, warm and cold, pain and pleasure, loud and quiet, still and moved. This world, it appears, is not divided into sets of opposites as is this description, which is divided thus because of the nature of language. During this preverbal, neonatal time, perceptions probably run together in a synesthesia. Moist sweetness, warm colors, and felt visions prevail. Perceptions may equally well fragment into unconnected bits of light, noise, touch, smell, and taste.

Even these poorly organized perceptions allow some connection to the environment. This early connectedness eventually evolves into complex relationships. Mahler referred to the well-known observation that each developmental phase blends into the next (Mahler et al. 1975). Earlier phases contain the anlage of the next phase, just as subsequent phases contain vestiges of previous development. In the autistic phase, there is only a small emotional investment in the external world; but there is some responsiveness to stimuli. "It is this fleeting responsivity to external stimuli that makes for the continuity between the normal autistic phase and later phases" (Mahler et al. 1975, p. 43).

Perhaps one reason adults find it difficult to conceptualize newborns as psychologically insulated is that adults themselves become so attached, or bonded (Klaus et al. 1972), to their babies. Any woman who delivers a child and sees its bright eyes and hears its voice and feels it placed wiggling and warm on her belly knows that bond. Any man garbed in the green gowns of the birthing room, who sees and hears a newborn emerge wet and squalling from the mother and then holds that youngster up against his chest, knows the oneness with his baby. In such circumstances, the adult enters a partial fusion state and attributes his or her own feelings of attachment to the baby. Close observation by less involved scientists indicates that even though the child may mold to some degree, the attachment is still largely one way—parent to child. This fact does not diminish the importance of the parent-to-child bond, for it is this connectedness that provides the matrix within which the infant eventually forms its own relatedness.

SYMBIOSIS (2 TO 6 MONTHS)

In Chapter 3, examples from clinical practice, the arts, and everyday life illustrated symbiotic experiences in adults. Mahler described this same symbiotic experience as the very stuff of the second through fifth or sixth months of life.

The child develops a "dim awareness of the need-satisfying object" (Mahler et al. 1975, p. 44) early in symbiosis. He begins to behave as if his mother and he were part of the same "omnipotent system—a dual unity within one common boundary" (p. 44). Freud (1930, p. 64) called this the "oceanic" feeling.

Dawning awareness of a two-person relationship derives from both gathering experience and a maturing nervous system. Neuro-physiologically, the ego functions of memory, cognition, and motor coordination are unfolding. They allow the infant to organize and remember the experiences of being hungry and fed, held and laid down, and of seeing, hearing, and smelling his mother's and his own body. These experiences provide a budding sense of self in relation to object. The child shifts from the one-person monadic system of autism to the bipolar self–other system of symbiosis. As yet, differentiation is not sufficiently complete to allow for development of a truly two-person relationship.

Not only do the ego functions allow for a budding relationship, but the relationship with a loving parent enhances the unfolding ego functions (Ritvo and Solnit 1958, Bell 1970, Mahler et al. 1975). If the child does not have such a relationship, if his mother does not adequately receive his cues about his needs and respond to them, the child's genetically programmed ego functions fail to develop. In the extreme case, as Spitz (1965) demonstrated with children raised in foundling homes, the child may return to an unrelated or autistic phase. These children, who lost their mothers, were left in cribs and fed with propped bottles. They were not held or rocked or fondled. With this lack of interaction, they began to lie motionless, staring, unattentive to their environment. Some of them wasted away and died of marasmus. Conversely, children who did have optimal interactions seemed to develop increasing abilities to perceive, process, remember, and respond to stimulation. There is a vital, circular interaction between the development of mother–child relationships and the maturation of ego functions.

The symbiotic relationship is heralded by the smiling response. Spitz (1946) noticed how the vertical, moving human face, or even a mask, releases a smiling response and visual following in the infant. This social smile is one of the first signs of a genuine relationship. While recognizing the importance of social smiling, Mahler emphasized the mother's holding her baby as one of the more important "symbiotic organizers of psychological birth" (Mahler et al. 1975, p. 49).

Mahler did not emphasize correct versus incorrect holding, but much like Winnicott, she focused on "good enough mothering" (Winnicott 1953) providing an adequate "holding environment" (Winnicott 1960) for a particular infant. A psychophysiologic equilibrium is attained by matching mother and infant interactions, as Brazelton (1969) also demonstrated. These patterns are called "mutual cuing" (Spitz 1965). Mahler (1965) filmed this cuing and molding of the mother and infant. She described how the infant responds differently to the warmth and turgor of its mother's body than to inanimate objects (Mahler 1971). She also demonstrated how infants can adopt or take in the holding pattern of their mothers. One child she observed during the weaning process, which followed a period of happy breast feeding, began to claw and tear at his mother's blouse. Wanting to soothe her baby and yet protect herself, the mother bounced him in her lap (Mahler et al. 1975, p. 49). Subsequently, this small boy learned to comfort himself, and even later to play a peek-a-boo game with this same bouncing pattern. The holding pattern which the child adopted when only partially differentiated from his mother laid the groundwork for a later constructive, adaptive, and more differentiated relationship pattern.

Not all is perfect even in the symbiotic phase. Infants experience cold, hunger, cramping colic, pinpricks, falls, and myriad other distressing events. Because of the baby's poor self–other differentiation, it experiences these unpleasurable events as encompassing its entire self and its world. When infants wail and scream, the whole world seems to be swallowed by their agony.

These unpleasant experiences also serve their developmental purpose. Mahler and Gosliner (1955) suggested that ever-increasing memory traces of unpleasurable (bad) emotional experiences in contrast to the prevailing pleasurable (good) experiences help define budding self- and object-images during the symbiotic phase and thereafter. Pleasure and pain, good and bad, become a second polarity around which the child organizes its world, along with the self–other polarity.

The infant gradually acquires an awareness of something out there, of someone holding and caressing and feeding him, in contrast to neglecting and leaving him. He can simultaneously feel himself to be the one caressing and feeding himself. The baby's poor self–other differentiation allows for this confusion. The infant can readily feel that when he moves his eyes, searching for the mother, she magically appears. When he moves toward her breast, it spontaneously approaches. When the mother of symbiosis is sufficiently present, the infant can associate his need, his wish, his hunger to be fed with her presence, as if the wish and fulfillment were one thing. Omnipotence permeates the baby's symbiotic world. As the baby moves, the world moves; as the baby feels, the world feels; as the baby breathes, the world breathes.

For parents, the symbiotic phase of their infants often fills them with joy. Both mothers and fathers can delight in the warm closeness of their babies, perhaps recalling their own infantile experiences. Nevertheless, feeding problems, sleeping troubles, and the requirement of being available twenty-four hours a day can wear on young parents. Occasionally, because of their own makeup, they may find the closeness of relating to a symbiotic infant threatening their own autonomy. Under such circumstances, they may retreat. Such efforts at distancing can take the form of imposing overly rigid feeding and sleeping schedules on the baby. Typically, however, parents enjoy the growing bond with their child.

Whereas mothers often find their parental role confirmed by their responsive infant, new fathers may at times feel displaced from this intense dyadic relationship between mother and baby. Some fathers nurture and support their wives in their new role, thereby participating indirectly in the symbiosis; and some mothers can share the symbiosis in this way. With more frequent sharing of direct child-care tasks, other fathers feed, nurture, and hold the baby themselves, thereby developing an intense symbiotic relationship of their own. In this case, the baby may experience the parents as one entity. The mother-father may thus become a partially undifferentiated other pole of the symbiotic dyad, though there is evidence that infants respond somewhat differently to different caretakers very early. Mahler did not study this parenting situation, but rather investigated only the traditional family constellation of middle-class Americans.

SEPARATION–INDIVIDUATION (6 TO 24 MONTHS)

Subphase 1: Hatching (6 to 10 months)

Symbiosis blends into the beginnings of the separation–individuation phase when the child is about 5 or 6 months old. The first subphase of separation–individuation is appropriately called hatching or, more technically, differentiation.

Whereas the child previously faded in and out of sleeplike states, directing attention inward or only attending to the me–mother unit, he now develops a look of "alertness, persistence, and goal directedness" (Mahler et al. 1975, p. 54). Mahler's staff members could consistently identify this look of attentiveness and would describe the child as "having hatched."

The child now seems to strain away from his mother's body while being held, apparently to have a better look at her. This tangible sign of differentiation contrasts with the previous molding of the infant in his mother's arms. As differentiation proceeds, the child increasingly explores parts of his mother's body, "pulling at mother's hair, ears, or nose, putting food into the mother's mouth" (Mahler et al. 1975, p. 54).

It is during this subphase that infants begin to derive increasing pleasure from a special blanket, teddy bear, or other soft, pliable object. Winnicott (1953) called these cherished possessions transitional objects. He considered them to represent both self and mother and, as such, to be residual from the omnipotent dyad of symbiosis. Yet the child seems to maintain an awareness at some level that the special possession is neither self nor other. Transitional objects will be discussed in more detail in Chapter 6.

The "hatching" child displays an increasing interest in the appearance of other people as opposed to his parent. The child seems to compare and contrast his budding mental image of the mother with everyone in his environment. Insofar as the father is intimately involved in child rearing, he shares this privileged position with the mother.

A young father in the grocery store carried his 7-month-old daughter in his arms. The little girl, in blue corduroy coveralls with a white embroidered puppy on the bib, leaned back from her father's shoulder, looking at his face, then staring at the passing people. Her wonderment attracted a friendly, gray-haired lady who approached her, smiling. Rather than indiscriminately smiling back at the kind woman, as a symbiotic child might have done, the little girl quieted down and clung closer to her father's chest. She peeked around his neck at the woman, fascinated and yet certain that this was not her object of attachment. She seemed to sink back into the symbiotic unity as she molded and clung to her father.

Many psychoanalysts have termed this differential response to nonparents stranger anxiety. Brody and Axelrad (1970) studied the variability of this reaction. Mahler preferred the term stranger reaction and considered anxiety too strong a word. She emphasized that the more secure an infant has been in his symbiotic attachments, the less anxiety and the more interest he will show in response to strangers. Aside from the strength of the response, most authors agree that stranger reactions demonstrate not only an increasing differentiation of self from mother, but also an ability to differentiate others from mother. The mother retains the self–object potential of a previous symbiotic relatedness, and thus the child clings to her. Simultaneously, he aggressively pushes away from strangers who might threaten the dual unity.

The child develops increasing motor skills as this subphase progresses. Improved mobility derives from maturation of both the musculoskeletal and nervous systems. This ego function of motor coordination serves the process of self–object differentiation by eventually allowing the child to go beyond straining back from his mother's arms. Eventually, this budding person can slide down from his mother's lap to play at her feet. Even if he learns to roll or drag himself along the floor, he tends to stay at his mother's feet. Emotional closeness and distance are visibly evident in terms of physical proximity between mother and child.

Most parents delight in the beginning differentiation of their children. A mother can now enjoy the presence of an emerging real person in her infant, thereby feeling both less alone and less enmeshed with her baby. She can enjoy the flattery of her child pulling at her ears and hair, exploring her face and clothes. The father, who may have been hesitant to intrude into the mother–child dyad, now often feels freer to dandle his child on his lap. He may hold the baby in the air above his head, cooing and laughing, and enjoying being pulled at and fed by the baby.

With any change come new problems. Even normal infants from time to time annoy their good mothers with intrusive explorations and demands. In addition to feeling a bit irritated, mothers also tend to feel some sadness as symbiosis gives way. Others are relieved of what may have been a burdening closeness for them. They may take this opportunity to wean their babies or return to work. Some mothers feel the need to become pregnant once again. In less healthy relationships, they may become so lonely and needy themselves, they cannot tolerate the baby's efforts at differentiation. They may alternately smother the child in love and then reject him, placing him in the crib alone for long periods when he fails to gratify their own needs for merger. Most frequently, however, the process of hatching takes place in a mutually satisfying fashion for the parents and the infant. A to-and-fro movement of closeness and distance—the dance of separation–individuation—has begun.

Subphase 2: Practicing (10 to 16 months)

The practicing subphase gradually emerges from differentiation. Mahler named it practicing, because the child aged 10 to 16 months or so seems to delight in exercising autonomous ego functions over and over, as if practicing new skills. A chapped-cheeked 10-month-old may play pat-a-cake again and again, howling with delight at each repetition. Although the fledgling child may enjoy lap games, he becomes most enamored of crawling, creeping and—finally—walking.

At first, this practicing remains rather subtle. The child's interest in his mother, which developed as he psychologically hatched, spreads to objects which she provides him. Early in this subphase, he may fondle and explore blankets, bed clothes, bottles, and toys. With wide-eyed wonder, he may turn a block over and over in his hands. One of these objects, such as a blanket or teddy bear, may become special to him—a transitional object.

The toddler's budding motor functions drive him to explore all aspects of the world. Soon, he can crawl or creep away from his mother, always checking back, at least visually, at first. He seems to orbit around his mother, who remains a "home base" (Mahler et al. 1975, p. 69); and he returns to her from time to time, as if for "emotional refueling," before venturing forth once again.

When upright posture is achieved, the child sees the world from a different perspective. Locomotion magically opens new vistas before him. He becomes "intoxicated with his own faculties and with the greatness of his own world. Narcissism is at its peak" (p. 71). The bright-eyed tyro is full of himself, toddling from here to there, exploring and mischievous. His facial expression declares his delight in each new discovery. Greenacre (1957) called it the "love affair with the world" (p. 57). Grandeur and omnipotence are the order of the day.

To-and-fro practicing games evolve into peek-a-boo. The baby covers his eyes and mother disappears. He opens them and mother reappears. Squealing with delight, he enjoys his mother's reciprocal pleasure. He covers and uncovers his eyes, omnipotently causing her to disappear and reappear, over and over again.

In catch-me-if-you-can, the toddler catches mother's attention and dashes off. He flees, certain he will be followed and swooped up in mother's arms and released. Mahler suggested that such games reflect the child's exhilaration, not only in exercising his new ego functions of self-direction and running, but also an "elated escape from fusion with, from engulfment by, mother" (Mahler et al. 1975, p. 71).[1] Like the Gingerbread Man of the popular children's story, the practicing-subphase toddler seems to taunt, "Run, run as fast as you can. You can't catch me, I'm the Gingerbread Man." Yet, he seems reassured that mother both will want to catch him and will put him down again after she does.

Mother typically accepts this further disengagement of her toddler. She remains present for refueling and enjoys the child's interest in the world outside the dyad. She often maintains involvement by watching her toddler and empathically delighting in his newly found delight in the world. This pleasure and confidence that the child can master his forays into the larger environment seems to be a trigger for the child's own feeling of safety. Most parents also become a bit anxious about the child's grandiose obliviousness. Children can fall down stairs, run into the street, play with sharp objects, insert

---

[1]This concern with engulfment and escape has been illustrated in the numerous trickster stories in which small animals are swallowed by and then escape their predators. The correlation of these folk themes and practicing subphase issues has been made with the use of clinical illustration (Hamilton 1980).

knitting needles into light sockets, and engage in myriad other disastrous endeavors.

The majority of parents can traverse these difficulties with a little effort, but some have great difficulty with this developmental phase, particularly mothers who have an exaggerated need for symbiotic relatedness. In Mahler's (Mahler et al. 1975) study, a few mothers pushed their child away during this phase, as if to avoid the pain of gradual separation. At other times, such a mother might interrupt her child's delighted practicing to pick him up and hug him, when she needed the closeness, not when her child needed it. In a few cases, it almost seemed as if the mother were practicing and refueling according to her own internal conflicts around separation, rather than responding in a reciprocal fashion to her child's to-and-fro behavior.

Mahler suggested that parents optimally respond to their toddler's moving away by giving them a gentle push, yet retaining emotional contact. They thereby provide a confident expectation that the child can master his new skills in an enlarging world.

Suphase 3: Rapprochement (16 to 24 months)

As the child's motor skills develop, his cognitive abilities also grow. The toddler seems increasingly able to comprehend his separateness toward the end of practicing and the beginning of rapprochement. Perhaps this growing awareness of his aloneness is what leads to his newly increased need for his mother's love. The practicing child's imperviousness to frustration and apparent obliviousness to mother fade. Spontaneous refueling and dashing away now evolve into a more deliberate search for and, alternatively, avoidance of physical contact. The difference between this behavior and that of the practicing youngster is more one of tone than tenor. Children in both stages move to and fro, but the rapprochement-subphase child seems to have a renewed awareness of vulnerability, and of dependency on the mother.

G.B., a 20-month-old boy, repeatedly searched out his mother, interrupting her while she was reading or folding clothes or working at her desk. He would climb into her lap, overcoming all obstacles, get her attention, and snuggle warmly into her lap. When she would put her arm around him, he would push it away and wriggle off her lap; but he would linger near her, looking a bit indecisive. During the practicing subphase, he had been content to play at her feet awhile and then dash off again, joyful and enthusiastic. Now, he seemed to need more closeness, but sought control over that closeness.

The child in the rapprochement subphase may shadow his mother. He may follow her with his eyes or actually follow along behind her for much longer periods than the brief "refueling" of practicing. This shadowing alternates with warding-off behavior, which is both more active and more conflictual than the dashing-off of practicing. In the earlier subphase the youngster delighted to move closer or run away toward some more interesting object. Closeness or distance now becomes conflictual. The child manifests dependency and needs for independence simultaneously.

This motoric approaching and avoiding is joined by other forms of communication. The child learns to say, "No!" He often becomes quite negative, indeed. This negativism is the verbal counterpart of physical pushing away. The child has a new, more modulated skill. He can maintain his separateness by standing still, by not obeying, by not coming when beckoned, by not snuggling, by not eating his food, and by saying, "No!"

The child also uses his utterances and facial expression to woo his mother. His fear of losing her becomes increasingly evident. Both boys and girls may now become demandingly dependent. Rather than accepting mother's warm embrace, her feeding, her help when she offers it, the child coerces her into giving help but rejects her spontaneous efforts. This odd conglomeration of newly found assertive powers and dependence appears to be an awkward solution to the conflict between growth toward increasing selfhood and a yearning to sink back into the bliss of symbiotic fusion.

M.S., a 24-month-old girl, pestered her mother in a most engaging way. When her mother worked on business accounts, M.S. dumped her teddy bear in her mother's lap, returned to her room for her rabbit, turtle, frog, another teddy bear, bed clothes, and a new jack-in-the-box. As soon as her mother set one toy down, or one fell off her lap, the child promptly and firmly replaced it. If her mother patted her, she turned away and brought more toys. When her mother ignored her to do her own work, the little girl imperiously pushed her mother's arm out of the way and rearranged the toys on her overflowing lap. If her mother put the ledger aside and picked her up, she would fend off her embrace. This toddler's mother at times felt her patience was being strained.

With the child's increased ability to influence his mother, to find her, to command her attention, to woo her, and to leave her, he develops a heightened awareness of the limits of his abilities. The child experiences a loss of magic power; grandeur erodes. A collapse of omnipotence is inevitable, because as the child's ability in other areas grows, his cognitive capacity to recognize and remember failures also develops.

The rapprochement-subphase child soon notices that his mother does not always want what he wants. He no longer seems able to relate to her as a home base or refueling depot designed solely to meet his needs. He must increasingly relate to her as a distinct person. Instead of dashing back to her, yanking on her leg for a few minutes, then dashing off, the child now seems more tentative and aware that his reception depends to some degree on his mother's mood. She may be at various times warm, distant, busy, or reflective. The mother's behavior is not magically controlled by the child.

Along with this increased awareness of separateness, smallness, and loss of omnipotent grandeur, the child becomes subject to fits of impotent rage and helplessness. He may throw temper tantrums when frustrated.

E.F., a 23-month-old boy, played much of the hour before dinner in his room. At the table he suddenly wanted his mother's undivided attention. He banged his plate with his spoon and messed his food whenever his parents discussed the day's events. When they turned their attention to E.F., he no longer wanted his food. He wanted his mother's food. She was glad to give him a bite from her plate, but he wanted the whole plate. He climbed down from his chair and up on her lap. She picked him up for a moment to hold him before returning him to his own chair. He grabbed her plate and attempted to overturn it. The mother retrieved it just in time. Twice more this interaction was repeated. Losing her patience, his mother sat him firmly on his chair and said, "No!" E.F. burst into impotent rage. He threw himself on the floor, kicked, and screamed. He was inconsolable for five minutes before calming, and finishing dinner.

In traditional families, tantrums take place more often with the mother than with the father, probably because rejection by the old symbiotic partner can hurt so much more. Fathers sometimes misunderstand this situation and think they handle their children better than their wives do. Such a misunderstanding may lead to discord between the parents.

The emotional swings of children during rapprochement can take on a characteristic pattern called splitting. The mother and another person may be treated alternately as all-good or all-bad.

When J.S.'s mother left him each morning at the baby-sitter's house, he would cry, cling to his mother, and shrink away from the baby-sitter, as if she were a bad person. His mother was the good object, and his baby-sitter the bad object. As soon as his mother shut the door, he would stop protesting and crawl into the baby-sitter's lap. He would rest his head against her before sliding down to romp in the playroom with the other children.

This process reversed itself in the evening. Upon his mother's return, J.S. would at first ignore her, then dawdle at the door as if ambivalent about leaving. Sometimes he would swat at his mother and say, "Bad Ma." His mother was now the bad object and the baby-sitter the good object. Once the door was shut behind them, J.S. would turn to his mother in the driveway, shouting, "Up, up!" She would lift him in her arms, and he would smile, hug her, and play with her hair until he was securely in his car seat once again, safe with his good mother.

This little boy had evidently developed an image of a good object who held him and gratified him and a bad object who abandoned him. Whether the mother or baby-sitter was the good or bad object depended on how she was interacting with him at the moment. This division of the object world into all-good and all-bad is called splitting. Who is good and who is bad in split object relations often flip-flops according to the child's mood and circumstances. Both intrapsychic and interpersonal splitting will be discussed in the next chapter.

Another aspect of the rapprochement crisis is the development of increasing attachments to transitional objects. Children at this subphase may insist on having their teddy bear or blanket with them most of the time. The blanket, which had a passing function as a trasitional self–object in hatching and practicing, now becomes the sole property of the child. He clings to his blanket and jealously says, "Mine," and grabs it back if someone else picks it up. Mother soon learns that cars are one space in which the child particularly needs a transitional object. Transitional activities and rituals also emerge. Parents and children develop ceremonies around the separation that takes place at bedtime. Shared activities such as looking at books or singing soothing songs seem to help the child develop a feeling of safety before moving from the presence of mother to the separation of being put to bed.

Struggles between closeness and autonomy gradually subside as rapprochement resolves. The child finds an optimal distance. The intensity and duration of temper tantrums decrease. Emotions become more modulated, and a new emotional repertoire emerges. The practicing child was elated and hyperactive; the early rapprochement child displayed some affective instability; the late rapprochement toddler can now display sadness, disappointment, and sometimes even concern. A capacity to empathize with the mother's moods emerges.

At this time the child can begin to play with children in a nearby room. He no longer needs his mother's visual presence. Symbolic activities occupy more of the toddler's time.

Language skills develop apace, increasing the child's sense of omnipotence and control once again. With a few words he elicits a specific response from his parent. He can now say "I" as well as "me" and can use simple sentences, such as, "I want ta' " for "I would like some toast, please." The use of "I" instead of the indirect objective case first person pronoun, "me," or the third person, "baby," to indicate the self as the subject of a sentence suggests an increased subject–object differentiation. The use of simple grammatical sentences demonstrates how the child now organizes his world into subject, verb, and object components. As mentioned in Chapter 1, this grammatical construction corresponds to the construction of object relations units in the following way:

Object relations unit:	Self	–	Affect	–	Object
	I		Love		Mother
Grammatical sentence:	Subject	–	Verb	–	Object
	I		Want		Toast
	I		Want		Up
					(in mother's lap)

Language behavior confirms that the child has a developing sense of being a self, a distinct entity, in relation to the world. This capacity to conceptualize self and others is further illustrated by children's recognizing and naming familiar people and themselves in photograph albums.

The child at this age rapidly increases his interest in dolls and other play figures. Favorite dolls are marched around the room, taken for walks, or bathed. Peek-a-boo with play figures and putting them in and out of containers are also common activities. This interest in toys going into and out of containers may parallel the child's own emergence from the engulfment of fusion and his longing for a return to merger. Playing with dolls suggests a growing richness of internal fantasy. It requires an ability to conceptualize aspects of the self and internal object-representations and to project them onto external objects, such as dolls or other figures. Play also requires an ability to maintain an "as-if" or "transitional" sense of internal being external without losing a true sense of boundaries; external symbols are used as if they were internal self- or object-representations without losing a sense of body intactness.

As the child grows in separateness and moves toward object constancy near the end of rapprochement, he takes in aspects of the people around him in new ways. Rules are one of the more obvious aspects of his parents which he internalizes.

> M.W. started to stick a spoon handle into an electric outlet. Frightened, her mother shouted, "No!" and slapped the little girl's hand, though she normally did not swat her children. That day, M.W.'s father put a new, child-proof cap over the outlet and said to her, "No, no, ouchy." The next morning, as she ate her cereal with a spoon, she caught sight of the electrical outlet by the toaster. Upending her spoon, she pointed the handle toward the receptacle. "No! No!" she said. She hit herself on the hand, saying, "No, no! Ouchy," over and over.

She had perceived her parents' admonitions. The previous diffuse closeness has given way to a new, more specific ability to take in aspects of the object without losing a sense of separateness.

This increasing sense of self includes a developing gender identity. Children discover their genitals early. In the practicing subphase, they can delight in touching their penis or clitoris. In rapprochement, they continue to develop an increasing awareness of the differences between the sexes—that some people have a penis and testicles and some have a vagina, labia, and clitoris. They begin to categorize themselves and others into male and female. A tangible manifestation of this categorization can be seen in their relation to the mother. When children discover, and show an interest in having or not having genitals similar to mother's, boys seem impelled toward greater differentiation—more distance and motor activity—whereas girls seem to move closer to their mothers. Sometimes this lingering closeness in girls is strikingly ambivalent. Mahler and colleagues (1975), like other psychoanalytic observers (Tyson 1982), have commented that some little girls tend to cling to their mother and yet manifest anger and disappointment in her when they discover she has not provided them with a penis.

The subject of penis envy is hotly debated. Some authors emphasize that it is not the penis or lack of it which plays a crucial role, but similarity to or difference from the mother (Chodorow 1974). Girls may maintain a closer bond to their mothers because they experience themselves as deeply and fundamentally similar, even in sensitive anatomic areas. Boys, on the other hand, must differentiate more thoroughly, because of their being different from their mothers. Chodorow (1974) has suggested that boys might differentiate too early for optimal development. Discussion over whether boys or girls develop optimally takes us out of the realm of object relations theory and into that of professional debate which often proves more destructive than helpful.

For parents, especially mothers, the rapprochement subphase holds numerous gratifications, but perhaps even more frustrations. The child may demand and reject help simultaneously. He may coerce and control the mother as an extension of himself. He may be negative and obstinate and throw tantrums. The demands on the mother are great. She is called upon to be available, and yet not controlling. She must restrain the child from actual dangerous activity without being intrusive. She must encourage separation without rejecting. Few mothers can remain so steady, so optimally close and distant, without feeling frustration, especially when the child places mutually exclusive demands on her, even small ones—such as insisting that his shoes be pulled effortlessly onto his feet, but that he be allowed to do it himself!

The mother may be going through an emotionally difficult process herself during this time. After fantasies of having a baby, she first has one within her, as an actual part of her body, for nine months. When the infant emerges from her, this physical unity is replaced by the psychological unity of symbiosis. As psychological birth progresses, the mother must go through a prolonged push-pull separation process at the child's pace and according to the child's needs, often with disregard for her needs for closeness and distance. The child's slowly developing capacity for concern and empathy toward his mother may be little recompense for the demands placed on her.

The mother who did not differentiate adequately often has the most trouble at this phase of her child's development. Because of her own anxieties over separation, she may do quite well with a symbiotic child who gratifies her need for closeness. During practicing, she may narcissistically enjoy the child's grandiosity. During rapprochement, though, she may experience anxiety as the child differentiates. She may cling to the child when he shows the slightest urge to separate, or cuddle the child when she needs it, not necessarily when the child needs it. The child is put down when the mother feels secure. Some mothers will actually reward closeness and punish separation with abandonment (Masterson and Rinsley 1975); that is, if the child shows a bit of independence, such mothers threaten to leave. They may be distant, often leaving the youngster alone for long hours. Alternately, when the child comes docilely to such a mother, she may wrap him in the warm embrace of fusion. This pattern is seen in the rewarding and punishing object relations units of borderline personality disorder to be discussed in Chapter 10.

Not all threats of abandonment, however, lead to psychological trouble. Even "good enough" mothers occasionally threaten their children with leaving them.

A young mother backed toward her car, facing her child, her arms full of packages. The obstinate 2-year-old clung to a shopping cart. She refused to be cajoled into entering the car. "Okay, Mommy go bye-bye. Bye-bye," the mother waved with her one free finger. The little girl stopped her play, quieted, and searched her mother's face. "Bye-bye," she repeated, struggling to open the car door. Her voice beckoned in its warm tones, rather than rejecting. The child looked at her once more, and then ignored her and climbed up a shopping cart. The mother stood up, sighed, put down her packages on the front seat, and said, "Oh, okay, have it your way." She walked over to the toddler, pried her chocolate-smeared fingers loose from the shiny cart, and carried her kicking and screaming to the car. Once strapped down in her car seat, the little girl accepted a grimy blanket her mother tossed her.

This mother, though seeming to threaten abandonment to coerce her child, did not actually do so. The tone of her voice betrayed her. Throughout, she was warm and beckoning. The child remained secure of her attachments.

Winnicott (1960) has stated that the child contributes to his own developmental process, obtaining much of what he needs from the environment. He does not need optimal mothering, only good enough mothering. Some children are more difficult to parent than others, just as some mothers have difficulties allowing distance and closeness when appropriate. Some children and mothers who might be otherwise adequate to the developmental tasks facing them are simply a poor match (Brazelton 1969). An energetic, ambitious mother who values autonomy and self-direction may have more difficulty with a calm baby boy who goes at his own pace. She may do better with an active, somewhat driven child who might be a challenge for another mother.

Fathers can take on new importance for their children during rapprochement, because of the push-pull struggle between mothers and children at this time. Throughout symbiosis or hatching, fathers may share the mother–child closeness. During rapprochement, the father's sharing usually shifts to a distinct role as a third party. This outside, yet special, person can help the mother and child disengage from the symbiotic dyad and from their consequent autonomy and control struggles. The father can foster the separation process by commanding the attention and emotional involvement of both mother and child as distinct people.

OBJECT CONSTANCY (24 TO 36 MONTHS AND BEYOND)

Signs of developing individuality and object constancy appear as the to-and-fro separating and returning of rapprochement wanes. Individuality entails an increasingly stable sense of who one is in various situations and moods. Object constancy means the ability to hold a steady image of the object, especially the mother, whether she is present or absent, gratifying or depriving. There is considerable evidence of developing individuality and object constancy in the midst of rapprochement. There is even more overlap between this phase and its predecessor than with the other phases. Furthermore, developing object constancy and individuality continue throughout life. This phase is open-ended.

The clinging and rejecting, demanding and dependent behaviors of the rapprochement-age child fade. He seems more secure, able to concentrate on his own tasks and to more or less ignore mother for long periods. Mahler and colleagues (1975) sought to illustrate this new-found security when they asked mothers to quietly leave their children in the playroom in order to see how they might react to an unannounced separation. A 26-month-old girl provided one example. She had had a solid first few months with a mother who was optimally available to her. When her mother left the playroom, this child played quietly without any concern about where her mother might be. She only became aware of her mother's absence as she grew very pleased with her drawing. At this point, she looked up and asked several times where her mother was. Mahler said the researchers believed the child wanted to share her drawing with her mother; but when no one answered her, she returned to her drawing and became happily involved in it.

To Mahler and her group this behavior suggested an ability to sustain a positive image of the mother. When this little girl wanted to share her pleasure with her mother, she asked for her; however, not finding her, she was sufficiently secure of her mother's ongoing interest and availability that she could continue concentrating on her own play. The fact that she was not merely disinterested was demonstrated by her looking up to show her mother her good work. This interest was further demonstrated when the girl's mother returned to the playroom, and she greeted her with smiles and brought her toys to show her. There was little demanding or running away, but a more modulated and secure response. It seemed as if the girl could reassure herself that her mother was there for her if she wanted or needed her.

This ability to hold an image of the good enough mother constantly in mind depends on both neurophysiologic development and interpersonal experience. Piaget (1937) studied the development of cognitive object permanence, which is a bit different from psychoanalytic or emotional object constancy (Hartmann 1952). Object permanence is the ability to seek hidden inanimate things after a lapse of time. Such searching suggests that the child can conjure up a mental image of the lost thing and hunt for it. Several psychoanalytic authors (Cobliner 1965, Fraiberg 1969, Lester 1983) have discussed the interrelationship of object permanence and object constancy. Since object permanence is the ability to search for hidden, inanimate things with the conviction that they can be found, object permanence is a prerequisite for constancy.

Emotional object constancy is complicated by feelings about other people. Because love and hate, hunger and satiation, can be so overpowering for youngsters, these feelings color experience. When angry or frightened, a child may have more trouble remembering that his mother exists as a good person than recalling a hidden toy when calm. Strong feelings can overwhelm memories of prior emotional qualities; thus, attaining a stable internal image of an emotionally charged object takes much longer than the mere development of knowledge that a misplaced toy still exists.

Bell's (1970) studies indicate that children with positive parental relationships develop "person permanence" before "object permanence." These studies do not contradict the finding that object permanence precedes object constancy. They merely demonstrate the importance of a stable and warm environment for the optimal unfolding of cognitive abilities. Children may be able to remember and look for a parent before they can do so with other things in their environment if they have a good relationship; but this ability is not emotional object constancy. Emotional object constancy is more complex than the cognitive task of remembering and looking for a physical person. It is the capacity to recall good feelings about a parent while seriously disappointed in them. Integrating emotions in this way takes longer to develop.

Before object constancy, the greatest emotional danger to the child was object loss. Now it becomes the loss of the love of the object. With a love object the issue is emotional consistency, not the mere presence of a nurturing thing.

Observations concerning object permanence and object constancy have convinced many psychoanalytic thinkers that a neurophysiologically determined ability to remember and form internal images is one prerequisite of object constancy. The other necessary ability is that of combining pleasant and unpleasant emotions in relation to the same person. This capacity to remain secure that the absent and therefore frustrating mother is the same one who admires and loves the child depends not only on being able to combine opposites intellectually, but also on an accumulation of a sufficient number of good experiences. There must be enough warm experiences available to the child that minor separations do not completely overwhelm his ability to call them to mind. When such good interactions are not adequately available, severe ambivalence develops. Highly ambivalent children show considerable anger and longing when their mothers leave, possibly because they cannot retain a positive image of the mother while she is actively or passively frustrating the child (Mahler et al. 1975).

The achievement of individuality usually goes hand-in-hand with the ability to form a more or less constant image of the object. Self constancy begins to coalesce. This increasingly secure sense of self allows for more purposeful activity. Because the child knows who he is and what he wants, even when mildly frustrated, he can now persist with tasks.

A sense of time and the ability to delay gratification mature along with the capacity to remember good things in the face of frustration. Children can now say they will see their aunt or uncle or another favored person tomorrow or in a little while. This increased sense of being a person in time and place is evidence of developing individuation, that is, a sense of being a cohesive individual with continuity over time, space, and interpersonal context.

As in all life-stages, children do not entirely leave their old struggles behind them during this phase. They often continue to betray doubt over their individuality by insisting excessively on autonomy in areas beyond their competence. For example, a little boy demanded that he be allowed to carry his own suitcase out to the car by himself, although he could not lift it. Negativism and temper tantrums also persist to a greater or lesser degree. Struggles over bowel control can sometimes suggest a need to reaffirm bodily separateness.

Parents begin to decrease slightly in importance at this time. The child can now fairly securely attend a preschool without evidence of overwhelming loss of a sense of mother or individuality. Fathers become still more important and can be seen increasingly to engage in organized play with their children.

The process of developing object constancy and individuality does not end in early life. Issues of learning who we are as separate individuals in relation to other individuals must next be negotiated in terms of the important oedipal conflict. Again in latency, adolescence, and especially when leaving home during young adulthood, these issues need to be reworked. Separation and identity concerns return for further resolution when we marry, when we have children, when our children traverse their own developmental stages, when we leave old jobs and take new ones, when we move to a different town, when our children leave us for their own careers, when we suffer illnesses, when we prepare for retirement, when we face the loss of our spouse or other loved one, and when we prepare for our own death. If we are fortunate, we spend a lifetime developing an increasingly complex and integrated sense of ourselves in relation to other people. This sense of identity becomes freer of wide swings determined by our moods or our circumstances.

In this chapter I have described how children develop an increasing sense of separateness and of individual integrity. While acknowledging the important work of others, I have focused primarily on the observations of Mahler and her colleagues as presented in *The Psychological Birth of the Human Infant* (1975). Her work has been of central importance to virtually all American object relations theories. Kaplan's book *Oneness and Separateness* (1978) is another account of personality development, largely inspired by Mahler's work.

Objects are irrelevant during the autistic phase (0–2 months); the child seems to remain in a psychological shell. As the child develops a budding awareness of self and object, the mother and child begin to form two poles of the dyadic unity of the symbiotic phase (2–6 months). Gradually differentiating from the mother, the baby enters the separation–individuation phase and its subphases: differentiation, practicing, and rapprochement. He becomes increasingly aware of his mother as a separate entity during the differentiation subphase (hatching) (6–10 months). Soon, increasing motor and cognitive skills seem to intoxicate the child with his own prowess, and he runs off from his mother, as if the world is all his. This subphase is called practicing (10–16 months). A growing awareness of his own separateness and helplessness ushers in the subphase of rapprochement (16–24 months). The child moves to and fro, separating and returning, demanding and yet dependent. As rapprochement resolves, the child displays an increased confidence in his mother's continued loving presence despite her occasional absences. Such an ability to retain an image of the mother as primarily gratifying but also frustrating is called emotional object constancy (24–36 months). The child develops a more stable and complex sense of individuality along with this increasingly stable sense of the object.

These observations of infantile phases and subphases are paralleled by a set of intrapsychic and interpersonal mechanisms observable as people grow and change in psychoanalysis and psychotherapy. The psychological mechanisms will be the subject of the next chapter.

CHAPTER 6
PSYCHOLOGICAL MECHANISMS

Many mental processes seen in psychoanalysis and psychotherapy strikingly parallel behaviors Mahler and her colleagues described in young children. Mahler (1971), Masterson and Rinsley (1975), Kernberg (1980), Horner (1984), and Adler (1985) have commented on the convergence of these two lines of evidence. Kernberg stated that Mahler's findings regarding the chronology of phase sequences provided evidence about the timetable of points of fixation and regression, which was difficult to determine on the basis of psycho-analytic work with patients alone. In turn, his work can "provide a psychoanalytic dimension from adulthood that reinforces Mahler's assumptions about intrapsychic correlates of developmental observa-tions in early childhood" (Kernberg 1980, p. 6).

It is important to have two lines of evidence about psychological development, one from psychotherapy and one from infant observa-tion. Infants cannot communicate their internal life verbally. We can only infer what they might be experiencing. On the other hand, memories and internal experiences of patients in psychotherapy may be condensed and reversed chronologically, leading to unfounded conclusions. Klein (1932), in particular, has attributed psychological processes in older, sometimes psychotic, children and adults to infants without data to support such speculations (Kernberg 1969). With the two lines of evidence, theoretical predications in one area can be confirmed or disconfirmed with information from a complementary body of information.

The mental processes found in patients that are pertinent to early development are differentiation and integration, projection and introjection, splitting, idealization and devaluation, projective identification, transitional object formation, developing object constancy, and identification. The object relations literature repeatedly refers to these concepts. Various authors use them differently. Here, I shall sort them out according to what is most generally accepted, useful in therapy, and consistent with the definitions of object, self, and integrative ego functions described in Part I.

INTEGRATION AND DIFFERENTIATION

Integration and differentiation are complementary ego functions. They pervade development from the beginning and persist throughout life. Integration means bringing two mental elements together meaningfully, whether those elements are perceptions, memories, representations, emotions, ideas, or movements. Differentiation means setting two mental elements apart.

The question of what motivates such basic psychological functions is currently the center of much theoretical controversy (Greenberg and Mitchell 1983), which will not be resolved herein. Freud (1940) related them to the drives, libido and aggression, and the associated feelings, love and hate. In his later years, he described eros as the instinct to establish "unities" and "bind together." Aggression, to the contrary, attempted "to undo connections" (p. 148). The American ego psychologists Gertrude Blanck and Rubin Blanck (1979) agree with this formulation, suggesting that libido is most usefully considered the drive to unite or integrate and aggression the drive to separate or differentiate. Other authors consider needs rather than drives as more important for growth and relate integration and differentiation to splitting and projective identification (Grotstein 1981a, p. 3). We can, however, explore what is known about these mental processes without maintaining a definite position concerning what causes them.

In psychotic disorders, we see basic deficits in integration and differentiation.

D.R. was a 28-year-old man with schizophrenia who had spent the last two years living on the streets of San Francisco. He had slept in alleys and doorways and Salvation Army shelters. He obtained food from soup lines when he was lucky. When he was not, he picked it out of garbage cans. His family eventually found him and enticed him back to their Tucson home with offers of shelter, food, and an education. Overstimulated by everyday home life, he felt as though his head would burst. Rather than allow him to escape once again to street life, his family cajoled him into hospital treatment.

Because he could not be committed against his will, the hospital staff members had to be tactful in order to keep him in the hospital. The psychologist and nurses who managed his daily care observed that he was sensitive to stimulation. He was unable to integrate and differentiate even basic auditory and visual stimuli. He soon felt assaulted by a chaotic sensory impingement if left in the usual hospital environment. Consequently, the psychiatrist allowed him to spend up to five hours at a time in his room. He was engaged in quiet talks every few hours and came out for meals and low-keyed, well-organized group meetings. With this regimen he slowly increased his tolerance for the world around him. It was weeks before he could allow his treaters to influence him so that he could take antipsychotic medications.

He gradually continued to improve. After three months, he could attend poetry classes, where he organized his experience into short poems, which became increasingly understandable. Eighteen months later, he still reported seeing fragments of colored lights and hearing roaring and buzzing sounds if the emotional intensity on his living unit heightened. He continued to have difficulty integrating and differentiating his experience at the rudimentary, sensory level. He could not integrate his perceptions into meaningful experience; he was unable to order his world. As he said, "I don't know what's happening. I see these colors, and these noises. I don't know what to make of it. I don't know where they are coming from or what they are. It doesn't make any sense."

He was also unable to differentiate himself from his surroundings. One day, he abruptly left in the middle of a ward community meeting. When the psychiatrist later questioned him about it, he said, "All that noise. It's a jumble. I get all mixed up with so much commotion. I had to leave." Evidentally, he could not listen to the somewhat chaotic group discussion without feeling chaotic himself. He could not distinguish the confusion in the group from what was going on inside him unless he physically left.

A family therapist and researcher with particular skill in treating schizophrenia helped the family reduce their expressed emotion level (Brown et al. 1962, Vaughn and Leff 1976, Goldstein et al. 1978, Falloon et al. 1982). With such changes in his environment, the patient could begin processing his experience a bit better. People around him helped by doing some of the integrating and differentiating for him, thereby serving as an auxiliary ego.

It is possible, though not common, for people who have retained a capacity to integrate and differentiate to suspend that ability for psychological reasons. Although they may not have a brain disease interfering with their integrative ego functions, they may still develop a schizophrenia-like illness, with fragmentation of experience (Hamilton and Allsbrook 1986). Searles (1959) has described a number of such cases. Bion (1959) called this process attacks on linking. He thought such patients were so profoundly disappointed in the rebuff reality had dealt them, particularly in their early object relationships, that they mentally attacked all logical connections with the world around them, even to the point of destroying their own integrative thought processes.

Psychological differentiation and integration in early development parallel similar processes seen in patients recovering from mental illnesses. Infants learn to distinguish sound from color, touch from smell, up from down, many from one. They learn to integrate a certain sound, sight, feel, smell, and taste as pertaining to one thing. They begin to recognize that the breast that feeds them has a characteristic smell, taste, feel, and appearance, which are all aspects of the same thing and not other things. Infants can eventually associate the feeding breast with their mother's face and can form a visual, tactile, olfactory, gustatory, and auditory image of the mother. Later in development, they can also form integrated images of themselves as distinct from the mother. These processes of differentiation and integration are complementary. One cannot integrate various elements that pertain to the same thing without differentiating them from elements that pertain to other things.

The smooth unfolding of differentiation and integration—which are perceptual, cognitive, and kinesthetic functions—can be interrupted by strong emotions in infants, as they can in adult patients. Longing, frustration, excitement, and contentment interfere with and alter the integrative ego functions, leading to projection, introjection, splitting, and projective identification. These later mental processes are sometimes called defense mechanisms because they protect the self-image from a catastrophic loss of a sense of well-being in the face of overwhelming frustration. Mental defenses attempt to insure the integrity of a sense of self and often provide the emotional richness and complexity of our lives. Without defenses we would be rather machine-like compilations of integrative and differentiating functions—all ego and no self.

The tendency to unite and divide is a basic biological as well as psychological process. A seed unfolds from its pod. The germ cell divides into multiple cells. These new cells in turn divide: they differentiate. Some of them band together to form coherent functioning units: they integrate. The roots, stems, leaves, and nutrient-transporting veins evolve from a single cell through differentiation and integration. All multicellular organisms go through similar growth processes.

Differentiation and integration are not simply primitive mechanisms, even though they are found in the tiniest infants, in the earliest efforts to recover from severe psychological disturbances, and, in fact, in all organisms. We rely on these functions throughout our lives. Debates over definitions of psychological terms, for example, are efforts to differentiate and integrate experience.

PROJECTION

Sometimes attempts to differentiate what is wanted from what is unwanted, good from bad, interferes with the differentiation of self from object. When one person attributes an unwanted aspect of self to another person, that is projection. It is clearest when the projection is onto an external object, but some theorists also refer to projection from the self onto an internal object.

Projection is an apt term, suggesting an analogy to a movie projector. The crucial elements, film, light, and lens, are inside the apparatus, but the image is cast outside, onto a screen to create the appearance of an external reality. In our psychological lives we can see that which is within us in others.

Projections are easily observed in clinical practice.

A.B. was a 31-year-old attorney who was the junior member of a prestigious law firm. He had begun psychotherapy because he suffered from excessive jealousy. He believed that his fears were unfounded, but they continued to interfere with his relationship with his wife. He also had difficulty with the senior partner in his firm.

One night A.B. dreamed that his boss sentenced him to jail. "He framed me," he said. "I know it was just a dream, but I think the guy is out to get me. He's mad at me now because of the M. case; but he's always had it in for me." The patient described in great detail all the evidence that his employer had it in for him.

The psychiatrist said, after several minutes, "And if you were the defense attorney for your employer, what would support his innocence. I'm not suggesting he is or is not innocent. I merely wonder what is on the other side of the question as you see it."

The patient recounted evidence that the senior partner was a benign authority who was providing guidance and holding his ambitious junior colleague in check so he might develop the skills needed to become a truly top-notch attorney. "And suppose his motives are selfish," the patient concluded, "they probably aren't personal. He has a right to guard his power and prerogatives so he can earn a living. I'll have my turn in a few years. You know," he said, pausing for a few moments, "maybe I'm the one who wants to send him to jail so I can get all the good cases." He laughed. "I've been madder than hell at him because he didn't give me enough cases so I could advance as fast as I'd like."

"Yes, you are an ambitious man," the therapist said, "and you see your ambition in the people around you."

"So what's wrong with ambition," A.B. challenged.

"Now you are worried I might be criticizing the very attribute which has brought you so far and given you so much success."

"I know what you are going to say next. I am a critical man, and I see my own criticism in the people around me."

"Do you think that?" the psychotherapist said.

"I'm ashamed of that quality. It's not good."

"You are criticizing yourself now. It will be interesting to learn how you came to be so hard on yourself."

A.B. had projected his aggressive competitiveness onto his employer. As he discovered, he was angry with him for not making success easier for him and thought that the senior partner was "out to get him." Later in the session, he thought the therapist was harshly critical when he was actually critical of himself. The patient attributed his own internal feelings and attitudes to people outside himself. He projected an aspect of himself onto them. The external objects may or may not have had the qualities he attributed to them. Even if his employer had been "out to get him" and his therapist had been harshly critical, the patient still would have been attributing his own attributes to them. He would still have been projecting.

People with paranoid psychosis or schizophrenia display extreme projection of hostile impulses. They may so thoroughly see their own aggressive impulses in the world around them that they become convinced there is a vicious plot against them. Anyone who argues that there is no such plot is suspect of complicity.

Aggressive impulses are not the only aspects of the self which are projected. Needs and self-images can be similarly externalized. Another clinical example will illustrate projection of a libidinal need: the need for nurturance and closeness.

One cold, rainy day, a disheveled man, wearing a torn sportcoat and shoes that did not match, wandered into the Westside Community Mental Health Clinic. A psychiatry resident interviewed him. He concluded that the man was psychotic, confused, and self-neglectful, and should be cared for in a hospital for a few weeks before returning to outpatient treatment. The patient refused hospitalization and medication, as he had over the past three years. He did not appear dangerous to himself or others, and thus the doctor could not hospitalize him without his consent.

"Okay, then," he said, "I would like you to come back again tomorrow, and I'll see if we can help you find a better place to live and some more to eat. That's what I'd like. What do you say?"

Although similar suggestions had been made and refused many times before, there was something different about the way this doctor offered help. He didn't order or prescribe or assert— he expressed a personal wish. This street person responded by saying, "Well, okay. If it will make you feel better, I'll be here. I don't mind helping you out." He kept his word. He was there the next day to get the food and shelter he had needed but refused for months.

The patient apparently forgot he wanted to feel better himself. He thought it was the doctor who would feel better if he had food and shelter. Although we could consider the use of the phrase "if it will make you feel better" to be mere coincidence, if a bit condescending, there is little doubt that the patient was projecting his need when he said, "I don't mind helping you out." It was the patient who had gone to the doctor for help, and now he thought it was the doctor who needed help. He had projected his wish for care and nurturance onto his doctor.

Some would argue that this projection was motivated by hostility, as well as by a wish to externalize unwanted needs and self-images. One could speculate that the patient enviously wanted to destroy the image of his doctor as secure and content and then wanted to repair the damage by helping (Klein and Riviere 1964). This explanation, I believe, gives undue emphasis to the theory that psychotic patients are overwhelmed by limitless aggressive impulses (Bion 1956); it overlooks the psychotic patient's capacity for concern and his wish to have others show concern for him (Hamilton 1986). It also introduces an extra element not necessary to understand the interaction itself, but only required to force the data to fit with the assumption that aggression motivates projection. It is much simpler and equally consistent with the data to conclude that the patient's needs were so great and so uncomfortable that he preferred to see them in someone else. One could even speculate that the projection helped him feel closer to another person.

The street person's statement did not solely reflect his tendency to project his wishes onto the psychiatrist. He also correctly, and rather astutely, described the actual situation, as is often the case with people suffering from psychoses. The resident did want his patient to return. Most psychiatrists need to succeed in helping patients in order to feel good about themselves as doctors and helpers. The doctor had said, "I would like you to come back again tomorrow," emphasizing his own, rather than the patient's need. This confused man found a ready recipient for his projection.

Projections often attach themselves to real objects and blend in with them, chameleon-like. Usually, but not always, people projecting find someone or something with a similarity to their projection. They attribute their own unwanted quality to that person or thing, exaggerating and distorting the similar quality. In nonclinical situations, such as administrative decision making, personnel management, and legal processes, the distinction between projection and perception of external events can be vital, but in the psychiatric setting it often does not initially make much difference. When the patient said, "I'll return if it will make you feel better," the doctor did not argue over who needed whom. He merely replied, "Yes, I would like that. Let's go up to the reception window, and I'll make you an appointment." He did not address his patient's need to project before the patient had a chance to get to know him.

There are similarities between projection in the clinical situation and various behaviors in babies. An infant puckering up its face and spitting out an unpleasant mouthful of pureed spinach is considered to be an early behavioral equivalent of projection—getting the bad out of the self. It can be speculated that the baby projects his hunger onto the object, as the disheveled man projected his neediness onto the psychiatry resident. Infants may bite the breast or their bottles aggressively, as if they have projected their hunger pains onto the nurturing object and then wish to punish it (Klein 1957a). An object relations view is that infants project their unwanted hungry, empty, and devouring feelings onto the breast or mother, and then, because of their self–object confusion, fear incorporation by the mother. Although we cannot be certain of infantile mental processes, the self–object confusion of late symbiosis and early differentiation would make such projections possible.

It is thought that during late symbiosis and the beginning stages of hatching, the child's sense of self as distinguished from mother clarifies itself. Accompanying the increased ability to distinguish self and other comes the ability to distinguish pleasure and pain. These capacities to differentiate and integrate experience, as previously mentioned, depend upon an orderly, neurophysiologic unfolding of ego functions in an environment which is neither physically nor emotionally depriving or overwhelming. Given this "good enough" (Winnicott 1953) environment, self and other and pleasure and pain sort themselves out. There is a natural tendency to prefer experiencing pleasure as self and pain as other. Good is retained in the self–mother, dual unity and bad is projected outward. Projection is an active and selective form of self–object confusion, relying on the ego function of differentiation.

Older children project unwanted feelings out of the mother–child dyad. Projections may play a part in stranger anxiety, whereby unwanted aggressive feelings are experienced outside the pair. Toddlers project when they attribute their feelings to stuffed animals. Later, they blame their transgressions on others: "Billy did it." Even healthy adults project unwanted feelings and attempt to externalize problems by passing the buck, or blaming, or by looking down on other people rather than acknowledging their own problems. Good can be projected as well as bad, but not as frequently. The saying "beauty is in the eye of the beholder" refers to the projection of desired qualities onto another person.

INCORPORATION, INTROJECTION, AND IDENTIFICATION

Introjection is most easily understood in relation to projection. Projection is a differentiating process. It begins when the child acquires a sense of not-me and purifies the self by removing unpleasantness to the external world or to internal objects. Introjection, on the other hand, is an integrating process. Although its roots precede differentiation of self and object, introjection, or taking-in, is present only after there is at least a nascent self to take into and an object to take in from.

There is confusion in the object relations literature concerning the terminology of taking-in processes (Sandler and Rosenblatt 1962, Schafer 1968, Meissner 1981, and Boesky 1983). In general, four terms have come to the fore as central to the discussion of taking-in. Internalization refers to any mechanism for including something new within the person. In the category of internalization are incorporation, introjection, and identification, in ascending order of complexity and maturity. The emphasis in this section will be on introjection, the reciprocal of projection. The more primitive incorporation will also be briefly discussed here. Identification, other than defining it, will be discussed in a later section of this chapter.

Incorporation implies a psychological "eating" prior to the development of clear self–other boundaries. The object is taken in and disappears inside the nondifferentiated self–other matrix. A physiologic analogy is an infant sucking warm sweet milk at the breast. Milk comes in and disappears into the baby–mother symbiotic oneness. Some of the cannibalism fantasies described by Freud in "Totem and Taboo" (1913a) refer to incorporation. I have discussed a visual analogue to incorporation in psychotherapy and compared this phenomenon to the observation of a child (Hamilton 1981).

In psychotherapy, a psychotic patient mentioned that he had seen a small boy walking with his father and adopting his father's exact posture and gait. "That's how the boy learns," the patient said. "The father osmoses into the son and they become one." The patient saw this interaction in terms of incorporation. The actual external boy was probably identifying with his father, that is, being like his father, rather than becoming him; however, the patient saw the interaction in more primitive terms. For him, the boy did not act like his father, but actually merged with him. The self and object lacked any differentiation. Clinically, this example illustrates incorporation, which is thought to parallel similar psychological processes that may take place in the suckling infant. As Greenberg and Mitchell (1983) described it, "Experiences of gratification give rise to fantasies of merger; experiences of frustration lead to the wish to expel, to separate. Merger fantasies, which involve ideas of 'total incorporation,' of becoming the object, are the foundation of all subsequent object relations" (p. 315). Fairbairn (1941) called this "primary identification," but I prefer to reserve the term identification for a more mature process, which Fairbairn calls "secondary identification."

As with other psychological processes, incorporation does not simply disappear in infancy and reappear only in troubled patients. Millions of psychologically intact Christians display incorporation when they take Communion. In the Bible, incorporation is described as follows:

For my flesh is meat indeed, and my
blood is drink indeed.
He that eateth my flesh, and drinketh
my blood, dwelleth in me, and I in him.

John 6:55–56

When introjection supplants incorporation, self and object are somewhat internally differentiated so the internalized object can be held as an object-image rather than merged with the self-image. Sandler and Rosenblatt (1962) assumed at least this degree of differentiation when they defined introjection as vesting object-representations with the real and fantasied power and authority of the actual external parent. An introject is an internal object-image sufficiently vivid to have emotional power in the internal world. It is an object-image that is taken in, embraced, and held intact, rather than devoured.

To place introjection in clearer perspective, it may be useful to give a brief description of identification, which follows it developmentally. In identification, valued qualities of previously introjected object-images are attributed to self-images. Unlike incorporation, self- and object-images are maintained intact, compared, and contrasted. Boesky (1983) has commented that "Sandler, Jacobson, and Kernberg are in approximate agreement about viewing identification as the fusion of self-representations and images with object representations and images" (pp. 579–580). Boesky would concur that he did not mean "fusion" in this passage to imply the primitive merger of incorporation, but coming together in such a way that self- and object-images become similar, yet separate.

Related concepts can be found in Kohut's (1971) discussion of transmuting internalization and Giovacchini's (1979) description of the assimilation of maternal functions into the self (see also Tolpin 1971).

Introjection is sometimes not as obvious in psychotherapy as is projection because it is directed inward rather than outward. Furthermore, introjects often are not manifest until they become integrated and differentiated into more subtle identifications. Although evidence of introjection can be observed, especially in less differentiated patients, we must keep in mind that the same patients often distort their introjects in a poorly modulated fashion. The internal object introjected does not exactly correspond to the external object, but is colored by projections onto the external object before it is introjected.

Cameron (1961), in his paper on introjection and reprojection, described a 25-year-old teacher who struggled for many years with incapacitating self-criticism. She grew to know her therapist over several years and gradually introjected his more benign attitudes, which eventually helped her modulate her own self-critical attacks upon her every action, feeling, and thought. She reported this process by saying, "I've taken you inside . . . I don't have hallucinations or anything like that. But . . . sometimes you say positive things, or seem to have a positive attitude" (p. 91). Even when her therapist was not physically present, she experienced his presence within her. He reminded her of the good aspects of herself. She was sufficiently well differentiated that she did not hallucinate his voice, but experienced his presence as an internal object, within her yet distinguished from her self. She had not yet integrated this introject as an abstract, internal value system, or attitude of her own, but still experienced it as an object, nonself.

B.J., a 20-year-old woman entered a long-term unit of the Menninger Hospital for help with overwhelming panic. Her anxiety had been so intense that she could not sleep away from her parents and would go to any length to sneak into their room and sleep at the foot of their bed. Exasperated, her parents locked their door, only to find their tormented daughter curled up on the floor outside their door. She had such a need for closeness that nothing helped, not psychotherapy, family therapy, medication, or short-term hospitalization. She was referred to a long-term psychiatric unit.

In the hospital, her ward psychiatrist met with her daily and listened to her carefully. He seemed to understand her loneliness and longing. The nurses cared for her and helped her groom herself. They kept her busy with constructive activities. The patient developed a great admiration and fondness for her hospital psychiatrist. She clearly wished to please him. She followed his directions and reported all her activities to him. She followed his advice in a rote fashion; she apparently had not internalized and processed his suggestions as they suited her needs, but had taken them within herself and uncritically adopted them, as if he were inside her, directing her. This phenomenon is introjection.

When her psychiatrist moved to a new position on a different unit, B.J. symbolized her introjection poignantly. For several days, she retreated to her room and lay still. She did not keep her appointment with her new psychotherapist, who went to her room, escorted by a familiar nurse. He asked the patient if she missed her old doctor, and communicated to her the idea that she did not want to see her new doctor because it reminded her that her previous psychiatrist was no longer there.

The patient quickly replied that she did not miss her doctor and had no need for a new one. Her beloved doctor was inside her, in her womb. He had magically impregnated her, she said, and his son would be born to her; he would be just the same as her doctor. The stress of separation had evidently led to a psychotic episode in which she symbolized her introjection of her first therapist as an impregnation.

B.J. was a sexually mature woman whose longings to take in her doctor had an erotic quality. The more pertinent aspect of her needs and wishes, however, had to do with a basic need for closeness. Her new psychotherapist, therefore, did not interpret her oedipal longings to be impregnated by her therapist, who probably represented her father, whose bed she had previously tried to enter. Neither did he confront her psychotic denial of the loss of her doctor. Instead, he interpreted the introjection of her doctor. He said, "Yes, you have taken in some important and valuable things from your doctor and will always have those things with you. I will be interested to learn about them."

It is not known whether B.J. eventually integrated the caring and understanding of those around her into herself in a way that allowed her to care for and understand herself. This thoughtful therapist, however, helped her feel sufficiently understood and cared about that she could go to his office to talk rather than remain secluded in her room.

A less clear example related to introjection was presented in a conference by a male social worker trained in psychotherapy. He reported that three of his patients in the past year had grown beards similar to his. All were young men confused about who they were and who they wanted to become. Some participants in the seminar suggested that these men had introjected and adopted their therapist's characteristic grooming as a way of keeping the therapist with them from session to session. Others thought that it was identification that had motivated the growing of beards, because the patients had adopted an aspect of the therapist as an aspect of their self. Yet others considered such behavior to be imitation, which requires no significant alteration of internal self- and object-representations. Mimicry may, in fact, indicate a warding off of the wish to take in from a therapist by keeping the similarities at the self–other boundary, that is, at the body surface. The seminar participants finally agreed they could not know a patient's internal self- and object-world from observation of the external person alone. They would need to hear about fantasies and dreams and observe personal interactions in the therapy.

B.G.—described in Chapter 2 as shifting identities almost daily—provides a complex and yet clear example of introjection in his report of a dream:

After 18 months of twice-weekly psychotherapy, he had gradually slowed down in changing religions and jobs. He began a session by describing a dream in which he had a terrible rash and was covered with fleas. He was very sick, he said. He then dreamed that his therapist rubbed a good lotion over his entire body and examined him, especially looking into his mouth. The therapist fed him medicine, and he vomited a black, seething mass of worms, terrible parasites which came from the eggs of fleas. In the dream, the therapist was not shocked or frightened by the foul sight, but was clinically interested and glad to help.

The patient said he felt the fleas and worms represented his illness, his depression and suicidal self-destructiveness, which were eating him up. One of his associations to the worms was the biting sarcasm with which his mother had attacked his internal sense of self-esteem. He felt he had taken the sarcasm inside of him. The worms represented an introjected, bad part-object, that aspect of his mother which was harmful to his sense of self as a solid person. He said he was now going to a doctor, and he listened to the doctor's words and was getting better. In the dream, he introjected the care of his therapist, which also may have represented the previous good aspects of his mother's care.

As suggested in this example, bad object-representations can be introjected, just as can good object-representations. The internal criticizer, which many patients describe, is a bad introject. Hallucinations of voices attacking the patient are more extreme examples of bad introjects. Soldiers after combat often experience introjection of the enemy in repetitive nightmares and flashbacks. They cannot rid themselves of these internal objects and therefore fight their war over and over again, until they accept their enemy as an aspect of themselves. Following car accidents, many people fantasize and dream about dangerous objects bearing down on them. The dangerous object is a bad introject.

These observations of adults have parallels in early development. Although children cannot describe their fantasies, we can observe behaviors that imply an introjective process. Brazelton (1975) filmed 10-week-old infants vocalizing in a way similar to the cooing of an adult. They seemed to introject and then project the patterns of their external objects, creating a brief moment of dual unity (Blanck and Blanck 1979).

Mahler (1971) described imitation at a somewhat later age which suggested that introjection played a part in the behavior of one of the subjects of her study. This boy was catapulted into the practicing subphase when he walked early, at nine months. He took into his early ego structure[1] certain aspects of both his mother and his father. She described him as emulating his father by the second half of the first year, acting like him, but in an exaggerated way. Using the more detailed descriptions of internal processes that patients provide, we can speculate that this boy felt an increased aloneness and vulnerability when his precocious motor skills prematurely separated him from his parents. In a manner typical of practicing-subphase youngsters, he compensated for his loss with grandiosity. Projecting his

---

[1]Mahler's use of the word ego implies elements of both self and ego as used in this book.

omnipotent fantasies onto his father, he made a hero out of him. We could conclude that he then introjected his heroic image of his father and tried to match his behavior to this internal image.

Less pleasant characteristics of introjected objects can also be exaggerated. A mildly scolding father can be internalized as an attacking monster until the child is old enough to moderate his internal images through processes of differentiation and integration. Because of this tendency of young children to augment their experiences in an unmodulated fashion, we must temper our conclusions concerning the attributes of their actual external parents when hearing them described in therapy or in other settings.

Klein (1957b) relied on her observation of patients to suggest that the good (feeding, warm, sweet, full, present) breast is the first object of introjection, as well as of incorporation. The infant takes it into himself and feels held by it and secure. Because he holds the image intact and separate, this process is introjection, not incorporation, according to my usage. The introjected good object is the basis for all subsequent good object relationships and also for the ability to care for the self in Klein's schema. She used the term good breast in a specific and concrete way, which seems overly anatomical to many object relations theorists today. As Mahler's work illustrated, it is not only the mother's breast which is introjected, but also her visual presence, her smell, her voice, her taste, and especially her holding. In our culture, not only are these qualities of the mother introjected, but children also increasingly have opportunities to introject aspects of the father very early.

Evidence of introjection, which is found in infants and patients, can be found in the arts and letters and everyday life. Somerset Maugham (1944), for instance, recognized the importance of internalization:

> For men and women are not only themselves, they are also the region in which they were born, the city apartment or the farm in which they learned to walk, the games they played as children, the old wive's tales they overheard, the food they ate, the schools they attended, the sports they followed, the poets they read, and the God they believed in. [p. 2]

Wordsworth described an introject when he wrote of the lasting effect on his life of seeing a host of golden daffodils—

> For oft, when on my couch I lie
> In vacant or in pensive mood,
> They flash upon that inward eye . . .

Memorizing favorite poems or other quotations is a process of introjecting valued objects. In times of pain or loneliness, we can call up these good introjects and remind ourselves that wonder still exists.

At a storefront church on the south side of Chicago, I once heard the congregation sing over and over again, "Open up your heart and let Jesus come in." Here, the heart represents the loving self, and Jesus represents the good object which is to be introjected.

Taking photographs of family members, friends, and places where good times are shared and pasting them in albums parallels the psychological introjection of the good object and holding and cherishing that good object. When people feel lonely, they may take out their albums to remind themselves of the goodness they have taken into their lives.

A 3-year-old boy displayed a capacity to introject and reproject when his mother spent several nights away from home. After his father had given him a bath and read him a bedtime story, he still had trouble settling down to sleep. He was disappointed that his father did not know all the same songs his mother sang to him. Tossing and turning in his bed, he wrapped himself tightly in his blue quilt. He turned one more time and then began to sing very quietly. He sang of a green field and the colored flowers blooming in the field. It was the song his mother sang to him. Although he did not get the words just right, he had the tone and melody exactly. A look of contentment crossed his face, and he drifted off to sleep.

He had introjected his mother singing the song. When he missed her, he could recreate the song, singing the words to himself, and reintroject it by hearing it again. As he heard his own soothing song, it reinforced his internal image of his good mother, comforting him to sleep.

When he was a child, a man now 41 years old, ate breakfast with his father every morning. His father always read the newspaper and played the radio at the breakfast table. He talked to his son, commenting on the news and the events to come for the day. The newspaper was crisp and his white shirt was fresh, and the smell of orange juice and coffee and eggs was rich. Once grown, the man still made the transition from sleep and rest to the work day by reading the newspaper and listening to music.

He internalized his father's habits, a structure, as some would call it. In his daily life, he recreated this introject in the external world. By ordering the newspaper and turning on the radio and pouring the orange juice, he recreated around him his father's world. He took it in again—reading the paper, hearing the music, and tasting and smelling the orange juice and coffee and eggs.

Introjection in the arts and letters and everyday life, as well as in psychotherapy and early development, allows us to take in valued and sustaining relationships. These good internal objects serve us well.

SPLITTING

Splitting joins with projection and introjection as a major mental mechanism of object relations theory. According to Kernberg (1980), splitting is the active "keeping apart of contradictory experiences of the self and of significant others" (p. 6). These contradictory internal elements remain conscious, but are separated in time or space, and do not influence one another. Although splitting does not come into its own until the rapprochement subphase (Mahler et al. 1975), its anlage is found in symbiosis (Kernberg 1980).

Splitting can be particularly obvious in the psychotherapy of patients with borderline disorders.

W.J., a 29-year-old receptionist, who usually dressed chicly, came to a session wearing jeans and a wrinkled blouse. She plopped herself down, curled her feet up under herself in the chair, glared sullenly for a few minutes, sighed, and began, "I feel horrible and alone. No one understands me anyway. What's the use? I don't even know why I come here."

The patient was in an all-bad self–other state. She described her self as alone or abandoned. Her affect was horrible or bad. She described her objects as not understanding or as emotionally absent. All bad object relations units of this kind are sometimes termed the mother-of-separation. W.J. had not truly regressed to the symbiotic all-bad experience of crying out with pain, because she still used words to describe her feelings; but there certainly are parallels between what this patient described and what a cold, hungry, abandoned baby must feel.

Her therapist suggested, "You must be disappointed in me. You hired me to try to understand and help you. But you still feel like no one understands you."

"No, no," she said. "It's not you. You are the only one who cares. I feel so much better when I'm here. It's that bastard husband of mine—and my mother."

When the therapist recognized her disappointment, she no longer felt misunderstood and abandoned, in relation to him, at least. Although previously she had explicitly included him as not understanding her by saying "Nobody understands me," and "I don't even know why I come here," she now changed her mind without acknowledging the change at all. She shifted from an all-bad self-object state to an all-good self-object state in relation to the therapist; but she still split her object world and saw her husband and her mother as villains. The therapist in such circumstances must be modest enough not to accept this state of affairs as reality, or he will end up with a patient who seems to be doing better and better in therapy while her personal life continues to deteriorate. The technique of handling splitting will be discussed further in Chapter 14.

In the case of B.G., splitting was also apparent. He was so fragmented that early in therapy he changed jobs, friends, and religions almost daily; but he eventually began to experience his world as more orderly. He did not gradually integrate the various contradictory aspects of himself and his object world bit by bit. Instead, his life rather rapidly arranged itself into discrete good and bad areas. In the second year of therapy, he divided his world into those who were for him and those who were against him. Increasingly, he idealized his therapist. He was convinced everything his therapist said was tactful, correct, and wise. Other people, who were trying to help him, he saw as hostile, or at best, neglectful and ignorant.

B.G. applied for vocational training from an agency, which assigned a sincere and interested counselor. When the counselor tried to help him persist with the frustrating tasks of work, B.G. became indignant. Session after session he railed at his therapist about how his counselor was unthoughtful, unhelpful, selfish, and professionally negligent. If the therapist pointed out the difficulty B.G. had recognizing his counselor's good will and efforts, the patient became enraged. If the therapist suggested that he had difficulty recognizing the therapist's limitations, B.G. similarly became enraged.

It was imperative for this patient to protect his therapy from any hint of disappointment. It was as if his good self-object experience was so tenuous that it had to be protected from any bad feelings, as if his bad feelings threatened to swallow up whatever good he was struggling to maintain.

This patient could be most destructive toward what he perceived to be his bad objects. He began gathering evidence to start a class-action suit against the agency. Fortunately, the therapist succeeded in helping the patient desist from this destructive act. The patient would have had no help with his vocational training if he had chosen litigation. He had not considered this problem because he had the fantasy that his all-good object, the therapist, would magically make the hard work of vocational training unnecessary. Despite the troublesomeness of this splitting, however, it did help him hold on to a sense of goodness and well-being in the therapy which he so desperately needed. It helped him organize his world a little better. At least he no longer had to jump from one thing to another daily. Later, he was able to start differentiating and integrating his good and bad experiences.

A particularly common type of splitting seen in therapy is between the good therapist and the bad spouse. Day after day, the therapist hears how understanding and helpful he or she is while the patient's spouse is portrayed as an insensitive, verbally abusive, and neglectful person. This form of splitting can be most difficult to sort out because the external situation may correspond to the internal split object relations to some degree.

In combined individual therapy and hospital treatment, the patient's split view of some staff members as all good and others as all bad has been well described (Burnham 1966, Adler 1977, Gabbard 1986). Frequent discussions among staff members and with consultants have demonstrated that even though differences among staff members do exist, they are exaggerated by patients, who have predominantly split internal object relations. These patients need to maintain the fantasy that there are totally good relationships available to them. To maintain this cherished belief, they must project unpleasantness outside their all-good relationships, thus splitting their experiential world in two.

In child development there are clear parallels to splitting observed in the treatment of adults. When a child feels warm, fed, and held, he seems to enter into those blissful merger states that correspond to the all-good object relations unit. Most authors focus on symbiosis as such a blissful unity of warm, nurturing closeness. During this period of dyadic unity, however, what happens when pain, hunger, or fear overwhelms the mother–child unit? Undoubtedly, the infant cannot differentiate self from object during pain states, either. If the child is racked with an excruciating middle ear infection, if his bowels churn with gastroenteritis, if the skin of his buttocks burns and itches with yeast infection, he must feel pain within himself and his undifferentiated surround. Since mother has become a major pole of his self–other experience, he probably feels this badness in her as well as in himself. Unpleasant symbiotic experiences are thought to be the basis for what later forms the bad object relations unit, whereas pleasant symbiotic experiences are thought to be the basis for what becomes the good object relations unit. However, it is not until self and object, pleasure and pain, good and bad are partially differentiated during rapprochement that splitting takes its complete form.

Mahler and colleagues (1975) described splitting as particularly common among rapprochement children whose mothers left them with observers. The observer might represent either the good or bad object. If the child happened to settle on her as good, he might cuddle up against her and mold into her. The mother's return would seem to interfere with the "good" symbiotic relationship under such circumstances and remind the child of the mother-of-absence, the "bad" or frustrating mother. The child might ignore or actively reject her. These parallels between rapprochement-subphase splitting and splitting among borderline patients have led to the conclusion that the former is the forerunner of the latter (Mahler 1971).

Kernberg (1980), among others, considers splitting to be characteristic of small children and severely disturbed adults. He has, however, commented that groups of people often show more primitive psychological functioning than do their individual members (Kernberg 1981). His finding may explain why evidence of splitting can be found so easily in entertainment, the arts and letters, religion, and public life. It is also possible that splitting is more common among well-adjusted people than was at first recognized.

A nursery rhyme describes splitting:

There was a little girl
Who had a little curl
Right in the middle of her forehead.
And when she was good,

She was very, very good,
And when she was bad, she was horrid.

The curl in the middle of her forehead symbolizes the divided self, and the little girl is described in all-good and all-bad terms.

Robert Louis Stevenson's *Doctor Jekyll and Mr. Hyde* provides an even more cogent description of splitting. In this tale the good doctor turns into a vicious and depraved villain and back again with little experiential continuity between the two states. Perhaps this story is fascinating because it describes in extreme form the reader's own archaic propensities for splitting.

Children in neighborhoods across the country have collections of six-inch plastic figures. There are potentially an infinite variety of them, but the youngsters categorize them into only two camps—good and bad.

"I've got Lizard Man. He's bad," one boy shouts.

"And I've got Hammerhead. He's good," another replies.

For hours, they can entertain one another with their fantasies about these figures. There are muscular, attractive heroes and voluptuous, powerful heroines. There are bat-winged heroes, spider heroes, mild-mannered heroes, queens of the ice, shooting star women, wonder heroines, and cyclonic powermen. In the bad camp, there are bone-faced monsters of incredible wickedness, alligator men, evil sorceresses, cat women, snake people, and all manner of troublemakers. There is no great difference between these games and the games of cowboys and Indians, tinged with racism, played by their parents. In the nineteenth century, children collected tin soldiers representing Yankees and Rebels, British and French, or Russians and Turks.

The good and bad objects in play evolve as children mature. Twelve-year-olds sometimes begin playing fantasy games, such as Champions. The characters are somewhat more complex and ambiguous than the plastic figures of the younger set. Good cannot be readily distinguished from bad, but it is the same principle: good us against bad them. Chess is a more abstract game, but it is still one side against the other.

I watched eleven boys chosen for a league soccer team. Although most of them did not know one another at first, they soon welded themselves into a functioning unit. It was "them against us," and wholesome bonds were formed. The boys took pride in themselves and one another and strove valiantly to defeat the opponent. The competition was intense. When the games were over, they were able to drop their rivalry with a created enemy. In sportsman-like fashion, they could shake hands and congratulate the other team.

With adults play is not always so clearly play. Sometimes the fans of professional soccer teams, divided into two camps equally loyal to their own side, forget they are watching a game. Violence and riots often erupt. Alcohol may impair their integrative ego functions. It is then that splitting gets out of hand.

Splitting the world into good and bad camps is not only motivated by inherent destructive tendencies. It is equally motivated by loyalty to good internal objects and the good people with whom we identify. This protection of the good object can always be detected in splitting. For example, during the week of February 16, 1986, when the residents of communities throughout northern California faced sudden floods, they joined forces. The Yuba, Feather, Mokelumne, Sacramento, San Joaquin, Napa, and Russian Rivers overflowed. Citizens of the valleys fought back to protect their families and neighbors. They rebuilt levees, evacuated the stranded, created shelters, and brought relief to the destitute. They were for one another and against the river. Some anger and resentment was directed against other people, such as the Army Corps of Engineers. Most of the initial efforts, however, were in the direction of banding together. It was not an appropriate time for speculating about how, in the natural course of things, rivers replenish and fertilize the earth by flooding across valleys. It was not time for the height of integrated thinking. It was time to take sides with the common good against a common enemy. This constructive behavior is akin to splitting.

During World War II, London suffered bombings. Men and women formed intense and quick attachments. When an external danger is so obvious, good and loving feelings become more available as the opposite pole of an all-bad object. Even in peaceful times, couples often cement their relationships by taking on a common adversary; they avoid the mundane world, because it intrudes on their good relationship. This is the "desert island" phenomenon of lovers. It shifts sooner or later. They support one another in establishing their careers and their family. They are in the world together, and to some extent against the world, because they must compete for jobs, security, and home, and must protect one another.

These loyalties to family, friends, and neighbors, to school and team, can apply to town, state, political parties, and countries, and even to ideologies and philosophies. It is Democrats against Republicans, liberals against conservatives, capitalists against communists, democracy against dictatorship. This divisive tendency stems from an adversarial position, but also from a loyalty to one's own choice. It is one of our deepest needs to attach to individuals, groups, or ideologies, and to protect that attachment by building boundaries against the outside, the foreign, the dangerous.

Splitting in the more global sense, then, is not only a destructive, infantile failure to see the larger picture. It plays an important role in the establishment of love relationships, family fealty, loyal friendships, patriotism, and dedication to a cause. Splitting both binds societies together and tears them apart.

Although splitting is a widely used term with numerous applications, some authors question its appropriateness as a technical term. Pruyser (1975) has pointed out difficulties in the application of this word to the ego and the self. Furthermore, while splitting of object relations units has been emphasized here, splitting can refer to dividing the object world into all-good and all-bad, heroes and villains, without reference to splitting the self-experience. Other times splitting can pertain to the self without reference to splits in the object world.

IDEALIZATION AND DEVALUATION

Idealization and devaluation are akin to splitting, but involve a slightly different arrangement of self- and object-experiences. As differentiation of self and other, good and bad take place, four potential units of interaction develop. Good self, bad self, good object, and bad object can be arranged in various combinations. In splitting, differentiation takes place along good–bad lines, with the good self and object combined as one unit and the bad self and object combined as another unit. In idealization and devaluation, good and self are combined as one unit and bad and object are combined as another unit, or vice versa.

Split Object Relations Units

Good Self – Good Object
Bad Self – Bad Object

Idealized – Devalued Object Relations Units

Good Self – Bad Object
Bad Self – Good Object

In therapy, the patient may at one time feel dependent, sick, and in need of help from a powerful, idealized healer who can bring him health. At another time, the polarity may reverse, and the patient may experience himself as having no problems and the therapist as unnecessary, or even worthless and incompetent. What distinguishes such shifts in idealization and devaluation from everyday fluctuations in valuing aspects of self and others is the extremity of the feelings. As the names imply, idealization refers to seeing self or object as perfect, and devaluation refers to seeing them as worthless. Because of its extreme polarity, idealization-devaluation is an unstable psychological mechanism, as is splitting.

In the experience of many therapists, patients have come to them complaining that their previous therapists were incompetent—but now they have found the only one who can help them. Regardless of the idealized therapists' external qualities, however, they will eventually come to be devalued by the same patients who idealized them.

M.J., a 26-year-old woman, met with a young female psychologist for the first time. She complained of occasionally feeling unreal and frequently feeling depressed and suicidal. She had been to three male psychiatrists. One had tried to give her medications, which she experienced as an insulting intrusion. The other two simply did not understand her. She did not want to go to another psychiatrist, because they were insensitive doctors who just treat crazy people. She didn't want to go to a male psychologist, because men could not possibly understand women's problems.

The psychotherapist warned the patient, "At some point you may become disappointed in me, too. That's sometimes a part of therapy. If that happens, you will need to discuss it with me and try to stick with your therapy if you can."

"Oh, of course," the patient replied. "I can talk with you about anything." Undaunted, she went on describing how wonderful the therapist was and how she would soon be feeling much better.

Such predictions as this psychologist made often help the patient stay in therapy. With M.J., however, it was not enough. Within six weeks, she declared that she was cured. She was going to quit treatment. Therapy had been interesting, but unhelpful. What had helped was a book on how to eliminate guilt feelings. Now she was free of guilt and her life was wonderful. New vistas opened before her—perhaps the psychotherapist could benefit from reading the book? The extent of how much she now devalued her therapy became manifest in her refusal to pay her bill. The previously idealized therapist was no longer worth anything.

On inpatient units, the vicissitudes of idealization and devaluation can be both painfully clear and unavoidable. Patients frequently come to the hospital afraid, hurt, depressed, and confused. Under such circumstances, they may idealize the psychiatrists and nurses. Soon, however, staff members must frustrate omnipotent wishes for security or pleasure, and the tables turn. Patients at such times can become superior and condescending. They no longer feel a need for anything from the hospital. They forget that not too long ago they were in desperate need of help.

F.D., a 34-year-old man, had made a moderately successful career for himself as an entertainer in southern California. He had become despondent when his addiction to cocaine and opiates resulted in loss of his wife and child and all his property. After a six-week treatment for addiction, he remained depressed and entered long-term hospital treatment. He said he had felt depressed and empty most of his life and used drugs to overcome these feelings. He needed extensive treatment. He chose a prestigious long-term psychiatric hospital with the firm conviction that the esteemed professionals there could help him with his feelings of depletion.

Within weeks, he began to wonder if he might need to supplement his treatment with a special physical fitness regimen. Although there were organized athletics at the hospital, they would not suffice. He needed to go to the best program downtown—why should he settle for second best?

The psychiatrist and other team clinicians at first agreed that the patient needed to stay within the confines of the established program. At this suggestion, F.D. became superior and condescending in patient meetings. He considered the other patients sicker than he was. He believed the doctors and nurses were deluded by a rigid theoretical system and did not realize that abstinence from drug abuse, attendance at Narcotics Anonymous, and a physical fitness program alone would help him. He was a drug addict, and he knew his illness best. Only other drug addicts could understand.

Rather than opposing the patient's wishes further, the psychiatrist empathized with his indignation. He feared that to insist the patient stay exactly within the prescribed program would lead to his feeling even more devalued. In turn, F.D. might have to try even harder to devalue his treatment and to idealize his own plan. The psychiatrist empathized by saying, "How disappointed in me you must have been when I didn't recognize how necessary it is for you to feel a bit special, as all people need to feel special at times. We have decided that it might be better to allow you to attend the program downtown, but I would like you to think about its implication for your treatment a few more days."

Within this intervention, F.D. returned to idealizing his psychiatrist. Only this psychiatrist and this treatment team would be thoughtful enough to correct a mistake. The patient thought it was now even more clear how especially humane the hospital staff was. He would defer to his good doctor's wisdom and wait not only a few days, but a few weeks until he was ready to go downtown to the fitness program.

By empathizing with the patient's reaction to what he experienced as a failure in empathy, an idealizing transference (Kohut 1971) was reestablished. F.D. had to go through several more cycles of idealization and devaluation before he could leave the hospital with his feelings of emptiness and craving for narcotics under better control.

As in F.D.'s case, cycles of idealization and devaluation are particularly common with narcotics addicts. They often describe how they feel so depleted, empty, and worthless without their idealized drug that they will throw away everything else to get it. Family, friends, work, money, and health are all sacrificed for the precious drug. After they get their intoxicant and extract the warmth and security they seek from it, they discard the container, the paper, syringe, or spoon, now empty and worthless. Sometimes the drug also seems worthless, and they may decide to stop using it. As soon as they begin to feel worthless again, however, the drug once more becomes the paramount concern in their lives; they feel valueless without it. The cycle continues.

Such a psychological explanation of idealization and devaluation is not at odds with the physiological understanding of addiction. Physiological changes have their psychodynamics, too. It is interesting, however, that many addicted patients, like F.D., continue cycles of idealization and devaluation even when they are not addicted. For such patients, one could speculate that their tendency to idealize and devalue led to the addiction. In the case of other patients, one suspects that idealization and devaluation are manifestations of addiction rather than causes of it.

Idealization and devaluing can be observed in rapprochement-subphase children.

> During a family gathering, a 2½-year-old girl first became crushed with rejection and then recovered from her disappointment. With a sparkle in her eye, she started to climb up the kitchen cupboards to reach a shiny vase. "No, no!" her mother called and took her down. Humiliated, she flopped on the floor, pouting and dejected. Within a few minutes, she began looking around, got up, walked to the living room, and deliberately sought out her bottle and blanket. Her eyes lit up when she found the valued objects. With eagerness she plopped down on the spot, sucking from the bottle and wrapping herself in the blanket. After a few moments' nurturance from her beloved bottle, she was finished. She stood up decisively, dropped her blanket at her feet, looked disdainfully at the bottle, and contemptuously flung it behind her. Full of life, she again started cruising among the guests, entertaining everyone.

In this example, the child saw the vase as a valued object. When her busy mother abruptly foiled her plans, the child's self-esteem seemed hurt. She threw herself on the floor as if devaluing herself. Apparently, she soon thought of her bottle and blanket as idealized objects, because her eyes lit up when she sought and found them, just as they had when she reached for the vase. After she had sucked for a while, her devalued self-image—which could be deduced from her humiliated facial expression—shifted. She again seemed full of vigor. She was the life of the party. The previously valued bottle was now worthless. With the contempt she had just seemed to have for herself, she now discarded the empty container.

By studying the vicissitudes of idealization and devaluation in children, Klein (1957a) and her students delineated the dynamics of envy. She described complex mental interactions between self and object at a mental age before the time at which children can readily distinguish self and object, as Mahler's studies indicate. Although her chronology is undoubtedly condensed, her insights into how children idealize and devalue the desired object have provided a framework for understanding many difficult therapeutic dilemmas. Typical of Klein, she described how a child can feel empty, hungry, and depleted. The self is devalued under such circumstances. While feeling this hunger and an aggressive wish to feed, the child sees the breast as full of warm goodness. It is idealized. According to Klein's schema, the child not only greedily wants to feed at the good breast, but also to project his unwanted pain and anger into it, replacing the good milk with badness, emptiness, and hostility. The badness of the self-image is exchanged thereby with the goodness of the object-image, so that the self is good and the object is bad, empty, and worthless. Idealization is replaced with devaluation. Klein actually claimed that children in the first few months of life feel they are replacing the good milk with bad feces and smearing it. Probably, however, children do not attain a fascination with feces and a sense of excrement as devalued until the second year of life, nor are they capable of such complex mental conceptualization as this vengeful scenario portrays. Thus, even though the idea of envy, with the exchange of idealization and devaluation, is useful in relation to older children and adults, Klein's chronology confuses information derived from the fantasies of older children with the chronology of normal development.

In various cultures, as Frazer (1890) described in *The Golden Bough*, a stranger would be selected to be a king or deity. This exalted personage was kept in the lap of luxury, pampered, and idolized, until it was time for the annual renewal ritual. He was then sacrificed and buried in the ground. Although we do not have access to the fantasies of such peoples, practices of this sort do strike one as alternating idealization and devaluation. In a less extreme way, most people become subject to fads. Throughout the history of civilization, people who could afford them have felt compelled to acquire the latest style of clothing, type of food or liquor, or model of car, only to find these quite outdated the next year. This behavior does seem similar to idealization and devaluation.

Even in the psychological sciences, there are fads. One year one set of theories is idealized, only to be devalued the next. I remember Dr. Ann Appelbaum, a child psychoanalyst, telling a group of argumentative psychiatry residents, "The reason many people condemn and devalue all of Freud's work may be that they have so idealized the innovator that they can't forgive him for not knowing everything. What they have idealized, they now devalue."[2]

PROJECTIVE IDENTIFICATION

In projective identification, an aspect of the self is first projected onto the object. Then, the subject attempts to control the projected aspect

---

[2]Appelbaum 1979, personal communication.

of the self in the object. By attempting to control his own attribute in the object, the subject betrays that at some level he is aware that the projected aspect of himself pertains to him. Projective identification is difficult to understand, because mental processes that, if considered logically, are mutually exclusive, take place simultaneously.

F.Y., a 32-year-old woman who entered all-good and all-bad self–other states (Chapter 3), began a session complaining that her psychiatrist had forgotten to refill her medications. She complained that her husband wanted her to stay home with the family on Saturday. Altough she had spent each evening in dance class, away from the children, she felt he would not do his share of the child care. Her Easter had been empty and unfulfilling. Her parents were dead. The cemetary caretakers had not trimmed around the graves. She felt neglected and abandoned.

The psychotherapist began asking for clarification of these issues in the latter part of the session. He asked her to look at her prescription bottle. She found five refills available, but still felt he should have reminded her. He decided not to tell her that he clearly remembered reminding her; instead, he merely said, "It sounds like you don't feel very cared for. It must have been hard for you. How long were you out of medicine?"

She mentioned that she had run out prior to the last appointment and had not mentioned it. Neither had she called. She had been so busy. Her children were demanding and ungrateful. They wanted her to pick up after them, feed them, entertain them, and buy them new toys when they did not even care for the toys they had. "Sometimes I wish I could be rid of them. I had such a wonderful time with my friend. She is single and doesn't have any children. I wouldn't feel that way if someone would help me out every now and then; but when I don't get any help, I feel like leaving."

F.Y. felt like neglecting others. She attributed this quality of herself to her husband and her therapist, which was a projection. She then reidentified with the projected aspect of herself and said that she did feel neglectful, but only because others were neglecting her. This process is projective identification.

The patient's therapist and husband both may or may not have been attentive at times; but evidence existed that they did provide some assistance to her. The husband had helped with the children so the patient could go to dance class. The therapist had prescribed refills and was available for phone calls. The patient ignored these actions and saw her own wishes to abandon her parenting functions as stemming from people around her.

Toward the end of the hour the patient said, "I won't be able to be here next week. I have a luncheon appointment with a friend. I suppose it doesn't matter anyway, because I will be on vacation the next two weeks. There's no harm in getting started a little early."

A feeling of dejection arose in the therapist. He felt cast off and unimportant. "If I'm the only one committed to this therapy," he thought, "it won't work. We might as well stop now." He realized that he was feeling precisely the way the patient must have felt. She had behaved in such a way as to elicit feelings of being neglected, which corresponded to her own, in the therapist. He could now more deeply empathize with how abandoned she felt and how she felt like discarding people because there was no hope for mutually gratifying relationships. He would need to wait three weeks, until she returned, to use this deeper insight.

Confusion over who is doing what to whom in projective identification has led to debate about the concept. Numerous authors, such as Klein (1946), Bion (957), Kernberg (1965), Ogden (1979, 1982), Grotstein (1981a), Rosenfeld (1983), Spillius (1983), and Hamilton (1986), have found the concept useful. Other authors, such as Meissner (1980), have preferred to divide projective identification into elements of projection and introjection. Spillius (1983) and Grotstein (1981a) consider all projections to be equivalent to projective identification. Kernberg (1976) distinguished between projection and projective identification.

For those who distinguish between projective identification and projection, in pure projection the unwanted aspect of the self is experienced as entirely alien. In projective identification, the denied aspect of the self is simultaneously experienced as part of the self. For example, a paranoid schizophrenic patient who projects his destructive potential onto conspirators does not feel any hatred. He will usually feel entirely innocent. On the other hand, a patient with borderline personality who engages in projective identification may feel that his friend is angry at him and simultaneously feel angry at his friend for feeling angry at him. Thus, in projective identification, there is some retained experience of the projected aspect of the self pertaining to one's own person.

Kernberg (1986) considers projection a more mature mechanism than projective identification. He believes the self–other boundary blurring and the intense eliciting of emotional reaction in the object during projective identification to be more closely related to symbiosis than to more differentiated states. Projection, then, implies greater self–object differentiation in Kernberg's view.

I hold the opinion, contrary to Kernberg's, that projective identification is a more mature mechanism than pure projection. This is based on both a theoretical and a clinical consideration. From a theoretical perspective, projection entails a firm, unshaken belief that an aspect of the self is in another person, without even dawning awareness that it is also an aspect of the self. In projective identification, the denial of an aspect of the self cannot entirely overcome an increasingly accurate sense that the unwanted aspect is still part of the self. This self–other haziness represents the part-self-, part-object experience of developing differentiation and integration. It can be related to transitional object formation during rapprochement, which will be discussed in the next section of this chapter.

On clinical grounds, pure projection is more often found in schizophrenic and paranoid psychotic patients, who are less differentiated, than in borderline patients. By contrast, borderline patients more often use projective identification than pure projection, and they are better able to maintain a conventional sense of reality than are psychotic patients. Since more differentiated and integrated patients use projective identification, the mechanism seems to be a more mature one. This point, however, is still controversial.

Clarification of projective identification has been furthered by Ogden (1979, 1982), who commented on both interpersonal and intrapsychic aspects of this phenomenon. The intrapsychic process takes place in the patient's fantasy and is consistent with the definition provided at the beginning of this chapter. The subject experiences within his own mind an aspect of his self in the object, and then tries to control that aspect of the self in the object. The interpersonal process is parallel to the intrapsychic phenomenon. Here, however, there must be another person involved. In the psychotherapy situation, a patient subtly behaves toward the therapist in such a way as to elicit certain affects in the therapist. The empathically attuned clinician may then find himself feeling and behaving in uncharacteristic ways. The patient actually elicits the unwanted feeling in the therapist. As Kernberg (1965), Grinberg

(1979), and others have pointed out, such feelings in the therapist can provide important information about the patient's deepest and most disturbing affects.

In the example of F.Y. who felt neglected and neglectful, as long as the therapist was benignly and empathically interested, the projective identification was intrapsychic. She saw her therapist, like her husband, as uncaring and unhelpful when he was not feeling or behaving in such a way. The patient wanted to escape her commitments to her husband, her children, and her therapy. Late in the therapy hour, the situation shifted. By then, she had elicited from the therapist an emotion corresponding to her own feelings. He felt for a moment as if he were neglected and should give up on the treatment. This latter process is interpersonal projective identification.

When discussing interpersonal projective identification, we must be careful to shift our phrasing. Klein (1946) used the phrase "projecting into" to suggest that patients actually fantasize putting something into the body of the therapist; therefore, "projecting onto" the therapist does not reflect the psychic reality of an intrusive fantasy. When we shift from Klein's description of a patient's internal fantasy world to an interpersonal process, however, using "projecting into" confuses the issue and smacks of a magical transfer of feeling states. For example, a psychoanalyst talking with a colleague said, "Actually, that was not my feeling. The patient projected it into me." The feeling being disavowed was, of course, the analyst's own feeling. The patient may have elicited it from him and may have been able to behave in such a way as to elicit such a feeling from most people, but it was still the therapist's feeling. Perhaps psychotherapists so commonly refer to patients projecting their feelings into clinicians because most psychotherapists are not comfortable with the intensity of emotions which can arise in many treatments. Furthermore, patients can interact with therapists in such a compelling fashion that the therapist's subjective experience is that of having something forcibly put into him. The patient is, however, actually eliciting an all-too-human feeling from the therapist rather than putting that feeling into him. This distinction is important because psychotherapists must take care to sort out within themselves what pertains to whom, especially when working with self–other disturbed patients. It is accurate to refer to a patient's eliciting feelings from therapists in interpersonal projective identification, while they may simultaneously have intrapsychic fantasies about projecting something onto the therapist.

Another example of interpersonal projective identification arose in a seminar on emergency psychiatry. One of the more accomplished and mature psychiatry residents described an interchange with a habitual visitor to the emergency room.

"Most of you know B.B.," he began. "He's back. He's been in the last three nights in a row. His needs seem urgent, yet nothing I do helps. I don't know what to try next."

The resident already conveyed a sense of urgency to his colleagues. He had even indicated that their suggestions probably would not help much either. One could suspect that the patient had induced these feelings of urgency and helplessness in the psychiatrist. This process would be interpersonal projective identification. The resident went on:

"B.B. launched into another tirade about how the hotel manager was poisoning him. You've probably heard the story; but as usual, he had to do something about it right then, that night, at two o'clock in the morning. He said I had to find him another place to stay, but not in the hospital. He had thought of going to his sister's, but she would make him go to the hospital. He had thought of killing the hotel manager while he slept behind the desk. But then, what was the use, he said, because 'the organization' would just send another minion to harass him. He was thinking of suicide, but he knew if he failed, he would end up in the hospital. By the time I had heard all this, I had lost my feeling that I could help. I get so discouraged with these guys. I have no idea what to do about patients like this."

During the ensuing discussion, all the participants described similar experiences of feeling drained, worthless, helpless, and stuck. These competent and normally effective doctors had taken on a feeling that would be more appropriate to their patients' circumstances than to their own. It was the patient who was psychotic, malnourished, ill-housed, and neglected; yet it was the doctor who was feeling dejected and discouraged.

As the discussion proceeded, the residents speculated that the patient may have elicited despair in the psychiatrist by repeatedly demanding help and then rejecting it. They decided it might be worthwhile to help B.B. recognize his own despair rather than try to assist him more directly.

Two evenings later B.B. returned to the emergency room. The resident listened to his story once again. When the patient paused, the doctor said, "I know, Mr. B., how discouraged and alone you must feel." The patient nodded slightly and looked down at his hands. The doctor went on, "I'm very sorry I can't help you as much as I would like. Perhaps I could try to understand your situation better, though. Could you come by my office tomorrow so I could give it a try?"

The patient sat back in his chair, looked perplexed a moment, and said, "Okay, but it won't help."

The next week, when the conference participants heard this report, they wagered that the patient would not keep the appointment. As it turned out, he did keep it, and he kept the one after that. Understanding the concept of projective identification had helped the resident overcome the discouragement which the patient had drawn forth from him. He was able to use an awareness of his sense of helplessness to make empathic contact with the patient and to help him with his despair.

Hostile feelings are most frequently described in relation to projective identification, perhaps because aggressive feelings are most noticeable and disturbing to psychotherapists. Projective identification can, however, also involve positive or loving feelings (Klein 1957b). I have termed this phenomenon *positive projective identification* (Hamilton 1986).

A.M.,[3] a 29-year-old man with schizophrenia, provided an example of positive projective identification. He had maintained the delusion of being a CIA agent for several years. Over the preceding few months, he had been able to forgo his delusion for as long as two days at a time. When not preoccupied with this exciting and frightening fantasy, he felt empty, alone, and meaningless. His only respite from these feelings came during brief periods in psychotherapy sessions. During those moments, he experienced himself as a disturbed and yet valuable human being who was positively regarded by his psychotherapist and who had hope for recovery.

As he entered the office one gray, spring day, his facial expression was downcast. He usually wore wrinkled fatigues; that day he wore pressed, new jeans and a sportshirt. His hair was neatly parted. His therapist greeted him in his usual fashion. The patient shook hands and sat down.

---

[3]A version of this example has already been published (Hamilton 1986).

The patient announced that he had not had delusions for two days. Immediately, he went on to say he did not like coming downtown. Since downtown was the location of the therapist's office, he thought this statement might be an allusion to the patient's disliking therapy, perhaps for playing a role in his giving up his cherished fantasy about the CIA. Allowing the patient to elaborate, the therapist merely said, "You particularly did not like downtown today."

A.M. described how, as he walked to his session through the busy streets, people would not look him in the eye. He felt worthless being downtown. If only people would look at him, he would have a chance. "When people look at you and you look them in the eye and smile and act friendly, they become the nicest little love dolls."

His affect was genuinely warm and engaging for a few minutes, although it was usually plastic. His eyes sparkled, and the therapist felt warm and caring in return.

"Yes," the therapist said, "you want to have some friends and to care about people and to be cared about in return."

The patient glowed. His warmth turned to adoration. Uncomfortable with the adoration and fearing he would fail the patient, the psychiatrist experienced a twinge of anxiety. Suddenly, the patient appeared confused.

As the psychotherapist quickly mastered his anxiety, the patient seemed to regain his confidence.

"I am learning to relate to people a little bit, aren't I?" the patient said.

"Yes, you are."

"I think I will get over this schizophrenia, maybe by next year," he added.

During the rest of the session, the patient discussed his concerns with the tasks of day-to-day living and his plans for the future.

The patient stated he had temporarily given up his frightening and exciting delusion about the CIA. This delusion had been the very stuff of his daily existence. The enemies of the CIA were the all-bad, persecuting objects. His self-concept as a secret agent constituted the all-good, omnipotent self. Having recently forgone this internal life of intrigue between the forces of good and evil, he had nothing left. He felt empty, meaningless, and alone. Yet, he had a spark of longing for love and companionship.

When he conceptualized himself as capable of friendliness, he projected this good and loving self-representation onto the passersby. That way, he did not feel quite so alone. Some object relations theorists would suggest that he projected his good feelings to protect them, to get them away from his all-bad, empty feelings, to keep them from being swallowed up by his emptiness. Some patients will describe feeling as if they are doing precisely that. In A.M.'s case, he was primarily motivated by his wishes for closeness.

While the patient projected his feelings, he also retained a partial identification with the projected aspect of himself. This blurring of self–other boundaries was evident when he said he could actually make the strangers become "the nicest little love dolls." The idea that one can influence the feelings of others just by changing oneself and without interacting with the other people indicates that the subject has confused altering the self with altering another person. This process was intrapsychic positive projective identification. It was the patient's fantasy; the strangers were unaffected by it.

In the therapy, however, the patient had a relationship. With his tone of voice, gestures, and facial expression, he elicited a warm feeling and response from his psychotherapist. This process was interpersonal as well as intrapsychic projective identification.

Projective identification is thought to play a part in the alternately affectionate and coercive behavior of rapprochement-subphase children. As they evolve out of symbiosis, they begin to distinguish self from object. They also distinguish pleasure from pain, good from bad. This differentiation is partial, as is the integration of their self- and object-images. Consequently, children can easily attribute their own feelings to their parent and try to control those feelings in that parent. Mahler and colleagues (1975) commented on such coercive behavior as characteristic of rapprochement-subphase children.

Projective identification may also play a role in the development of a capacity for sympathy at this age. The child may see a parent's sad facial expression. Identifying with the parent, he or she too can call up a sad feeling. Perhaps the parent is conveying the feeling to the child through projective identification at this point. If the child is sufficiently differentiated at this age, however, he realizes it is his parent who is sad. He may then reproject his own sad feeling onto his parent and attempt to control it by consoling the love object. Thereby, children learn to sympathize. Similarly, projective identification can be seen to play a part when children, or adults for that matter, share in one another's happiness. This capacity for emotional responsivity begins during the rapprochement subphase.

We can also see evidence of projective identification in our everyday lives.

A dark-haired, bright-eyed 12-year-old girl wrote secretly at her desk while her teacher drew a map on the blackboard. She composed two notes. One she slipped to Jennifer, the other to Edward. "Eddie told me he likes you," Jennifer's note said. The other note claimed, "Jenny told me she likes you." Although Edward and Jennifer had not previously thought of one another romantically, a mutual infatuation soon blossomed, much to the delight of their friend who had passed them notes.

The matchmaker started a process of mutual, positive projective identification between Jennifer and Edward. She sent a positive expectation to each. It is understandable that they would take in this good news, augment it with their own capacity for fondness, and return one another's presumed affection. When each thought that the other had feelings of fondness, that feeling was projected onto the other person. They acted in such a way as to elicit a return of positive emotion. This process is projective identification. The example is complicated by the matchmaker acting as a go-between and possibly projecting her own infatuations onto her friends, or at least eliciting those feelings.

Numerous self-improvement books have emphasized the power of positive attitudes in human affairs. Norman Vincent Peale (1952) described the power of "positive thinking," and Dale Carnegie pointed out the usefulness of commenting on people's strengths in his book *How to Win Friends and Influence People* (1936). In his text on public speaking, Carnegie (1926) suggested that the speaker assume the audience is interested in what he has to say and that they like him. He should even imagine an important and approving friend or relative in the audience. He should speak to that person, because when you behave familiarly and positively to your audience, they respond in kind.

In Carnegie's example, the friendly person whom the speaker imagines in the audience is an approving and confirming *selfobject*, to use Kohut's (1971) term a bit loosely.[4] The speaker projects this

---

[4]Kohut's term "selfobject" usually refers to an external person who fills a vital function for the subject's self, such as supplying confirmation, approval, and esteem. On the other hand, in this book, "self–object" refers to an aspect of the self-image blurred with aspects of an internal object-image; the role of an actual external person is not emphasized. The two terms, selfobject and self–object, are brought together in a way that may, at first, be a bit confusing. Here, the fantasy friend or relative is an internal object in that he represents a person who is not present. However, this imagined person also represents the speaker's own ability to approve of himself.

fantasy aspect of himself and his internal objects onto the audience and behaves accordingly. Members of the audience experience themselves as good selfobjects and respond accordingly to the speaker. Such a process is positive projective identification.

Actors and actresses must present themselves with self-confidence and excitement to their audience. Stage fright can sometimes be allayed by assuming a mirroring response (Kohut 1971). Gabbard (1979), who studied stage fright from a psychoanalytic viewpoint, observed that "some performers consciously identify themselves with their audiences." He said, "Their thinking runs like this: 'All these impressive, sophisticated people have come to see me perform, clearly conveying their confidence in me. They're not worried about me, so why should I worry?' " (p. 390). This process is positive projective identification (Hamilton 1986) in that the performer projects his confidence onto the audience and then reidentifies with it, hoping to control his own feelings and the response of the audience.

Salesmen, politicians, skillful administrators, religious leaders, healers, teachers, and all those who influence other people through persuasion rather than force are practiced and adept at projective identification. Confidence men, seducers, and sychophants employ projective identification, although their underlying intentions are not consistent with their overt behavior. People who are duped often project their own positive expectations onto the deceiver to such an extent that they are blinded to his true intentions.

Projective identification is the basis for our deepest affections and attachments. Lovers describe themselves as giving their love. They give their selves and hearts to each other. These common expressions of love are examples of projective identification—imagining a loving aspect of oneself to be actually inside the other person, and acting accordingly.

A husband coming home from work felt particularly fond of his wife that evening. He had accomplished an important task at work and felt good about himself and those around him. Thinking of his wife, he looked forward to seeing her and remembered how she loved him and was considerate of him. He stopped along the way to pick up a bouquet of wild irises. She

---

Because these elements of internal self and internal object are both present, the approving person is a self–object. However, the audience is actually there as an external object and is used for its confirming and approving capacities, so it is also a selfobject in Kohut's sense. Thus, the friend–audience is both selfobject and self–object.

had had a rather routine day at her office. When he presented his wife with the flowers and smiled, he fully expected that she too would feel the fondness he felt. His behavior elicited from her a warm emotion, which corresponded to his own. Such interchanges are positive projective identification.

This mental mechanism of projective identification can also have destructive aspects.

A professor at a prominent university envied the success of a male colleague and a female colleague and decided to bring about their downfall. She confided first to one and then to the other that each of them was spreading malicious gossip about the other's sexual propensities. She planted the seeds of suspicion, which started a mutually destructive projective identification. Their negative thoughts of one another were projected onto one another, and elicited the expected hostility.

This process is negative projective identification. As in the previous example of children passing notes, the third party, who started the activity, may have been projecting her own feelings onto her colleagues and eliciting those feelings from them.

Individuals often declare that they only hedge on their taxes because other people do. "If I don't follow the custom, they will be cheating me," the argument runs. Actually, the majority of people do not cheat on their taxes. The hedger is projecting his own exploitive tendencies onto his fellow citizens, then identifying with them, and committing the very acts he sees in them. He is projecting and identifying with his own greed at the same time.

In societies where bribery is condoned, this mechanism of negative projective identification is common. Citizens justify their own corrupt behavior by perceiving it in others and claiming that they must act in a similar fashion to protect themselves. Just because the people onto whom the projection is cast are actually corrupt does not mean that projection is not involved.

In our society, we have heard football and basketball coaches rationalize their unscrupulous recruiting practices. "I am really an honest man at heart. It is the other coaches who cheat, because of their excessive competitiveness, so I must cheat." In fact, the coach who uses such a rationalization is undoubtedly excessively competitive, and perhaps ruthless, himself. He chooses to see this aspect of himself in the other coaches and to identify with it.

A more constuctive form of negative projective identification is also used by athletes. I once heard a college wrestler talking with a friend in the locker room.

"When I get tired, so tired my gut aches and my eyes are about to pop, I tell myself, 'If I'm hurting this much, the other guy feels just as bad. Every bit I exert myself and I hurt just that much more, that is just how much more he hurts.' So I pour it on even harder until he turns over on his back."

The wrestler had projected his fatigue and pain onto his opponent and attempted to defeat and conquer it in the other man. This is a creative use of one's own pain in the service of legitimate competition.

In our adversarial legal system, a similar use of negative projective identification can sometimes be detected. Attorneys often assume that the opponent, whether plaintiff or respondent, is responsible for all the damage. They argue that their client was wronged and exploited by the other party. Their own understandable exploitive wishes to gain a legal or financial advantage are projected onto the other person and attacked, adding fuel to the fires of righteous indignation. This conviction in the rightness of their cause and in the wrongness of the other side can allow an advocate to work that much more convincingly for the client.

This aspect of the adversarial process motivates both sides to explore vigorously and thoroughly the facts that support their side of the question. The judge or jury performs the integrative function of weighing both sides of the question. This is a more civilized and adaptive process than the ancient practice of trial by combat in which adversaries literally attempted to project deadly objects, such as swords and spears, into the body of their opponent to prove their own innocence and goodness.

Terrorist attacks can be viewed as projective identification. The behavior of Middle Eastern factions, ethnic separatists, local fanatic groups, and others indicates that they experience their aggression in other people. In their view, those they attack are murderers and exploiters. The terrorists then murder innocent victims, while experiencing themselves as victims. As in other forms of projective identification, they elicit corresponding murderous rage in the objects of their projection. A vicious circle of victimization is begun. The victim becomes the victimizer and vice versa. The fantasy becomes a reality. Where it all began becomes difficult to determine.

An obvious and frightening negative projective identification is the nuclear arms race between Russia and the United States. Each side depicts the other as a threat to humankind. From time to time, both sides issue volleys of irrational, one-sided statements about the other side's being entirely responsible for the danger posed to humanity, as if destructive capabilities and even intents were not apparent in all peoples. Unlike the courtroom situation, there is no judge backed by superior force to sort out the merits of the case. Fortunately, both governments at present are attempting to modulate this tendency through a process of discussions.

Examples of projective identification from group behavior or from individuals in everyday interactions are not entirely satisfactory because we do not have access to internal fantasies as we do in the psychotherapy situation. Nevertheless, the parallels are clear.

Projective identification is the mental mechanism of attributing an aspect of the self to the object and then attempting to control or abolish that aspect in the object. Although projective identification is more obvious and extreme among rapprochement-subphase children and patients with borderline and psychotic disorders, it remains an important element in all relationships.

TRANSITIONAL OBJECT FORMATION

Projective identification plays a role in transitional object formation. A transitional object is neither self nor object, and yet it has qualities of both (Winnicott 1953, Grolnick et al. 1978). A blanket or teddy bear, for instance, may be treated as if it is the beloved mother and simultaneously as if it is the beloved self. Winnicott (1953), who developed the concept of transitional objects, said they form "a resting-place for the individual engaged in the perpetual human task of keeping inner and outer reality separate yet inter-related" (p. 90). They inhabit "an intermediate area of experiencing, to which inner reality and external life both contribute" (p. 90). In addition to transitional objects, there are transitional phenomena such as songs, lullabies, gestures, or mannerisms, which serve the same function.

Transitional objects and transitional phenomena often reveal themselves in the psychotherapy situation. They particularly play a part in the treatment of seriously disturbed individuals. Many patients with schizophrenia have described the importance of their stuffed animals as they improved and sometimes recovered from their illnesses.

D.E. was a 23-year-old woman from an upper-middle-class family in Wisconsin. She had been preoccupied with hallucinations and delusions for one-and-a-half years. Her illness had made completion of her college work impossible.

Her pattern was to begin treatment with one psychiatrist, keep appointments for a few sessions, take the prescribed medicine, begin to improve, and suddenly leave treatment. Her symptoms would worsen within a few months, she would become desperately frightened and lonely, enter another hospital for brief hospitalization, and begin treatment with a different psychiatrist.

The psychiatrist at one general hospital told D.E. that he would ask a psychologist and a social worker with a special interest in problems like hers to help with her treatment. The social worker contacted the family and provided them with information about schizophrenia and what they could do to help. One necessary element of the treatment would be a consistent treatment relationship. The family decided they would provide financial support for this treatment team and encourage their daughter to stay with it.

The patient was slow to warm up to the psychologist with whom she met twice weekly. It was three months before she clearly described how lonely and frightened she became in her apartment at night. She would increasingly attend to hallucinations. They made her feel a little less alone, but she would become increasingly confused and isolated when attending to the voices. They were her only consistent companions. She revealed that she sometimes stopped taking the medication because it made her hallucinatory companions go away.

D.E. expressed increasing dependency feelings toward the therapist as she talked of her isolation and preoccupation with internal object relations. She now became hesistant to leave the office at the end of treatment hours. The psychiatrist and psychologist decided that periodic brief hospitalizations might help the patient with her isolation. She began bringing a teddy bear to the hospital with her. She would not tell the nurses about her feelings, but her teddy bear would. The nurses indulged this fantasy and talked back to the stuffed animal. It seemed a step up from preoccupation with hallucinations.

She began bringing the teddy bear to therapy sessions and

continued to do so for two years. She said he remembered everything that was said in sessions; he would repeat it to her verbatim at night when she was alone. That way she did not feel so isolated and did not need to stop taking her medication so she could hallucinate.

In the third year of treatment, she felt ready to take another step. She discussed with her therapist the possibility of giving up the bimonthly, week-long hospitalizations which had become an important part of her treatment. She said she would miss the nurses and the occupational therapist, but it was time for her to develop other relationships. "My teddy would miss the hospital too much. He said he doesn't have to grow up. He's not a person. I'm a person, and I have to grow up; but he doesn't have to, because he's a teddy. He said he won't be too lonely without me if I leave him in the hospital. I can go ahead and grow up without him. He'll be all right."

"You're going to take him to the hospital and leave him there when you say good-bye to the nurses?"

"Yes. I'll bet they keep him, too. I know and they know that he didn't really talk; but everybody likes a teddy bear, even grown-up nurses. I'll bet they miss me a little bit, too. I think they will want to keep the bear to remember me by."

"I'm curious why you don't want to keep your bear to remember them by?" the therapist asked.

"I like to think about my teddy in the hospital so I don't have to go back. It's like a symbol. I'm not quite sure. Maybe there is a part of myself that will never grow up and always need to be taken care of. I need to set that part aside and get on with things. I was very sick, and I needed that teddy. I'm doing better now."

"It sounds like you're still a little worried you might have to go back to the hospital."

"I might. I don't think I will, though. There are other things in my life now. I won't promise the nurses I'm never coming back. I am going to say good-bye and tell them I don't think I will need to come back."

She did tell the nurses good-bye. They were glad to keep her teddy; and she did not need to return.

The teddy bear was a transitional object. The patient had moved from the internal and isolated world of hallucinations toward other people. The teddy bear represented the self, the baby who wanted to be held and nursed. It also represented the good object who told her bedtime stories in the form of verbatim repetitions of therapy sessions. She had brought the bear into the hospital and therapy sessions at a time when she was making a transition from the self–other confusion of hallucinations to the self–other differentiation of relating to actual people. She provided a buffer zone between herself and the nurses by having the teddy bear speak for her for several months.

She gave up the teddy bear at another transition time. She was now relinquishing her need for a stuffed animal to act as an intermediary between herself and the object world. For the first time, she spoke of it as a symbol. Until that day neither the patient nor the therapist had raised the issue of whether or not the teddy bear was real. She could now say on her own that it was not real but had been an important symbol to her. This transition away from fantasy and toward relating to people as potential sources of gratification was confirmed when, within a few weeks, she began to date again. She had not dated in five years.

Another patient, B.G.—the 30-year-old man with profound identity disturbance described in Chapter 2—also had a teddy bear, which he called Denny. He loved and cuddled and talked to Denny. If anyone questioned the teddy bear's importance, the patient put him in the backroom where he was safe. It was only slowly that he could reveal how deeply he loved his teddy bear and how, in turn, the stuffed animal helped him with his profound loneliness. When he went home, despairing of human companionship, feeling empty within, he could comfort and be comforted by Denny. Through projective identification, he attributed his need for comfort to the stuffed toy. He also projected his own soothing function onto it, while simultaneously retaining that capacity within himself. When he hugged and soothed his bear, he, too, felt hugged and soothed.

The autoerotic roots of teddy bear love revealed themselves in this patient's associations. He thought of diapers and the feel of them against his skin. He also fantasized the warmth of his own feces. With some embarrassment, he recalled reading about homosexuals who were aroused by wearing diapers and defecated in them in front of their sexual partner. These associations revealed a primitive root of the transitional object. The stimulations offered by diapers and warm feces against the skin are called autoerotic phenomena. It may have been this infantile experience that eventually evolved into the patient's pleasure in relating to a transitional object. Although transitional objects first develop with the heightened oral and skin awareness that accompany hatching and practicing, they remain important into a period of greater interest in anal sensations, as the patient's associations illustrate. Further evolution of the transitional object into creativity and productive work eventually takes place in children. After several more months of therapy, the patient also took this step in psychological growth. It was then that he began to make and sell stuffed animals for profit.[5]

Most adults do not relate to inanimate objects in as openly an infantile fashion as these two sensitive and talented patients. Many less severely ill patients, however, retain appointment slips, pens, or even bills from the therapist as a kind of transitional reminder of a benevolent person.

Scott (1984) has suggested that adults often use alcohol or other drugs as transitional objects. They may have a favorite brand of liquor, which they must keep on hand. They love their whiskey or beer. They feel soothed by the very presence of a full bottle of a known brand in a safe place. Simultaneously, they identify with the liquor, with the warmth and strength associated with alcohol. Enticements to alcohol play upon this association. They typically represent people relaxing after work, being seduced before bedtime, sailing into the sunset, or similar transitional activities. One could argue that alcoholics ingest their alcohol as a real substance, and it makes them feel good in a physiologic way, and thus cannot be transitional. Although alcohol does have a physiological effect, it also has a psychological meaning. Scott might be correct in his observation that many alcohol abusers treat their liquor as they would a transitional object. Even the physiological effects of this drug suggest such a

---

[5]Although the patient made only a modest profit with his stuffed bears, the history of marketing these toys attests to the widespread preoccupation with transitional objects. In both 1984 and 1985, stuffed bears were among the ten best-selling toys in the United States.

Care Bears are modern versions of the Teddy Bear, which was introduced in 1903 by Morris Michton of Ideal Toy Company. Michton named his stuffed bear after Theodore Roosevelt when Clifford Berryman, a *Washington Post* cartoonist, celebrated Roosevelt's refusal to shoot a captured bear. The famous cartoonist simultaneously teased Roosevelt for his preoccupation with hunting. The President had been frustrated on his bear hunting trip in Mississippi and had not found his quarry. Local guides, wishing to oblige the great man, captured a bear for him to shoot. Teddy declined to do so, saying it would be unsportsmanlike.

In 1903 Margaret Steiff of Geingen, Germany, first sold stuffed toy bears in America. By 1908, Steiff manufactured one million of her now famous bears.

possibility. Ingesting alcohol leads to poor self–other differentiation and the nearly symbiotic experience of intoxication. Perhaps such states of mind, themselves, are transitional in their nature, existing between symbiosis and object relatedness.

In childhood, the blanket or comforter carried about, sucked, caressed, held, and cuddled is one of the best examples of a transitional object. A blanket is held, and yet it holds. It receives warmth from the child and returns that warmth to him. It even acquires odors and returns those odors. Such smells can become so important to the child that he protests if his precious blanket is washed. Although the toddler usually projects warm, close aspects of himself and his internal image of his mother into the blanket, the child can sometimes bite, hit, or mutilate his transitional object. This evidence of negative projective identification into the blanket is rarer than a positive interaction.

Although Winnicott (1953) originally stressed how the child creates the transitional object through his own active imagination, the mother and child create it together. The child treats it as special and comforting, sharing mother's omnipotent glow. Mother, for her part, confirms the specialness by making sure the child has his blanket in times of object loss. Many parents will go to great lengths to make sure their children have their "blanky" at bedtime, when they shut their eyes on the external object world and curl up within themselves to sleep. When children travel in the car, visit relatives, or are left with the baby-sitter, parents make certain the blanket is handy. They do not question the special properties of this child–blanket relationship. Parents acknowledge what Winnicott termed the realm of illusion. "Of the transitional object it can be said that it is a matter of agreement between us and the baby that we will never ask the question, 'Did you conceive of this or was it presented to you from without?' The important point is that no decision on this point is expected. The question is not to be formulated" (p. 95).

Transitional objects play a role in the rapprochement subphase, though their formation begins earlier. Toward the end of rapprochement, this intermediate zone of experience provides an arena for fantasy games and other as-if functioning. Eventually, this play diffuses into music, art, religion, and the sciences. It becomes, as Winnicott (1953) stated, "spread out over the whole intermediate territory between 'inner psychic reality' and the 'external world as perceived by two persons in common,' that is to say, over the whole cultural field" (p. 91).

Tolpin (1971) suggested that transitional object formation plays a crucial role in the developmental line (A. Freud 1965) of self-soothing . Originally, the infant in its symbiotic merger experiences soothing as an omnipotent self–other happening. Upon becoming differentiated, about 6 to 8 months old, an increasing awareness of need for something outside himself to comfort him is developed. It is then that he creates a self-soothing object, a blanket which comforts by virtue of his attributing special importance to it. Eventually, this self-soothing function of the transitional object becomes internalized, so that the child can soothe himself. Tolpin (1971) suggested this process as an example of what Kohut (1971) has called transmuting internalization.

As children grow older, their transitional relatedness evolves, but they do not give it up entirely, even in adulthood. To illustrate this concept, some examples from everyday life are provided.

A 60-year-old man sat in a certain worn chair while he read by the fire at night. He cantankerously opposed his wife's suggestion that the faded chair could be reupholstered. He felt comforted by his old, worn, and slightly pungent chair. The chair was a transitional object.

A 30-year-old woman cuddled up with her pillow each night. Its feathers had long since lost their fluff, but she preferred this pillow to all others.

A 43-year-old Japanese-American man would stare at his grandfather's samurai sword as he meditated each evening after work. During this transition time between work and family, he gazed on the setting sun reflecting on the old sword, which he had held in his hands so many times. The entire tradition of samurai and duty and a feeling of belonging would return to him as he meditated.

A 38-year-old social worker carried a print of a Rembrandt self-portrait to her new office and hung it on the wall without delay. She was not comfortable without it. It was the same print she had in her college dormitory room. Although her taste in many other areas had changed over the past several years, she still preferred this print to all others.

These examples represent adult residuals of transitional objects or phenomena which begin with differentiation and become prominent during rapprochement.

DEVELOPING WHOLE OBJECT RELATIONS

If goodness is taken as goodness,
Wickedness enters as well.
For is and is-not come together.

Lao Tzu
[translated by R. B. Blakney, 1955, p. 54]

The ego eventually integrates good and bad aspects of self-representations and good and bad aspects of object-representations. When all-good and all-bad object-images are brought together, it is called developing object constancy. Simultaneously, all-good and all-bad self-images come together so that identity is consolidated. We can see ourselves as essentially good, but we also acknowledge some less desirable qualities. Similarly, we experience the object as primarily good, but also as having some unfortunate aspects. The world is no longer seen in black and white. With this new integration, split object relations give way to whole object relations.

M.W., a 28-year-old psychologist, reported to her therapist how desperately sad she had felt the previous evening. Normally a pert, self-confident, and bright-eyed woman, she had begun therapy in the midst of a divorce. She described how she had felt alone and had sunk into despair. She felt shut away and sad. Worse than that, she felt she was a bad person. She wept bitterly in the session, tears smearing her carefully applied makeup. As she stopped crying, she said, "When I get that sad, I hate myself. I feel like smoking cigarette after cigarette. I feel like smoking all day long, smoking and smoking until I turn my lungs black and burn myself up from the inside out." Suddenly, she stopped, shook her head, and laughed slightly at her melodramatics. Her perkiness returned. "I guess I really don't feel that way," she said smiling at herself.

Her therapist commented simply, "You were the one who said it."

She quieted. She no longer felt either despair or amusement. "I guess I did," she said. "I guess at some level I really do feel that bad; but I can also feel good at times." She was calm and reflective for the rest of the session, exploring the depth of her despair, anger, and loss and, simultaneously, her ability to be cheerful, strong, and persistent. This bringing together of good and bad, sad and glad, represents the development of a more integrated self-image and more thoroughly integrated self- and object-relationships.

B.G., the 30-year-old man with shifting identities, interests, religions, and friends, began to organize his self- and object-images into all-good and all-bad units during the first two years of treatment. He at times described his mother as a rigid, cold, rejecting person more interested in her own personal beauty and the cleanliness of her home than in the emotional well-being of her children. He elaborated fantasies of killing her by poison or starvation. Other times he wanted to move back into her home. She was a bright, wealthy, interesting woman who would provide for him nicely. He composed elaborate poems about an idealized woman in the style of early Renaissance sonneteers and collected rare editions of love poems, some of which he sent to his mother as gifts. In the transference, he idealized his therapist most of the time, while vilifying other helping professionals. The polarity shifted when his therapist was on vacation. He thought he wasn't receiving any help and became suicidally despondent.

The patient slowly developed more integrated feelings about the people around him. In the last half of the third year of therapy, he went through a period of several months during which he was predominately angry at his therapist who could do nothing right. One day, he said, "It seems like I've been in a one–sided argument with you for months. I've being going through this fight in my mind. I used to think you were next to God, but you aren't. You are just a regular person, like everyone else. It's kind of sad to get so angry at someone I care about. You have helped me. I guess I've been so annoyed because you couldn't make things easier for me."

The idealized mother and idealized therapist had been part of the all-good self–object unit. The devalued mother and professionals had been part of the all-bad unit. The patient had been unable to think of the less agreeable aspects of the therapy and therapist, probably because he needed an all-good object upon whom he could depend early in his treatment. As he grew more self-confident, he could explore his negative feelings about the therapist, but could not simultaneously think about his positive and negative feelings until late in treatment. At that point anger gave way to sadness. He felt remorseful that he had been destructively angry at the same person about whom he cared. His feelings were now both positive and negative at the same time. He was developing whole object relations.

He developed similar complex feelings about his mother. A blood clot had broken loose from a varicose vein and lodged in his mother's lung. He visited her in the intensive care unit and during her recovery. When he returned, he said, "It was odd to see her so hurt. I had been seeing her as so powerful—either malignant or helpful—but she looked hurt and frightened in the hospital. I realized she is a confused little old woman. I don't need to be so angry or admiring anymore."

"Now that you are grown up; but what about when you were a child?" the therapist asked.

"Even then," he said. "I was a little kid, and I couldn't think about it this way then. She was my whole world; but when I look back on it, I keep thinking how lonely and insecure she must have been to need a little kid's admiration so much. What an upbringing she must have had!"

"You can still remember your anger, though," the therapist said.

"Sure, I can, but I can forgive her now. I had trouble relating to people when I came to therapy. I was lucky to have someone help me get over it; but my mother didn't have anyone to help her. I feel sorry for her. I wish I could help her, talk her into getting into therapy or something, but that would hurt her feelings. She would feel criticized if I told her she needed treatment. I'm afraid I can't help her. It's too bad."

The patient could see his mother as a whole complex person, not merely someone who either gratified or frustrated his desires and needs. She had a history of her own. When people develop a more integrated image of others in their lives, they learn to empathize and have genuine concern. At the same time, this patient could be more detached. He no longer needed to flee her or seek her. He could be concerned and interested from a psychological remove. This greater emotional distance paradoxically allowed him to be more genuinely and accurately understanding and to relate to her as herself, not as the person he needed her to be.

Forgiveness depends on the acquisition of whole object relatedness. One must be able to hold two emotionally contradictory images in mind, one of the object as frustrating or harmful and the other of the object as valuable and loved. It is then that forgiveness is possible.

B.G. demonstrated this when he learned to forgive his mother after he began to see her in a more well-rounded fashion.

I described in Chapter 5 how children, following rapprochement, develop an increasingly stable sense that mother is a gratifying presence and occasionally a frustrating one. The child also develops a growing sense of being a complex yet stable individual. The splitting of all-good and all-bad self- and object-experiences evolves into whole object relationships. This ability depends to some extent on neurophysiologic capacities to remember, compare, and contrast, that is, on the development of integrative ego functions. Piaget's (1937) studies, as mentioned, revealed the orderly sequences in which these mental capacities unfold. These studies complement those of Mahler (Fraiberg 1969, Mahler et al. 1975, and Lester 1983) and Spitz (Cobliner 1965). In addition to neurophysiologic capacities, however, the child must acquire enough good experiences to be secure that frustration will not entirely destroy his inner equanimity. Erikson (1950) called this the development of basic trust.

In adult patients, loss can lead to such strong feelings that the ego's capacity to integrate is temporarily overwhelmed, even in people who have otherwise intact egos. Children are even more vulnerable in this regard. If chronically frustrated, there may be a stunting of the integrative ego functions. That is, their environment can be so overwhelming that their capacity to compare and contrast emotional experience fails to develop; they remain stuck in a split, all-good and all-bad self- and object-experience.

Hartmann (1952) and other ego psychologists have called the increasing ability to modulate emotions that accompanies object constancy neutralization. Integration, however, seems a better term, because it implies the creation of something new, rather than the canceling out of energies. As Greenacre (1957) has said, "I find neutralization so difficult in this connection. To me neutralization, borrowed presumably from chemistry, has the natural connotation of something which has been rendered inert, or at least temporarily ineffective" (p. 69). The integration that accompanies development of whole object relations does not lead to a balancing act to cancel out dangerous impulses, but to new sources of gratification.

Klein's (Segal 1964) term for the coming together of the good and bad self- and object-worlds is the depressive position. Her phrasing, like Hartmann's, implies a loss of zest, which seems inaccurate. There is a kind of sadness that comes with integration of the good and bad self- and object-images. The grandiose self-images and omnipotent object-images do recede into the realm of fiction, mythology, and dreams. Salvation no longer beckons, but damnation no longer threatens. Knowledge of both good and evil together does result in a loss of paradise. Yet, the term depressive position implies too much helplessness and too much lack of progress for such an important and creative developmental step. Consequently, integration and developing whole object relations, as Mahler describes it, and establishing a cohesive self, as Kohut (1971) suggests, are more apt terms.

In everyday life and in literature, there are numerous examples of integrating good and bad self- and object-images.

On May 14, 1986, a wall of wind and water capsized the clipper *Pride of Baltimore*, sinking it within minutes. The first mate, John Flanagan, struggled to inflate a defective life raft. While they worked on the raft, he and eight others helplessly watched two of their shipmates drown. They did not know the whereabouts of two others. After surviving the stormy seas for five days, Flanagan and his companions were rescued. When he was asked to act as spokesman at a news conference, he told members of the press, "It's very hard to explain the grief of losing shipmates and the joy of being alive."[6]

This capacity to acknowledge and tolerate mutually contradictory emotions simultaneously is whole object relatedness.

Shakespeare's lines in *All's Well that Ends Well* also portray integration:

The web of our life is of a mingled yarn,
Good and ill together.

Act IV, scene 3, line 83

A similar integration can sometimes lead to humorous tolerance of conflict. Mark Twain once stated:

It were not best that we should all think alike; it is difference of opinion that makes horse-races.

Pudd'nhead Wilson's Calendar

---

[6]This story was written by Saundra Saperstein and Barbara Vobejda of the *Los Angeles Times–Washington Post News Service*; it was published in *The Oregonian*, Thursday, May 22, 1986, p. 1.

Here, Twain acknowledges both the conflict and pleasure of disagreement.

Another successful integration and differentiation, awareness of gain in loss, is reflected in Wordsworth's lines:

Though nothing can bring back the hour
Of splendour in the grass, of glory in the flower;
We will grieve not, rather find
Strength in what remains behind

"Ode on Intimations of Immortality
from Recollections of Early Childhood"

In these lines, Wordsworth is commenting on the strength that follows awareness of the loss of innocent unity in infancy.

The contemplativeness of Proust's *A la Recherche du Temps Perdu* suggests the meaningfulness of reflecting upon past events, valued and yet gone. Similarly, the nostalgic pleasure of sitting at one's desk at twilight, sipping tea in the quiet solitude and recalling bygone days with love, sadness, and longing is different from depression; it is acceptant and meaningful. It reveals the capacity to long for something and to value it, even in its absence.

The integration of remembering a shred of good in the midst of misery can steel one to seemingly impossible endurance. At a time when a classical education was more common, soldiers in the frozen mud of the trenches of World War I consoled themselves with Shakespeare's phrase:

Come what come may,
Time and the hour runs through the roughest day.

Macbeth, Act I, scene 3, line 146

When he received the Nobel Prize, William Faulkner sang out from his late-life alcoholism to inspire a younger generation of authors with his own style of integrating the good and the bad. He spoke of the writer's job, saying:[7]

It is his privilege to help man endure by lifting his heart, by reminding him of the courage and honor and hope and pride and

---

[7]*The Faulkner Reader* (1954). New York: Random House.

compassion and pity and sacrifice which have been the glory of his past.

Here there is no splitting off or canceling out of emotions, but a mature and resolute combining of multiple possibilities in human life, for good or for ill.

Our most intimate relationships—those which involve a loving sexual union—also require a bringing together of contrasting impulses, not a toning down or canceling out. As Freud (1940) pointed out, mature sexual relations require a certain amount of aggressive energy as well as libido or love. There can be no ecstacy, no passionate coming together, if there is not at least a modicum of aggressive seeking, as well as loving longing.

It is this bringing together of opposites in a meaningful way that constitutes the development of whole object relations.

IDENTIFICATION

As integration and differentiation become free from influence by the vagaries of mood swings, stable self- and object-images develop. The acquisition of object constancy, however, does not imply that we no longer change. We still continue to take in aspects of our love objects and alter our self-images accordingly. This process is called identification.

Identification is more selective and refined than incorporation or introjection. Introjection implies taking in the behavior, attitude, mood, or demeanor of an external object. This introjected object or part-object remains relatively "unmetabolized." As the powers of integration and differentiation develop, these introjected object-representations become metabolized and transformed into new mental representations. Identification is the attribution of aspects of object-images to self-images (Sandler and Rosenblatt 1962).

M.N. was a 25-year-old teacher who initially complained of depression. She had been a compliant child and followed the clear social guidelines of her upper-class Midwest family. In college she became infatuated with a professor. That relationship broke off after one year, and she became attached to an ambitious and somewhat narcissistic man her own age. They married after one year.

M.N. enjoyed her verbal and often exciting husband, but was

increasingly dissatisfied when his attentions turned to academic pursuits. Several of her friends told her of their interest in the writing of William James. His description of a vivid interior world fascinated her and partially filled the internal void she felt. She tried to look closely at her own internal world, but found a deep feeling of depletion and emptiness. It was with this loneliness and sense of inadequacy that she began treatment.

The second year of treatment she explained how she called an image of her therapist to mind when she felt lonely or inadequate. "I feel drained by the students between classes. They suck me dry. They are so demanding I don't think I can do it. Then I say to myself, 'What would Dr. D. say?' It's like I hear your voice saying something along the lines of, 'It sounds as if you feel you must meet all of their needs rather than just some of them.' I feel so much better then. I know it is my thought, but I can hear the tone of your voice as clearly as if you were in the room with me."

M.N. had introjected her therapist as a good internal object who helped her modulate her harsh and self-critical demands that she be a perfect nurturer and teacher. Her self-image remained clearly differentiated from the image of her therapist.

Several months later she announced her plan to return to graduate school and work toward becoming a psychotherapist. She was beginning to attribute aspects of the object-image, her therapist, to her self-image and to act on this new internal sense of herself. She identified with her therapist in more subtle ways also. She more easily maintained her sense of self-esteem. She no longer called up the image of her therapist to soothe her, but reminded herself of her adequacy. When her husband pointed out the drawbacks to her returning to school, she asserted herself in a challenging way characteristic of her therapist. She bolstered herself with indignancy, one of her therapist's less fortunate qualities, which revealed itself even in the treatment situation.

Introjection had given way to identification at this point. M.N. attributed aspects of the object-image to her self-image. She learned to experience herself as a confident, assertive, and sometimes indignant person similar to but different from her therapist. She did not return to the self-object merger of symbiosis, but selectively adopted some aspects of her therapist.

This therapy did not turn out well. The therapist was unable to help her understand the defensive aspect of her identification with him. Neither did he have a firm awareness of his own shortcomings. The patient became increasingly assertive, denying her attachment and dependency feelings and identifying with a false self-confidence which her therapist encouraged. She precipitously left her teaching career, angrily divorced her husband, and fell into financial straits which forced her to discontinue treatment. She had to give up graduate school and find a new, less favorable teaching job. It was several years before she could begin therapy again.

She identified with this therapist too. He was able to help her examine her identification with him more closely. This work allowed her to select what aspects of her identification were most suited to her own talents and situation. What she retained of most importance from this second therapy was an image of herself as someone who could reflect upon what was best suited to her own talents and needs. Selectively is the hallmark of mature identification.

M.N. began a relationshp with a new man near the end of her second therapy. She related to him in a fashion consistent with the roles available to her during a time of expanding possibilities for women. Her concerns, conflicts, and trial solutions in this area of how to be both independent and intimate in relation to a man were appropriate to her background, her biology, and her new social circumstances.

Her autonomy, her wishes to be her own person and to suit herself, had always been respected in her second therapy. This respectful attitude toward her capacity to discover and create her own meaning and purpose in her own life became internalized as a part of her identity. Identification for her had become less personalized than with her first therapist. It became generalized as a set of guiding principles. Some theorists call this process structuralization.

Most psychotherapists believe that all therapies, including psychoanalysis, are aided by identification with the therapist. Even fairly mature patients take in their therapist's interested observation and acceptance of the human condition. They alter these attributes as suits their needs. For example, it is not appropriate that patients should merely wonder at their feelings, as many therapists do, without taking any action. Patients need either to take action on their feelings or to delay action. Thus, as patients finish therapy, they combine enlightened and benign self-observation, which they have internalized, with a self-confident ability to make decisions and take action.

In child development, identification, as opposed to introjection, becomes increasingly obvious when whole object relations mature. At this time, the formation of triadic, or oedipal relations, gives a developmental boost to identification.

Many object relations theorists, like Mahler, discuss issues of separation and individuation more than oedipal concerns, although they take care to note that oedipal conflicts are important. Rather than deny the influence of these sexual and aggressive concerns, they merely assume that previous work, beginning with Freud (1900), has already elucidated this important developmental issue. Others, like Jacobson (1964), trace the processes of introjection, projection, and identification right through the oedipal period and into adolescence.

During the oedipal period, boys pay increasing attention to their similarity to their fathers. They observe their genital structure. They also mention their wish to possess and be close to their mothers. They consequently feel rivalrous toward the father. Having increasingly whole object relations, they simultaneously feel small, dependent, and unable to compete with their fathers. One solution to the wish to vie with their father for their mother's attention and avoid conflict with the father is to identify with him. In this way, they can experience themselves as big and as possessing the mother, the way they imagine the father possessing her. This identification is useful to boys because they generalize it and also learn to work diligently, assert themselves, obey rules, and cooperate with groups. It is not until adolescence and young adulthood, when they establish a social standing of their own and search for a woman companion of their own, that they give up this partial solution to their wish to possess the mother. At this point, they are free to develop new identifications.

The oedipal relations of girls are slightly different (Tyson 1982), because they identify with their mothers, with whom they originally had the greatest self–other unity, whereas boys have to give up their early identity with their primary object and establish an identification with a new person, the father. Through the process of differentiation, girls learn that they are separate from and yet similar to their mothers. Soon, they enviously wish to have the good things which mother has, such as the special attention of father and the babies he can give her. Unable to compete successfully with mother for father's full affection, girls reach the solution of reidentifying with their mothers.

Anna Freud (1936) described identification with the aggressor in both children and adults. For example, prisoners often take on the characteristics of their captors. In their helplessness, they have a greater need for closeness, nurturance, and gratification of dependency. Their deprived state and resultant increased need open them to internalizing authority figures as they did when they were small children. By identifying with the aggressor they can deny their helplessness, telling themselves that they are not the victim, but the powerful victimizer. Thus, captives are prone to identify with those who take care of them, however cruelly.

Identification with the aggressor may explain why abused children are so likely to abuse their own children when they become parents. When a child is hurt, he has an increased need for those upon whom he depends. Consequently, he may cling even more fiercely to the very parent who harms him. The need for closeness leads the child to firmly introject the abusing parent and then identify with the powerful figure. The child no longer experiences himself as small, helpless, and hurt, but as big, powerful, and strong. Thus, the abused child often becomes an abusing parent. In normal development, with caring and well-modulated parents, identification with the aggressor also plays some role. The unavoidable oedipal situation, as described above, has elements of identification with the perceived aggressor.

Identity formation does not end in early life. In adolescence, we again differentiate from parents and use peers and teachers for role models. When we enter careers, we identify with our superiors, learning their ways and adapting them to our own needs. In old age, we learn from other people how to form a role appropriate to our new station in life. Through taking in aspects of new relationships and experiences, we never become a thing, but always remain a process, an interaction of self and object.

In the Christian tradition, identification with good aspects of the object was extolled as a virtue when Christ, preparing for his departure, said:

This is my commandment, That ye
love one another; as I have
loved you.

John 15:12

In this passage, the disciples are encouraged to identify with Christ's love of them and to love one another.

Many artists will call to mind the techniques of masters when working. They describe imagining themselves as being that master, until they mature in their own identities as artists. Resident surgeons, who learn by assisting senior surgeons, identify with their mentors. They often adopt the mannerisms and attitudes of the colleagues with whom they spend so many hours. As one neurosurgery resident said to a medical student who asked his advice about where to do an internship, "Where you do your training is very important, because you play ball like the people you play ball with."

In the forested mountains of the Northwest, toward the end of one snowy day, when the loggers' hands and feet were numb with cold and frost hung off their moustaches, a young crew leader made an error in rigging. He sent the wrong cable five hundred yards downhill. His comrades threw up their hands in disgust—they would have to work at least an hour more, dragging yards of steel cable uphill to be ready to log in the morning. The crew leader tried to save face by retrieving the line himself. He worked his way downhill. He saw his superintendent plodding bull-like uphill with the line over his shoulder. His tin hat had fallen off. Steam blew from his nostrils as he panted in the cold air. The younger man would not have blamed the superintendent if he had fired him, though he was one of the steadier employees. He would not have been surprised if his boss lost his temper, shouted, or even struck out at him.

When he reached his boss, the older man stopped and looked up at him. His eyes blazed hatred and disgust, but he only said, "Well, I suppose a man can stand anything for an hour. Let's get finished." The two men, hurt and exhausted, hauled on the line for an hour until it was hooked up and ready to go for morning.

Later, walking up the frozen road to the warm trucks, the superintendent put his arm around the younger man's shoulder and hugged him. "I'll never forget," he said, "when I was barely a man, just a boy, really, and I'd have to go out with Pa to cut one more tree before supper, he'd always remind me, 'A man can stand anything for an hour.' I've never forgotten it." The superintendent walked off toward his pickup truck and headed for town without looking back.

Identification is the ability to call up the memory of the good object, the encouraging father whom the superintendent carried around inside him, and to act according to that father's principles. In turn, the crew leader identified with the boss. He learned to pass on the same encouragement to his crew members.

Identification is the ability to maintain a feeling of being distinct from important objects and yet attribute aspects of the object-image to the self-image. Throughout life, identification is a way to remain open to other people and allow them to influence us and help us change.

The observation of adults and children in therapy has provided important information on the mental mechanisms that help us establish our sense of self in relation to other people. There are striking parallels between the interactions of patients in therapy and the behavior of healthy children in relation to their parents. The increasing capacity to differentiate self from object and to integrate good and bad experiences helps both children and adults move from the less refined mechanisms of projection, introjection, splitting, and idealization and devaluation, through projective identification and transitional object formation, to object constancy and mature identification. Although these mental functions can be placed on a continuum from less to more mature, none of them disappear from our psychological repertoire. Each retains some utility throughout life.

PART III
THE OBJECT RELATIONS CONTINUUM

> *Lovers and madmen have such seething brains,*
> *Such shaping fantasies, that apprehend*
> *More than cool reason ever comprehends.*
>
> —William Shakespeare, *A Midsummer Night's Dream*
> (Act V, scene 1)

INTRODUCTION

Philosophers and scientists have organized and reorganized, classified and reclassified mental disturbances (Menninger et al. 1963). These efforts have relied on various combinations of empirical observation and theoretical principles. Hippocrates (Adams 1929) used empirical observation when he discovered that the sacred disease, epilepsy, could be classified with other brain diseases. Although most Greeks at the time assumed that the gods afflicted people with seizures, Hippocrates noticed that they were often associated with brain injuries, so he reclassified them as physical rather than spiritual problems. Even his empirical work, however, led to classification based on a theory: either anatomical or spiritual changes cause functional disturbances.

In medieval medicine, the Greek theory of the four humors along with the Arabic astrologers' predictions served to classify and explain various problems. Aggressive outbursts, for instance, could be categorized as an excess of the bodily humor choler and an influence of the fiery planet Mars.

In nineteenth-century European medicine, scientists strove toward as pure an empiricism as possible. Physicians made detailed observations of various psychic disturbances and classified them according to their surface manifestations. Kraepelin (1919) eventually organized the resulting multitudinous disorders into mood and thought disorders, thereby creating a dualistic theory of psychopathology, which continues to play an important role in psychiatry today.

At the turn of the century, Freud organized empirical observations of patients' reports of their psychic experiences. Using this source of data, he discovered that there are unconscious thought processes and infantile conflicts which repeat themselves in adult psychopathology. His observations led to theoretical principles, which have been used to classify various problems according to the infantile developmental difficulty most prominently involved. Freud's theories continue to be an important factor in the classification of mental disorders today.

According to the classical system of psychosexual development (Fenichel 1945), the addictions repeated oral cravings from the first year, obsessions repeated anal-sadistic conflicts of the second and third years, and hysteria repeated oedipal concerns of the third, fourth, and fifth years. This fixation theory maintains that conflicts in later life rearouse similar, unresolved problems from early life. These earlier difficulties and defensive attempts to avoid them manifest themselves as symptoms. There remains much controversy even within psychoanalysis about fixation theory, and most present-day authors place fixation theory within a more complicated psychosocial–biological matrix.

Since Fenichel's time more has been learned about severe mental disorders, such as the psychoses and borderline conditions. Simultaneously, studies of early infant–mother interactions have resulted in delineation of the stages of separation–individuation. Numerous clinicians and researchers have noticed similarities between the problems of patients and the developmental struggles of children at various phases of development. Blanck and Blanck (1979), two ego psychologists who rely heavily on Mahler's work, have used this information to help them dispense with diagnostic labels. Instead of making formal diagnoses, they delineate specific accomplishments and unresolved developmental problems in their patients. They call this process descriptive developmental diagnosis (p. 64).

Most object relations theorists do not go so far as the Blancks. They still use labels to some extent to describe constellations of symptoms. When they correlate these entities with early developmental tasks, they achieve a continuum of psychopathology arranged according to stages of separation–individuation (Kernberg 1970, Rinsley 1982, Horner 1984, and Adler 1985). Here is such a schema.

Developmental Stage	Diagnosis	Level of Personality Organization
Autism	Autistic psychosis	Psychotic organization
Symbiosis	Schizophrenia	
Hatching		
Practicing	Bipolar affective disorders	
Rapprochement	Antisocial Schizotypal Schizoid Borderline Narcissistic	Borderline organization
Whole object relations	Obsessive Hysterical Normal-neurotic	Neurotic organization

Such schema are always being refined and revised. As Sandler and Rosenblatt (1962) described psychoanalytic research, "There is a constant interaction between our clinical material and our theoretical formulations, an interaction which seems to us to be an essential constituent of all scientific procedures" (p. 128).

In casual conversation, many clinicians will describe a patient as having split object relations, as if the patient had psychologically remained a rapprochement toddler. The object relations continuum, however, does not imply such an oversimplified theory of causation, nor do most clinicians subscribe to such a stripped-down theory of fixation when they are actually questioned. Most are careful to point out that an adult's separation–individuation problems may be similar to those of a child, yet are more complicated, because the adult has passed through oedipal conflicts, latency development, and the identity reformation of adolescence (Blanck and Blanck 1979).

Many psychotherapists, because of their interest in personal interactions, emphasize disturbed early relationships as causing difficulties, although different factors can cause object relations disturbances. Congenitally deficient integrative ego functions, present in some learning and attention-deficit disorders, can result in an inability to integrate good and bad self- and object-representations. Such failure can result in a persistence of split object relations units into adult hood. Similarly, an adult who had previously developed integrated whole object relations might become brain-damaged, so that his integrative ego functions deteriorate. This adult might return to split object relations in currently emotionally charged interactions, while retaining old memories of whole relationships when calm and secure. Thus, it can be seen that object relations theory, although an essentially interpersonal construct, does not imply an exclusively interpersonal theory of the causation of psychological problems.

If this theory of infantile development and psychopathology does not predict causation of illness, what is its usefulness? The key to this question lies, I believe, in the general biological observation that growth takes place in an orderly sequence, with more differentiated and integrated structures and functions emerging from more crudely organized structures and functions. This process holds true for the development of increasingly complex species in evolution, as it does for development of increasingly complex organ systems in embryologic development. This phenomenon is reflected in the famous dictum ontogeny recapitulates phylogeny.

Jackson (1884), the great nineteenth-century neurologist, similarly considered the mind to evolve from less complex to more complex, from less voluntary to more voluntary. During illness, the progress of dysfunction takes a reverse direction, from most complex to less complex. Jackson thought of it as "undevelopment." Following Jackson's notion, people who suffer psychological injury, whether from biological or interpersonal causes, dedifferentiate, or regress, and reorganize according to more primitive principles. Therapists who have a knowledge of psychological development can help patients take the next step needed in the processes of integration and differentiation in order to resume their psychological growth. The development of children holds the key to the sequence of those steps. Developmental diagnosis is the most appropriate diagnostic system to guide psychotherapeutic interventions, although other kinds of diagnosis, such as that in the American Psychiatric Association's (1980) current *Diagnostic and Statistical Manual* (DSM-III), may be more appropriate for guiding pharmacologic interventions.

In this section, some representative psychiatric disorders will be discussed in object relations terms. They will be presented in the order that they occur on the object relations continuum: autism (Chapter 7), schizophrenia (Chapter 8), mania (Chapter 9), borderline personality disorder (Chapter 10), narcissistic personality disorder (Chapter 11), and neurotic and normal personalities (Chapter 12).

CHAPTER 7

AUTISM

In 1980, I interrupted my study of narcissistic, borderline, and psychotic adults at a private psychoanalytic hospital to explore the object relations of severely retarded children. When I entered the ward at Kansas Neurological Institute, one stunted 10-year-old girl with the features of Down's Syndrome ran forward and thrust her arms around my neck as I leaned over to greet her. Another child stopped his hallucinatory muttering to look up, and then returned to his preoccupation. One child, 4 years old, a dark-haired girl with averted brown eyes, did not even notice the nurse or me.

"Who is this one?" I asked the nurse.
"That's J.J. She's autistic," the nurse replied. "Don't touch her. She bangs her head or bites if you do."
J.J. stared at a crack in the linoleum tile. She gazed intently, running her finger up and down the crack. I approached her carefully, knelt beside her, and positioned my face to make eye contact. An eerie feeling overcame me when, as I invaded her normal zone of privacy, she did not notice me. She remained absorbed in running her finger up and down the crack. I was not only nonhuman, but seemingly nonexistent. I quietly retreated.

We often observed this 4-year-old autistic girl during the coming weeks. One day, we watched an attendant approach her. J.J. was staring at her toe, wiggling it back and forth. When he got so close his image must have crossed her visual field, she turned her head suddenly away. She seemed to avoid the attendant's intrusion by flapping her fingers in front of her eyes to make the sunlight flash. When he softly spoke her name, she screamed in terror and cringed, covering her ears with her hands. She had reacted as if her solitude had been suddenly pierced by the shriek of a fire engine's siren, rather than by a soothing human voice.

The next day, I once more quietly invaded her privacy and sat perfectly still. When by chance her eyes met mine, she stared through me, as if I were a thing rather than a person. She did not even have the visual following response of an 8-week-old infant to the human face. She remained in her nonhuman world, without object relationship.

Individuals with autism do not make normal human contact. They seem unable to make the first symbiotic attachment. Mahler termed these problems "autistic infantile psychosis" (1952, p. 289), and Rinsley called them "presymbiotic psychoses" (1972, p. 169). Using a knowledge of how infants develop object relations, one can hypothesize several causes of autism. It could be due to lack of an adequate symbiotic partner. At one time such a theory was widely held (Eisenberg and Kanner 1956). The parents of these children were sometimes informally referred to as "refrigerator parents." They contained the basic supplies of nurturance, but they had a cold, nonhuman exterior. They could not hold their children, the theory suggested. The child's inability to mold to people and interact was considered to be a problem inherent in the parents. Further studies revealed that the parents of these children did have the capacity to hold their infants (Rutter 1971); the babies had an inherent incapacity to respond to their parents.

Most clinicians now believe that autism arises from congenital problems within the child. Using Klein's ideas concerning projection of the death instinct, one could consider autism to result from an excess of destructive drive which is projected onto the external world so it seems an inhospitable or even dangerous place. Such an environment could cause retreat into autistic preoccupation. This explanation does not seem adequate because it suggests that self–other differentiation has already taken place. A person cannot retreat from the external world into an internal world if there is no prior self–other distinction. Such a retreat, at any rate, is not autistic, but schizoid.

Another explanation is that neither the object-world nor the impulses within the patient cause the self–other problem of autism. It could be the integrative ego functioning which is deficient or distorted. Mahler (1952) leans toward this hypothesis. She observed that nearly all children with autism have severe congenital problems with their autonomous ego functions. This finding is consistent with the observation that autistic children have trouble filtering perceptions and attending to pertinent stimuli. They may not notice a truck coming down the road, but may recoil in terror from a gentle touch. They also often have trouble molding to their mother's arms. They do not form transitional objects, and they have particular difficulty with all communication, by facial expression, gesture, and later with words.

The likelihood is that autistic children have severe, congenital ego deficits or distortions which do not allow them to perceive, organize, and interact with the environment in such a way as to establish object contact. They are presymbiotic, in a state where self and object, even as a dyadic unity, are irrelevant.

Not all autistic children remain in such a bizarre state. Particularly those with high intellectual endowment in some area may function in everyday life, though their manner remains unnatural and their social life devoid of intimacy.

C.E. had been diagnosed as being autistic when he was a child. He entered a private psychiatric hospital in New England when he was 22, following the loss of his job as a computer programmer. He had become clinically depressed, with lack of appetite, early morning insomnia, and suicidal ideation. His depression improved rapidly with antidepressant medication, but he remained socially withdrawn and odd in his behavior. His blond hair was cropped close at a uniform length. His portable computer was his only cherished belonging.

His first ward psychiatrist diagnosed the patient as having residual childhood autism. He structured a safe environment to help the patient make human contact. For six months, C.E. remained in his room. He refused to go to group meetings, despite his nurse's encouragement. It was fine with him when he didn't receive privileges to go off the ward, eat in the dining room, attend activities, or shop at the store—he could not be coaxed out of his room with these enticements. He vehemently asserted that he would never condescend to participate in group discussions of people's "petty concerns."

He refused to meet with his nurse. He claimed to hate his psychiatrist, because he had to meet with him. He felt controlled and attacked by him. He finally did consent to see a psychotherapist off the ward, but would go to his office only if he was allowed a weekly trip to the computer store to buy needed equipment. His psychotherapist remained excluded from his interior life.

After six months, his ward psychiatrist left the hospital to take another position. When his new psychiatrist entered C.E.'s room daily, the patient protested that she had no right to invade his space and that she was as bad as his previous doctor. He had nothing to tell her or any other "mortal." He maintained an aloof facade in interpersonal contacts, apparently harboring an internal autistic, objectless emptiness. Perhaps he was autistic, the psychiatrist thought, able to relate only to numbers and a computer, which are inanimate. His previous psychiatrist had remarked, "He relates to things, so you may have to relate to him through things."

For days, he refused to speak or acknowledge his doctor's presence. He continued to work at his computer, as if the intruder were nonexistent. In a few weeks, the new psychiatrist learned to observe the computer screen instead of the patient. There were incomprehensible combinations of letters, numbers, and patterns. "You are telling me that you have some orderly and elegant message within you, but I can't comprehend it yet," she said.

"I am not telling you anything," the patient countered. "I am working on my project just as I did before you invaded my room like a barbarian."

C.E. was not entirely in an objectless, autistic state, as he had been as a child. He distinguished self and object, but he had a protective shell of isolation around himself. When people entered, he felt invaded.

His psychiatrist learned from the nurses that the patient spent long hours playing computer games which he had created. One day the patient showed her a game. In the dimly lit room he peered into the computer's green screen to find good figures guarding a circle of good space and bad forces invading the defender's territory. The defenders shot out rays to destroy the invaders. Indeed, he had good as well as bad objects in his inner world. The boundaries also indicated a sense of self–other differentiation.

An object relations theory of development indicated that the patient had shifted from autism to hatching processes, bypassing symbiosis. He could intellectually distinguish self from environment, but he had never been able to merge into a warm, symbiotic relationship. Perhaps his early fusion experiences had been with inanimate objects, rather than with people. He apparently had never had the ability to form warm dyadic relationships. He seemed to experience such relationships as attacks, as J.J. seemed to do when she screamed and recoiled from the soothing voice of her attendant. This observation confirmed the previous psychiatrist's suggestion that one must always be careful to relate to this patient through things, not directly as a person.

The next day, the patient had two parallel sets of symbols on his display. The light in his room was a little brighter. "Two languages?" the doctor asked.

"Yes," the patient said. "I'm writing a new program to translate my computer language, which is really superior, to BASIC."

"So you made up your own language, and you're translating it so other people can understand?"

"No. I could care less about people. My computer becomes more powerful if its language can draw upon information in other languages."

"Yes," the psychiatrist said. She did not want to intrude too much by reminding him that perhaps he was ready to start using his computer to feel understood by other people.

Within weeks his computer seemed to become less an inanimate object to be manipulated in an autoerotic fashion. It was now an intermediary between self and object. He could use it to relate to others in his own odd way. In a few more weeks, he showed his doctor programs he had packaged. He accepted encouragement and sent the programs off to computer companies. Evidentally, his communication was received by other people, because they bought his programs and even offered to hire him to produce more of them. He spent hours at the computer store, talking with other programmers, a few of whom had a similar need for emotional distance.

In six more months, he reached out to the larger world. He

sent resumes to prospective employers. Two months later, he had a job with a large computer company in North Carolina and prepared to leave the hospital.

C.E., who had been autistic and unable to form symbiotic object ties, never was able to go back and pick up this developmental step. It may have been this inability that made it impossible for him to enter into the ward groups. Groups often represent a symbiotic oneness, a dual unity into which one enters. He had to bypass group therapy and work on job skills.

He seemed able partially to bypass symbiosis and use inanimate objects and mathematics as an intermediate zone, a buffer between his internal self and the world of external things. He could then create a niche for himself in the commerce of everyday relationships. Although the hospital staff members did not help this man develop warm, loving relationships, he was able to tell them he appreciated their efforts to help him.

Autism as a clinical entity parallels the autistic phase of human development in that the patient seems to live in an objectless world. There are no self–object relationships with emotional significance. Some patients with autism are able to learn to relate to people, but most often, only by using their cognitive skills and impersonal things as means for communication.

CHAPTER 8

SCHIZOPHRENIA

Schizophrenia is a complex set of illnesses. Mood disorders, seizures, personality disorders, minimal brain dysfunction, organic mental disorders, and drug abuse, as well as rarer conditions, can all contribute to schizophrenia-like syndromes (Hamilton and Allsbrook 1986). In this chapter, I will not attempt to divide schizophrenia into discrete diagnostic entities. Instead, I will describe the object relations of patients classified as having this disorder according to conventional usage.

The most current and accepted diagnostic schema, found in the *Diagnostic and Statistical Manual of Mental Disorders*, Third Edition (DSM-III) (American Psychiatric Association 1980), lists six major criteria for schizophrenia. To be classified as schizophrenic, a patient must meet at least one of the criteria. Five symptoms have to do with various kinds of delusions and hallucinations, and the sixth with incoherent speech and bizarre behavior. All these problems can be understood as disturbances in the relationship between the self and either internal or external objects.

Hallucinations are perceptions of a fantasy or idea. Something that normally would be experienced as self seems to be an object. Auditory hallucinations can sometimes be attributed to external objects, and are heard outside the person; sometimes they are attributed to internal objects, and are heard inside the person but still experienced as nonself, another presence. Several patients have mentioned that they hear different kinds of voices: (1) coming from inside the head; (2) coming from outside the head, but not perceived by other people; and (3) coming from outside and heard by others. The first two of these categories are hallucinations, and the third, normal perception. Psychotic patients do not distinguish the three in terms of realness, but sometimes mention that the outside voices also heard by others, that is, normal perceptions, are the least pertinent to their lives.

If a therapist confronts a patient with the "unreality" of his hallucinations, the patient often vigorously protests that he trusts his own perception of reality—why should he accede to an authoritarian statement or a democratic consensus when he can see with his own eyes and hear with his own ears? The problem is not only that the patient has vivid fantasies attributed to the object-world, but that he also gives preference to his internal world at the expense of an orderly relationship to the external world. Simultaneously, such a patient may desperately seek contact with other people. He may intrusively and inappropriately insist on talking about his innermost fantasies as if they were part of the external object-world that everyone can see and hear. Such talk is often very disconcerting.

With delusions, the preference given to internal data over and above external relationships is equally clear. A common definition of delusion is a fixed, untrue idea. In object relations terms, a delusion is the confusion of a vivid idea with a correct assessment of the nature of external events. One begins with an inner conviction and then interprets all external events in relation to that conclusion.

Each morning before class a college student talked with the delusional owner of a coffee shop in a small city in Oregon. The shopowner told him how newspaper articles contained a coded message from the pope about a Communist party plot to take over the world. If one began with the inner conviction that there was an organized plot, that the pope in Rome had a special relationship with a shopkeeper in Oregon, and that all the forces of civilization revolved around this one, seemingly insignificant shopkeeper, then each explanation seemed logical and convincing. The problem for this man was that no one else shared his assumptions. He did not open himself to taking in new data or interpretations other people might offer. Luckily, his customers were primarily college students who enjoyed and humored him.

No one shares the beliefs of schizophrenics, and they are in conflict with everyone else about the ideas they hold most dear. For them, these beliefs are often a life-and-death issue. Thus cut off from others, they have no avenue for checking and altering their inner life. Consequently, their fantasies, which may initially seem complex because of their idiosyncratic nature, often reveal themselves to be stereotyped, empty, and lifeless. No new influences are allowed to disturb and renew the old ideas.

Incoherence and bizarre behavior are also disturbances between one person and others, because these qualities are defined from the outside. That is, one person, the clinician, judges another person, the patient, to be unusual because the patient does not relate, speak, or act in a readily comprehensible manner. It would be easy to assume that such bizarre or incoherent people contain within them a disturbed sense of self, which is reflected in their external behavior. This conclusion, however, would not be warranted; it confuses the person viewed from the outside with the self viewed from the inside.

Language provides a glimpse into the internal life. People with bizarre speech, who may be judged as incoherent, actually do not produce utterances at random. Certainly, they do not speak according to the logic psychoanalysts call secondary process thinking. Their ramblings, however, even in extremely loose associations, do follow a set of principles, termed primary process thinking (Freud 1911, Brenner 1973). In this language of dreams and fantasies, opposites have no relevance and negatives do not exist. Part of an object can stand for the whole, and the whole, for the part. Symbols, such as words, can be treated as if they were the object which they symbolize. Time and sequence do not exist. It is the language of mythology, poetry, and madness.

Because, in primary process thinking, opposites have no relevance, there is an absence of stable self- and object-distinction. Self and object can only be defined as opposites in a dichotomy, yet in primary process thinking, opposites do not exist. Thus, it can be seen that people who speak incoherently or, more properly, according to primary process principles, do suffer from self–object confusion.

Dr. Peter Novotny (1980), of the Menninger Foundation, used the following example to illustrate this kind of thinking:

> A 50-year-old, schizophrenic man, Richard, appeared ashen and weak one day as he came to talk with his psychiatrist. "I feel fine, today," the patient said as he sat down. "I am Richard the Lionhearted." His astute psychiatrist saved his patient with his interpretation. "Can you guess what it was?" Novotny asked.

After several minutes of hemming and hawing, one of the residents guessed, "He's having a myocardial infarction. It's Richard the *lyin' hearted*, not Richard the *Lionhearted*. He doesn't feel fine today at all."

The sounds of the words "lion" and "lyin' " were fused together, and both meanings applied. Because there are no opposites in primary process thinking, there is no exclusiveness of meaning. On the one hand, Richard was lying about his heart by saying he felt fine when he was having chest pain. On the other hand, Richard did conceptualize himself as lionhearted, because he wanted to be strong of heart and courageous,[1] particularly at a time when his heart felt weak and he was afraid. "Lionhearted" could also refer to someone who felt physically as if a lion had attacked his heart. All these meanings were true and superimposed one on another with no exclusivity of opposites. Richard had so much trouble distinguishing his hurt, somatic self-image from his ideal object-image of King Richard I, that he did not behave appropriately to his situation of having a heart attack. His unusual language and behavior were both determined by his primary process thinking, which does not allow for opposites and does not distinguish self from object.

An example of bizarre behavior caused by the self-object confusion of primary process thinking is seen in this case:

A 48-year-old woman wore an aluminum foil hat bobby-pinned to her graying red hair. A resident internist nudged his psychiatric colleague. "Schizophrenic," he said. He somewhat precipitously concluded from her unusual dress and demeanor that she had a thought disorder.

When the psychiatry resident examined the patient, she explained that she had had unwanted thoughts beamed into her head for years. In the past few months, since she had discovered the solution of reflecting the thoughts back out with the aluminum foil, she had been able to live a much more stable life.

She confirmed the resident's presumption that her odd behavior reflected the self–other confusion of schizophrenia when she explained the thinking that went on behind her unusual appearance. She believed that unwanted thoughts were coming from outside her,

---

[1]The word courage is derived from the French *coeur*, and before that from the Latin *cor*, both of which mean heart.

and thus attempted to ward them off by placing metallic wrap on her head. This barrier could be seen in primary process terms to be a symbolic attempt to reinforce the faulty boundary between herself and the world around her. In all unusual schizophrenic behavior and speech, evidence of similar self–object confusions can be found.

The major symptoms of schizophrenia entail both self–object fusion and fragmentation. Hallucinations involve the perception of fantasies as if they derived from objects. This self–other confusion is always accompanied by fragmentation, because the hallucination, which pertains to the self, is split off and experienced as nonself. Delusions function in the same way. Here, ideas are confused with external events. This entails a blurring of self–other boundaries and also a splitting of the self into aspects which are experienced as self and different aspects which are projected into the object world. Bizarre talk and behavior also involve the fusion and fragmentation of primary thought processes.

Because schizophrenic symptoms can be thought of as deriving from self–other confusions and fragmentations analogous to those in symbiotic and hatching infants, these disorders are placed at that level on the developmental continuum. Some authors (Mahler 1952, Rinsley 1972) have described what they call a symbiotic psychosis. Placing schizophrenia at the symbiotic level of development does not mean, however, that these issues for schizophrenics are exactly the same as those for infants, nor does it mean that patients with schizophrenia never rise above the symbiotic level of relatedness. It does not necessarily imply that their adaptation prior to the outbreak of illness was only "as-if" or a pseudo-adaptation. It is entirely possible that some schizophrenic patients develop adequately integrated personalities by early adolescence. They may then acquire a brain disease which interferes with their integrative ego functions. Deprived of their previously adequate abilities to differentiate self and object, they may regress and reorganize along symbiotic-like lines, dealing with primitive issues of fusion and separation. Because they are adults, with adult sexual and aggressive interests, they have a bizarre symbiosis, strangely similar to, but different from, that of an infant.

Other schizophrenics with congenital minimal brain dysfunction (Hartocollis 1968, Bellak 1979, Hamilton and Allsbrook 1986) may adapt well until they face the adolescent demands for abstract thinking and ambiguous sexual and competitive relationships. At this time, they also face separation from the family. All these stresses at the same time may overwhelm their tenuous integrative ego functions. This group probably includes the largest portion of people suffering from schizophrenia.

P.W., a 22-year-old man, was typical of patients with schizophrenia in that he had a family history of the disorder and had been diagnosed as having attention deficit disorder and dyslexia as a child.[2] His parents did not believe the teachers and school psychologists. They insisted that he was a uniquely gifted child and that his teachers did not understand him. Nevertheless, his cognitive and visual–spatial organizing problems persisted; in late adolescence, his coping abilities failed him. He became preoccupied with bizarre religious ideas.

He initially refused treatment, because he did not believe himself to be ill. He was convinced he had special powers. Later, he agreed to talk with a psychiatrist about his troubles. During the sixth month of treatment, he confided how Unity, his delusional friend, had described the history of the earth. Originally, the earth was perfectly symmetrical and was surrounded by a circular layer of water. Moisture diffused the light so there was a uniform and moderate temperature. There were no seasons, because the earth was not tilted; neither was there precession of the equinoxes. In time, Sin, including the knowledge of good and evil, led to the flood. The waters from above were poured down onto the earth. The world split. The continents drifted apart. The oceans formed. The perfect balance was upset, and thus the world wobbled and reeled, leading to seasons and consequently the passage of time and the problems of deterioration and death.

Fortunately, he said, the angels were now aligning themselves at the four corners of the world to right things in the year 2000. All would again be in harmonic balance. We would once again be enveloped in a watery layer which would warm and protect us.

P.W. talked of how he felt about this story; it became clear that he longed for the protection and stability of being enclosed in womb-like waters. He longed to be in harmony and at one with his good object, represented by Unity. If only he could find an

---

[2]Prospective studies of children at risk for schizophrenia indicate that many of them have scattered learning and perceptual-motor difficulties (Mirsky et al. 1985). This finding does not imply that the large group of children with attention deficits, many of whom have learning disorders, are at statistically significantly greater risk for schizophrenia (Cantwell 1986). Similarly, people with albinism have blue eyes, but it is rare for someone with blue eyes to have albinism.

ideal relationship, he said some weeks later, if only someone would understand him, he would no longer be considered sick. The world would be right again. He thought perhaps his therapist would understand him in such a thorough way.

This patient apparently felt out of balance. He experienced his discord in the world around him, as well as in himself. His ability to comprehend and organize experiences was overtaxed, and he hoped that the understanding he longed for could come from outside, from his delusional symbiotic friend, whom he experienced as outside, or from the therapist. Whether or not his cognitive and perceptual-motor deficits caused his wishes to retreat into symbiotic oneness, these problems with integrative ego functions certainly did not make his struggle any easier. Many patients with schizophrenia have such impairments in ego functioning, and it makes theoretical sense that a failure of integrative functions could result in regression to a symbiotic personality organization.

A small number of patients diagnosed as schizophrenic potentially have neurophysiologically intact integrative ego functions. These patients' self–other confusion probably dates back to the earliest mother–child relationship. Such problems may be rearoused in adulthood during times of separation or loss.

A bright schizophrenic woman, J.W., fell ill when she graduated from high school and moved to a college town 100 miles from her mother's home.

As a child, she had had difficulty forming a secure symbiosis with her mother. Her father had been killed, and her mother seriously injured in an automobile accident shortly after her birth. The patient had been unharmed. Her mother could not hold her for months because of her injuries, yet she insisted on doing the parenting without help, despite having adequate financial resources to hire assistance. Her mother, who may have suffered some brain injury during the accident, claimed to be able to read her daughter's mind. While she was growing up, she was told by her mother what her feelings were, how to dress and even where to sit. Her mother often kept her home from school but would require that she sit silently for long hours. This odd combination of intrusive closeness and simultaneous rejection probably predisposed her to an eventual symbiotic psychosis in her late teens.

The patient was sufficiently well endowed constitutionally that she responded to this odd home life by reading voraciously and attending school whenever she was allowed. She did not have close school chums, but became the favorite of several teachers. When she faced the loss of familiar teachers and her mother, and found herself in an impersonal university, her longing for and fear of closeness rearoused her old symbiotic wishes and fears. She developed delusional figures who cared for her perfectly or else threatened her with nothingness. To ward off feelings of annihilation by abandonment, she compulsively masturbated.

J.W. was an intelligent woman with no signs of brain dysfunction on cognitive and visual–spatial tests. She was among the minority of patients who could entirely overcome her two-year-long psychosis by talking with someone, primarily about learning who she was in relation to other people.

Such symbiotic longings are characteristic of patients with schizophrenia of whatever type. Searles (1959) found symbiotic longings at the core of schizophrenia in patient after patient. He believed these problems usually derived from disruption in the early parent–child relationship. Recently, investigators have found that congenitally impaired integrative ego functioning in patients can cause disruption of parent–child relationships at least as often as dysfunctional relationships interfere with ego functioning.

In schizophrenia, symbiotic preoccupations and self–other boundary confusions dominate thinking. Consequently, schizophrenia is placed at the symbiotic level of development on the object relations continuum.

CHAPTER 9

MANIA

Patients with bipolar affective disorder have extreme mood swings, the elated pole of which is called mania. Their self–other boundary problems are not as severe as those of patients with schizophrenia, although at times they may become quite confused. When manic, bipolar patients display the omnipotent, world-is-my-oyster mentality of a practicing-subphase toddler. There is a pressured quality to their activities, as if they must exert greater and greater effort to ward off the realization that the world is not their oyster at all. Inwardly, these patients feel hopelessly insignificant.

E.H. was a tall, thin 45-year-old man, from Chicago, who attended group therapy. His dated suit coat flopped open in front of him, and his shirt tail hung out. Two weeks earlier, he had received a ten thousand dollar insurance settlement for mental disability.

Bustling into the meeting, he opened his briefcase and rummaged through impressive-looking documents. While other members talked of their troubles, hopes, and fears, he busied himself with more important matters. He looked up from time to time, and finally handed a document around the room for the

141

group to admire. He had just started a new business. Letterhead paper proudly displayed his title: President, Universal Opportunities, Incorporated. He intended to make a fortune and help mankind by turning the disabilities of all people into a human resource.

The next week, he announced that he had taken in a young, destitute woman. He was certain he could help her and planned to make her vice-president of Universal Opportunities. When his fellow group members questioned him, he interrupted, shouted them down, and talked faster and faster, insisting that if they understood, they would agree with his plan. When they persisted with their doubts, he announced he did not need the group as much as they needed him, and he left the room, only to return in a few minutes.

The following session, he explained again how no one had ever cared about this 18-year-old woman. Because he really cared about her, she would thrive. Sure, he said, it was disconcerting that money was disappearing from his house, but she would improve. He was not so worried about the flattery and companionship of this relationship. He wanted to help this woman. He wanted nothing for himself. He was a giver.

Within three weeks, he had lost his young friend along with five thousand dollars she had taken with her. Rather than grieving, he redoubled his efforts. He was impervious. He had made a mistake, he said, but he knew he could do good for the world. Others would sooner or later recognize how right he was.

At this point, he decided he no longer needed medication. He slept only two or three hours a night, because he was too busy to waste time resting. He drafted manifestos for his nonprofit corporation. He solicited donations, and a month later, another young person who had been living on the street, moved in with him. Two weeks later, his new partner moved out with the patient's furniture. It was beneath him to notice this loss. He was going to take care of the weak and homeless of the world.

He proclaimed his intentions even louder. When group members argued that he was manic and needed help, he became furious. He would help people. He needed no help for himself. All efforts by the psychiatrist to persuade him to go into the hospital or take his medication regularly were summarily rejected as insulting to his dignity.

Some group members appealed to his sense of entitlement instead of to his reason. They did not point out how he might hurt someone nor how he was needful. They told him he was a valuable person who was entitled to hospital care and help from his fellow human beings. He had worked and had paid for his medical insurance; he had a right to hospitalization if he wanted it. They were not telling him to enter the hospital because they thought he was sick or crazy or incompetent. With this approach, he allowed himself to be hospitalized. He also began taking lithium carbonate again.

It was fortunate that he could accept the group members' help. Otherwise, his psychiatrist might have had to try to hospitalize him forcibly. Using the police might have humiliated this vulnerable man even more, causing him to redouble again his already taxed efforts at demonstrating his omnipotence.

Like a practicing-subphase toddler, the patient was elated, determined, and impervious to setbacks. He had an I-will-do-it-myself attitude and used the group only for emotional refueling. He was not sensitive to the needs of other patients in the group, but came there to have people listen to his ideas. When they made suggestions, contradicted him, or otherwise frustrated him, he left, only to return later. This to-and-fro behavior seems very much like that of a toddler running off from and then returning to his mother. These similarities between manic behavior and practicing-subphase characteristics suggest that it can be placed at 10 to 16 months on the developmental continuum.

In addition to describing the obvious grandiosity among practicing youngsters, Mahler and colleagues (1975) pointed out a subtheme of insecurity, smallness, and a wish to return to mother's total care. While enjoying his newfound prowess, the child simultaneously reacts against his dependent longings, feelings of smallness, and fear of the larger world. E.H. displayed a similar reaction in his manic behavior.

After he was discharged from the hospital, he was able to describe his elated episode. He had been happy to get his disability settlement. Here was ten thousand dollars, just handed over to him; but he felt insulted too. Was he actually considered that sick? Did he have ten thousand dollars' worth of mental problems? Was he that needy? No, he was not the needy one. It was other people who were in need of his help, and to prove it, he would save them. In fact, he would save everyone.

Authors of the British school of object relations (Winnicott 1935, Klein 1940, Guntrip 1962) have described how manic-depressive patients deny feelings of helplessness by turning them into their opposite, omnipotence. They have noted a major difficulty in the therapy of these patients, namely, their tendency to experience help as an insult. If the therapist assists them, it implies they must be hopelessly dependent. Unmodulated affects do not allow manic patients to feel valuable and strong in certain areas and in need of help in other areas. Instead, they swing back and forth.

The object relations view of serious mental disorders does not stop with pointing out behavioral similarities to various developmental subphases. It also provides an understanding of the ways in which internal mental mechanisms are used to rearrange self- and object-experiences. For example, upon receiving his settlement, E.H. felt small, helpless, and defective. To deny this view of himself, he split it off from his self-image and projected it onto others. He was not helpless, others were. He was not desperately lonely; the people he took in were desperate. He did not need group therapy; the group needed him.

Splitting the self-image was involved to the extent that strong aspects of the self were experienced as entirely separate from any weak or dependent aspects, and the related mechanism of projective identification was involved to the extent that the split-off feelings of being defective were projected onto others. The patient then attempted to control and eradicate his dependency needs by meeting those needs in others. In the group, interpersonal projective identification could also be observed. Through his tirades, he elicited helpless feelings in group members by demonstrating his need while rejecting their efforts to help him. He then tried to enlighten them and reassure them, as a way of controlling his own feelings. Fortunately, the group members were able, with some encouragement and support from the psychiatrist, to contain his tirades.

Many patients with bipolar disorders have well-integrated personalities when they take lithium and are between periods of elation or depression. They can modulate affects, be considerate of others, see the mixed good and bad aspects of complex human interactions, and tolerate ambiguity and stress. During psychotic episodes, however, their extreme moods take them back to poorly integrated, grandiose, or hopelessly despondent self-images. This pattern indicates that most patients with bipolar disorders have traversed the difficulties of practicing, rapprochement, and even oedipal, latency, and adolescent periods quite well. When their biologically driven mood swings dominate, their behavior deteriorates along predictable lines to a level consistent with practicing behavior. Other bipolar patients seem to have a lifelong history of personality disorder, even between episodes. These patients often display a predominance of envy, which is yet another kind of turning an unwanted feeling into its opposite. These patients not only have mood swings, but also vacillate between idealization and devaluation (see Chapter 6).

Klein (1957a) described envy as a normal and marked aspect of child development during a period that corresponds to the development of practicing and early rapprochement issues. She used the relationship to the breast as a prototypical case. According to her account, a hungry child feels empty, pained, and angry inside himself. When his mother prepares to feed him, he sees the breast as full and rich, containing all the good supplies he wishes he had inside him. Angry at the breast for withholding good supplies, the baby wishes not only to share in the goodness, but to empty, deplete, and punish the breast. He wants to replace the fullness in the breast with the hungry emptiness inside him, while replacing the badness inside him with the warm fullness inside the breast. This intention can result in aggressive feeding and sometimes biting and pulling at the nipple, so typical of practicing-subphase youngsters. The child described in Chapter 5 who did not want to eat off his own plate, but wanted to mess and dump the food on his mother's plate, may have been showing envy.

J.E., a 35-year-old accountant with bipolar affective disorder, showed pronounced envy in his interactions. Even when nonpsychotic, he insatiably demanded repeated medication changes. He saw his doctor as the idealized container of coveted remedies. When his physician agreed to the changes, the patient contemptuously derided the ineffectiveness of the new regimen. In other matters, he took in the advice of his doctor and devalued him, returning contemptuous sneers. His psychiatrist felt stymied, sometimes doubting his own competence.

Neither was J.E. satisfied at work. His psychiatrist had prevailed upon an enlightened businessman to hire the patient, who was a bright accountant. Although his supervisor was positively disposed toward him initially, the patient felt insufficiently appreciated. He soon began criticizing his employer's personnel practices. When he eventually berated his boss's incompetence in front of other employees, he was threatened with termination. The patient was outraged that his boss would have the power to fire him, and he set out to prove that he was not important. He initiated a lawsuit on the grounds of discrimination against mentally disabled persons. This behavior occurred when his mood was relatively stable.

A circular pattern revealed itself. J.E. experienced himself as weak and devalued by others, who appeared to be omnipotently withholding perfect care, medications, or approval and recognition. In object relations terms, he split the self- and object-world along good–bad lines. Self was experienced as neglected and in need of help (bad); the object was experienced as powerful and filled with available supplies (good). He then put all his considerable effort into reversing the polarity of the idealization–devaluation. Through interpersonal projective identification, he elicited feelings of helplessness in the people around him. By defeating their efforts to help him, he triumphed. In this way, he denied his own feelings of smallness and aloneness, turning them into feelings of power and independence. Envy is related to the manic defense of turning despair into elation and of not needing anyone else.

Manic defenses are not always associated with malignant envy, or with psychosis. Many normal people use similar defenses to cope with sadness, loss, fear, and fatigue. The giddiness felt by students studying all night for a final examination or residents working twenty-four-hour shifts in the emergency room is psychologically a manic defense against tiredness, although it undoubtedly also has physiological correlates.

Some people who do not have bipolar affective disorder use a manic defense against serious depression.

M.M. had seen a woman psychiatrist four times. She listened, talked with her, and recommended lithium carbonate. When the patient refused to take the medication, her psychiatrist, while agreeing to continue seeing her, asked for another opinion about the medication. She referred her for consultation.

The patient was 5 feet 4 inches tall, weighed 180 pounds, and sat upright, thrusting her plump chest forward. She wore bright-red lipstick and gold jewelry. With rapid speech, she told the consultant she had calmed considerably since meeting with her psychiatrist over the past four weeks. She had just been worn out. She sang in two choirs and had been busy singing at funerals that summer. She pressed on to list an astounding number of activities she had been involved in the past few months, including driving the Meals-on-Wheels van to bring food to elderly people.

The consultant deftly interjected into her torrent of words, "You sing at funerals. How interesting. What is that about?"

"Oh, I've been terribly busy. I sang at three funerals this summer. Plus, I had choral practice. One funeral was for a church member. I have to take care of everyone. When my little brother died, I took care of the property; and when my sister died, her husband didn't know what to do, of course, poor thing. Singing at the funeral, that's my way of making a contribution. You see, I'm a fine singer. My mother used to say . . ."

"Mrs. M.," he said, "I think perhaps you are singing at a funeral right now. You are chirping away as if you don't have a very deep sadness within you, as if you wouldn't be heard anyway if you spoke of your sadness."

She stopped short and then said calmly, "Well, he was the first of my generation; and then my sister the same year. You know, when older people die you expect it; but when your own brothers and sisters start dying . . ." She could not go on. She wept.

M.M.'s mother and father had died when she was 7 years old. She had helped to raise her younger siblings. When she was 20, the world was at war. She spent her young adult years in a support unit for combat soldiers in London. After the war, she married a young soldier. She took care of him, his dying mother, his four younger brothers and sisters, and then her own four children. She thrust herself into activities, taking care of others. When her brother and then her sister died in the same summer, she redoubled her efforts to appear happy and demonstrate that she needed no one, but that others needed her. She could not accept her psychiatrist's advice— she felt she did not need medication. She had felt, however, that she had been listened to, and by the time she went to the consultant, she already had some awareness of the sadness underlying her elation.

M.M. did not have a classical bipolar disorder. Psychodynamically, she had a manic defense against depression. Since early childhood, she split off the dependent, needy aspects of herself and projected her dependency onto others. That way, she did not feel helpless. She was the provider of care and needed no help. When she felt sadness about the loss of her brother and sister, she did not mourn. She denied her own wishes to be held and comforted, and this led to feelings of abandonment. Her efforts to deny her feelings had to be redoubled. Soon she could not sleep, sit still, or slow her speech. It was not until her psychiatrist listened to her rambling story over and over and sent her for consultation that she could allow her grandiose defense against depression to diminish. After the consultation, she returned to her psychiatrist and talked about her losses for six more sessions. She was discharged improved.

Individuals with bipolar affective disorder, or with more common manic defenses of a less extreme kind, display many of the interpersonal characteristics of practicing-subphase toddlers. They deny their weaknesses and develop a sense of omnipotence. They attempt to do everything themselves and have difficulty accepting help. When frustrated, they can fly into tantrums or tirades.

CHAPTER 10

BORDERLINE PERSONALITY DISORDER

Extensive study of borderline personality over the past two decades has played a crucial role in the development of American object relations theory. Borderline disorders display issues of the rapprochement crisis (Mahler 1971, Kernberg 1975, 1980, Masterson and Rinsley 1975, Adler 1985).

For decades, "borderline" referred to a group of patients who had features of both neurosis and schizophrenia or who seemed to shift back and forth between the two. As Wong (1980) has catalogued, various diagnoses were included in the classification borderline, including as-if personality (Deutsch 1934), borderline neurosis (Stern 1938), ambulatory schizophrenia (Zilboorg 1941), occult schizophrenia (Stern 1945), schizophrenic character (Schafer 1948), pseudoneurotic schizophrenia (Hoch and Polatin 1949), abortive schizophrenia (Mayer 1950), subclinical schizophrenia (Peterson 1954), and psychotic character (Frosch 1964). It was not until Grinker's (Grinker et al. 1968) work that these patients were studied empirically. Later, Kolb and Gunderson (1980) introduced the Diagnostic Interview for Borderline, facilitating further empirical studies.

Kernberg (1967, 1975) offered the most comprehensive psychoanalytic understanding of what he termed borderline personality organization. As he described these patients, they had certain symptoms, character structure, and developmental features. Furthermore, he argued that borderline patients had a specific and stable, though in some areas dysfunctional, personality. They were not merely in a transient state fluctuating between psychosis and neurosis.

As Kernberg described their symptoms, these patients are often impulsive, angry, prone to addictions, sexually promiscuous or perverse, psychosomatically concerned, phobic, and chronically racked with diffuse anxiety. They are also prone to dissociation, paranoid thinking, and obsessions.

Structurally,[1] borderline patients have ego weakness, specific defensive operations (splitting, projective identification, idealization, and devaluation), and split internalized objects. Ego weakness refers to problems similar to those originally found by Knight (1953). These dysfunctions consist of inability to modulate anxiety or other affects, lack of impulse control, and poor ability to sublimate, that is, turn sexual and aggressive impulses to other, socially appropriate activities. Sublimation requires the ego function of integrating the demands of impulses with the benefits of conforming to more complex social standards.

The characteristic development, according to Kernberg's formulation, turns upon an increase in aggressive drive. Either because they are constitutionally predisposed to aggression or because they are excessively frustrated, these individuals need to protect internalized good objects by splitting off and excessively projecting bad (aggressive) objects. This combination of splitting and projection leads to an inability to integrate good and bad self- and object-images during the rapprochement subphase.

Understanding borderline personality organization in terms of a psychoanalytic theory of personality made this category a broad one. It included most other serious personality disorders, such as schizoid, paranoid, antisocial, passive–aggressive, and infantile personalities, because all of these disorders display similar internal object relations. Diagnosing in terms of intrapsychic issues casts such a broad net because all people still have within them, at some level, residuals from all the stages of development they have traversed. Consequently, everyone, whether more integrated or more fragmented, has some

---

[1]The psychoanalytic theory of structures refers to id, ego, and superego functions (Freud 1923). Structure in general can be defined as a set of functions which have a slow rate of change.

evidence of ego weakness and primitive defensive operations, such as splitting, projective identification, idealization, and devaluation.

Current diagnostic criteria have become somewhat less broad than Kernberg's conceptualization (Gunderson 1982, Hamilton et al. 1984, Fisher et al. 1985). This narrowing of definition took place, not by discarding Kernberg's ideas, but by translating them from psychoanalytic abstractions into more descriptive and behavioral terms. Extensive empirical work (Spitzer et al. 1979, Sheehy et al. 1980, Kernberg et al. 1981, Kroll et al. 1981, Soloff and Ulrich 1981, Gunderson 1982, McGlashan 1983, Hamilton et al. 1984, Fisher et al. 1985) helped in this evolution.

The DSM-III criteria include impulsivity, intense unstable relationships, inappropriate anger, identity disturbance, mood instability, intolerance of being alone, self-destructive acts, and chronic feelings of emptiness or boredom. All these symptoms reflect their roots in Kernberg's formulations and can be understood in terms of split internal object relations and a failure to achieve object constancy. This splitting, with poor object constancy, is characteristic of rapprochement-subphase children (as described in Chapters 5 and 6). Before looking at the possible causes of borderline disorders, I shall indicate how each DSM-III criterion for this condition reflects a failure of integration, which results in poor object constancy and split internal object relations.

The impulsivity of many adolescent and adult borderline patients resembles that of toddlers. Without considering consequences, they may rush toward what seems like a gratifying object, forgetting the currently frustrating object.

D.L.'s employer took him aside and suggested he learn a more efficient procedure for routing mail. His boss valued him and was trying to help, but D.L. could not perceive the help while simultaneously having to tolerate the frustration of accepting criticism and needing to learn something new. He forgot that he was a valued employee who had recently been advanced. He impulsively quit his job. He drank, listened to music, and sought out friends. After a few days, he returned to work, hoping to get his job back. He was lonely, bored, and broke. His life away from work had now become a frustrating object, and the job again looked good.

Patients like D.L. often turn to drugs or alcohol as a gratifying object. When the drugs cause pain or lowering of self-esteem, they will suddenly quit using them, only to return. This is similar to the movement of a rapprochement child toward and away from its mother. This to-and-fro behavior extends to treatment also.

> D.D., a 25-year-old borderline patient, sought treatment to escape "aloneness and emptiness." Initially, she felt safe in treatment and less alone. A few weeks later, when therapy became frustrating, she forgot its good aspects and terminated. She returned two months later.

Hospital staff members may find it particularly vexatious when borderline patients sign into the hospital, only to sign out again the next day.

In these examples of impulsivity, the patients could not maintain a stable object-image of an essentially good relationship. When something was frustrating, it suddenly seemed all bad, a thing to be avoided for fear it would make the self bad also. When drugs or a new relationship were experienced as good, they temporarily seemed all good and were sought, only to be discarded shortly. Impulsivity in borderline patients results from these shifting all-good and all-bad splits, with little ability to hold a steady image of something as primarily good, but also bad.

This same shifting of the self- and object-world leads to impulsivity in relationships. Because borderline individuals may experience a new relationship as gratifying, their infatuations can be intensely exciting, like an all-good, symbiotic attachment. This boundary blurring of the all-good self–other experience can just as quickly turn to all-bad self–other hatred, because there is a lack of object constancy, that is, lack of the ability to remember the presence of the good object in the face of frustration.

When these patients feel alone or unloved, they attempt to alter their feelings by manipulating others. Through projective identification, they believe they would feel good if only the other would make it happen. When ungratified, they throw tantrums, threaten, cajole — even make suicide attempts — in efforts to force the return of the all-good object and to punish the all-bad object. They are unable to conceptualize that the person who is ignoring them at one point in time is the same person they felt loved by at a previous time. Such intense emotions often lead to the promiscuity or other serial relationships described in DSM-III.

The anger of borderline individuals similarly derives from internal splits and a tendency to enter all-bad self-object states while forgetting their love of the object. Because of their poorly established self–other boundaries, they easily become involved in negative projective identification.

I consulted with J.A., a 33-year-old borderline woman who had just completed an unsuccessful psychotherapy. When I asked her what had gone amiss, she complained that her psychotherapist got angry at her "all the time." Then she would get angry at him. She tried to calm him down, but he was intractable, and so she had finally felt compelled to quit. When I questioned her further about her own problems with anger, she admitted she did have some such difficulty, but felt she could not improve when her therapist had the same problem she did. Further interviewing revealed that anger and self–other boundary blurring, resulting in an all-bad self-object experience, was characteristic of all her relationships.

In the therapy situation, as in her other relationships, J.A. could not tolerate the hostility she experienced when she was frustrated. Thus, she would project this hostility into her image and perception of the therapist. She would then reintroject it into her self-image, saying, "I am angry because he is angry." Thereby, she split off her anger. Through the use of projective identification, she entered an all-bad self-object state, resulting in the intense and inappropriate anger in the DSM-III for borderline disorder.

Identity disturbances found in borderline personality derive from poor object constancy and splitting along all-good and all-bad lines. Some patients actually describe themselves as having a good self and a bad self. Although borderline patients do not have multiple personalities, they often feel like a different person depending upon whether they feel accepted or abandoned.

R.O. reported that when she was alone, she would sink into a black abyss and verge on ceasing to exist. She was terrified of aloneness, fearing she could lose her sense of self, her identity, at a basic level. On the other hand, when she was with people, and involved in constructive activity, she felt confident and creative.

Many borderline patients are severely impaired and cannot work consistently, because of their shifting identity. Others function quite well in the work place, as long as their role is clearly defined for them.

R.O. could work as a physician in a structured institutional setting, if her tasks were clear and her supervisor supportive. On weekends, she suffered feelings of loss of identity and desperately sought contact and soothing through drug abuse, promiscuity, dangerous activities, and compulsive athletics.

A borderline patient's moods can be so dependent on the external environment that they constantly shift. Lacking good object constancy, such people may not be able to maintain a feeling of well-being if relationships are temporarily frustrating. They may not be able to remember that life is generally gratifying and people care about them when they are deprived or alone. With a pleasant and supportive person, they may feel wonderful. The extreme, all-good and all-bad self–other states of people with borderline disorder, then, lead to mood instability.

These patients are dependent on gratifying external objects in order to feel good internally. They have a poor tolerance for being alone, unlike most people who can enjoy being by themselves or accomplishing something on their own, and do not feel abandoned, but experience themselves as if they have a good, caring object within them. Borderline disordered individuals lack a constant, gratifying internal object to accompany them when they are alone. They do not have that "still, small voice" within them whispering to them that all is well. When alone they forget that anyone has ever been there for them.

> One of my colleague's patients told him that she thought he was a good therapist who helped her during the week, but over the weekend she thought of him as uncaring and cold. Each Sunday, she decided to announce in the Monday session she was quitting treatment; but when she actually saw him on Monday, her discontent vanished, and she remembered how she felt helped in therapy.

It is this lack of object constancy, this dependence upon the actual presence of the good object to remind them that they are valued, which leads to the intolerance of being alone described in DSM-III.

The all-bad self-object state can go to the extreme of stimulating self-damaging acts.

> A resident psychiatrist described a 27-year-old woman who felt rejected by her boyfriend. They had an argument, and she told

him if he did not love her and take care of her, she would leave home, perhaps even kill herself. She packed her suitcase and walked and walked in the rain. She crossed the Morrison Bridge over the Willamette River and thought of how angry she was at her lover. She felt an urge to jump off the bridge. She later described how she imagined herself sinking into the dark waters, never to return; at that point, her boyfriend drove up and stopped his car in the middle of traffic. She started to walk off, but he grabbed her suitcase, dragged her into the car, and drove her to the University Hospital emergency room.

The resident learned that she had taken overdoses of medicines under similar circumstances. When he examined her, he found scars on her wrists from self-inflicted lacerations. The resident formulated the object relations of this patient when he described her in conference. As her loneliness plus her rage at her boyfriend grew, her self–other boundaries dissolved. She entered an all-bad self-object state. Convinced she was unloved, she felt abandoned. In retaliation, or perhaps because of self–other confusion, she abandoned her lover. The dark, empty feeling within her seemed indistinguishable from the black nighttime waters of the river that she felt drawn toward. She succeeded in threatening her boyfriend sufficiently that he turned into the semblance of an omnipotent good object so that she no longer had the need to harm herself.

Many borderline patients learn that they can relieve tension and resolve their physical boundaries by cutting themselves.

R.O., the physician described above, told her therapist how she would feel bad, empty, and worthless, her physical boundaries dissolving into nothingness. In desperation, she would roll up her sleeve, sterilize her forearm, and use a scalpel to slice a fine line in her skin. The slight pain and the sight of red blood oozing through her white skin reminded her in a tangible way of her self–other boundary.

Chronic feelings of emptiness or boredom also relate to a tendency to enter all-bad states and an inability to call up the good self and good object. To feel empty is to feel that the self is depleted. The external equivalent of emptiness is boredom, that is, to feel that the world is depleted and devoid of interest. By way of contrast, some people with well-established object constancy do not become bored even under the most extreme conditions of deprivation. Rudyard Kipling was sent from his warm, loving home and mother in colonial India back to England for his education when he was barely of school age (Pollock 1985). Forced to live with a harsh woman who kept him locked alone in a barren room for long hours, he created elaborate and fantastic tales, neither succumbing to the boredom and emptiness of abandonment nor to the delusion that his imaginings were real. The borderline disordered person does not have this capacity to call upon inner resources. There is a constant need to seek the good symbiotic mother in the external world to ward off feelings of emptiness and boredom.

All the DSM-III criteria for borderline disorder can be seen to derive from lack of object constancy and split internal object relations. Because these characteristics of borderline patients are also typical of rapprochement-subphase children, borderline disorders are placed at the rapprochement level in the object relations continuum. The cause of these problems has most frequently been related to an internal, constitutional excess of aggression (Kernberg 1975), to a reciprocal deficit of loving impulses (Federn 1952, Rinsley 1968), or to a lack of consistent, confirming, and modulating care by the parents (Masterson and Rinsley 1975, Adler 1985).

If he has an excess of aggression or a deficit of loving impulses, the rapprochment child must use increasing projective mechanisms to protect the fragile good internal object from being overwhelmed by hostility. This age group cannot integrate the good and bad self- and object-images and cannot develop a stable, internal, good enough object-image; children at this stage must constantly seek supplies of warmth and concern from outside themselves.

Since children internalize what they perceive, and not necessarily what is characteristic of external objects, they may project their own excess aggression onto their external objects and then introject hostile objects even when their actual parents are benign. Subsequently, they must split off and project these newly reintrojected hostile objects. In this way, children who, according to this theory, have excessive aggression enter a vicious circle of projecting hostility which leads to the need to split and to project further hostility.

There is an alternative view, that borderline disorders are caused by a deficit of maternal soothing. As Adler (1985) has described, children whose parents cannot adequately empathize, soothe, and confirm do not have an opportunity to internalize this function. Consequently, they do not learn to listen to themselves, to soothe themselves, and to modulate their complex positive and negative affects. Masterson and Rinsley (1975) have described mothers who need to cling to their children to meet their own previously unmet dependency needs. These mothers offer approval, support, and emotional supplies for symbiotic, clinging behavior. They are threatened by separation and become "attacking, critical, hostile, angry, withdrawing supplies and approval in the face of assertiveness or other efforts toward separation–individuation" (p. 169). This reinforces the infant's all-good and all-bad split object relations. It leads the child to feel abandoned if he behaves maturely, and to constantly seek good symbiotic objects.

The splitting and lack of object constancy in borderline patients need not necessarily be the result of increased hostility and decreased love in the internal or the external object-world, but can also be due to faulty integrative ego functions. If the ego is not able cognitively to bring together, compare, and contrast good and bad self- and object-images, split objects and poor object constancy will persist. This factor leads to the as yet inadequately explored clinical finding that mental retardation and minimal brain dysfunction are associated with borderline personality disorder.

Adults with previously developed fairly well-integrated personalities may suffer a brain injury which impairs their integrative ego functions and results in a change of personality. The resulting organically damaged personality may be indistinguishable from borderline personality, with impulsivity, chronic anger, intense, unstable relationships, mood instability, and even self-damaging acts. As suggested earlier, these patients often remember their previous relationships in a detailed and integrated fashion, because their long-term memory is spared. Their current relationships reflect their split all-good and all-bad object relations and their inability to integrate experience.

It is not only brain injury that can cause a return to rapprochement-like functioning in adults; extreme experiences at certain life phases may result in a similar regression. It has been well observed that veterans of the Vietnam War with posttraumatic stress disorder are often indistinguishable from patients with borderline personality. Brende (1983) has described how war, particularly the Vietnam War, could lead to the predominate use of splitting and projective identification as defense mechanisms.

Many soldiers who fought in Vietnam were from 18 to 22 years old. During this life phase of late adolescence, adult identity is consolidated and new intimacies are established (Erikson 1950). As a part of this process, the separation issues of rapprochement are reopened and reworked. This is a time when young adults separate from parents and function independently in work and social worlds. The earlier separation issues reappear. College-age late adolescents often rework these separation and attachment issues by moving in and out of the parental home repeatedly. They are still at times dependent on their families.

When young men of this age group were sent off to war during a life phase of identity reconsolidation, they were placed in a most unfavorable circumstance. Their task was ambiguous; because it was guerrilla warfare, there was no home territory to control; political and emotional support for the war and for military leaders broke down. This lack of support contributed to feelings of loss, if not abandonment. Furthermore, as in any war, splitting and projective identification were often used—one's comrades were good, and the enemy was bad. One's own hostility was projected onto the enemy, and then controlled and subdued through aggressive attacks. The war reopened partially resolved rapprochement issues for this age group. Splitting and projective identification could cause a rift in the internal object world of these men, so that their personalities could be permanently and significantly damaged.

Borderline personality disorder can be understood in terms of split internal all-good and all-bad self- and object-representations, and inadequate object constancy. Because these same factors are central to the rapprochement subphase, this disorder is placed at that level of the object relations continuum. These difficulties may begin during the rapprochement subphase itself, or may be rearoused during later development.

CHAPTER **11**

NARCISSISTIC PERSONALITY DISORDER

Individuals with narcissistic disorders are preoccupied with grandiose schemes, crave attention, and tout their own perfection. Underneath this facade, they feel insecure and dependent. They can make a fairly clear distinction between self and object, but retain some uncertainty about this issue in crucial areas. Particularly, they tend to attribute the internal function of maintaining self-esteem to those around them and to enter partial merger states with people they idealize. In the area of integration, they have difficulty bringing together grandiose and devalued aspects of the self. The grandiose (good) and devalued (bad) aspects of the self are not experienced as part of the same thing. According to Kohut's terminology, they have an "insufficient consolidation of the self" (Ornstein 1974, p. 137).

Narcissistic patients can sometimes maintain an inflated sense of their importance and uniqueness for days or weeks at a time. When this grandiose self prevails, they have little awareness of whatever hurt, sad, and devalued self-images they may retain. Should they suffer an insult or defeat that penetrates their narcissistic shell, they may feel crushed, small, inadequate, and worthless. They do not remember their previous good opinion of themselves and integrate it with their present experience of humiliation. When they feel better again, they once more forget their small, hurt self and involve themselves in further grandiose endeavors.

Patients with narcissistic personality alternate between the extremes of idealization and devaluation of others. They may admire and emulate a famous person and consider his flaws to highlight assets. "He is so good," they may say about an idol, "he doesn't have to cover up things that would be a mistake for other people. He is such a genius, it all fits together." When they experience some real disappointment in relation to their idealized star, they can suddenly consider that person worthless and "ready for the ash can." They have little ability to recognize and integrate previously held high opinions of the admired person with their new awareness of the person's shortcomings.

Borderline and narcissistic categories overlap on the diagnostic continuum; many narcissistic patients have some borderline features. Narcissistic individuals, however, are above the borderline in level of personality organization. There is indication of a more advanced self–object differentiation in narcissistic patients, who seldom have the brief psychotic episodes to which many borderline patients are susceptible (Kernberg 1975, Kolb and Gunderson 1980, Chopra and Beatson 1986). Hallucinations, delusions, and loss of a sense of reality constitute psychotic episodes and are manifestations of severe boundary disturbances, and narcissistic patients only infrequently have such severe boundary disturbances, unlike their borderline counterparts. Psychologically, they are more separated.

Narcissistic patients tolerate frustration better than less integrated patients do. They are not as impulsive as borderline patients. They can distinguish themselves from other people, conceptualize them clearly, and manipulate them consistently. Unlike borderline patients, narcissistic patients do not endlessly seek the object itself as a physical entity. It is the attention and admiration of the object that they crave. They seek praise, like addicts need drugs. When someone fails to deliver the required adulation, these patients avoid loss of self-esteem by projecting their feelings of worthlessness onto the object. The depriving person becomes worthless and scorned. "I did not need him anyway," the patient tells himself. "What do I care about the opinion of a fool?" When such defense mechanisms fail, the grandiose self comes tumbling down.

Narcissistic patients have difficulty empathizing because of their preoccupation with their grandiose self. Their indifference and disregard for the integrity of others can make them seem especially independent. This appearance is belied, however, by the observation that their locus of self-esteem regulation remains outside them. Since the ego function of assessing their own performance in relation to their goals is attributed to the people around them, they remain dependent on praise. Although their self- and object-images have fairly distinct boundaries, it is in this area of self-esteem regulation that their boundaries are most permeable. Thus, they are dependent on people outside of them for self-esteem regulation. Kohut (1971) calls the external objects who help narcissistic patients maintain a sense of self-worth "selfobjects."[1]

Narcissistic patients often cannot empathize with and soothe themselves any more than they can empathize with other people. If they suffer criticism or defeat, they cannot reflect on their difficulty and recognize their own sadness or pain. They cannot tell themselves, "You have fallen down in this area, but you really made a credible effort, and you do quite well in other areas." The failure to empathize with themselves thus leads to a need for outside approval. The more adaptive often drive themselves toward acclaim, allowing their grandiose self total domination, neglecting the need for rest and companionship. They can be their own cruel task masters, demanding perfection. Less adaptive narcissists must settle for attention of any kind in place of acclaim.

The following example illustrates some problems with integration of the grandiose and devalued self and regulation of self-esteem and self-soothing.

D.C., a 23-year-old man, came to the hospital from Belaire, California, because he used cocaine, drove recklessly, and achieved opportunities in his budding acting career, only to fail by engaging in wild pranks.

His latest disaster occurred the night before he was to begin a small but respectable part in a television series. Instead of resting or preparing for the next day's work, he caroused all night and searched for a source of cocaine. When three drug dealers, who were carrying weapons, robbed his friend, spat in his face, and refused to hand over the agreed-upon cocaine, he took it upon himself to rectify the situation—he would save the day. Overestimating his physical prowess, he attacked one of the hoodlums. As he swung around to confront the other two dealers, an iron bar met him in the face, fracturing his zygomatic arch. He fell to the ground and suffered a severe beating.

---

[1]See footnote on p. 96.

D.C. refused the advice of the doctor in the emergency room. The next day he dragged himself to the studio. Perhaps a broken face would stop some actors, but not him.

He fell into a depression following the first filming. The part was not good enough. The famous actors ignored him. He felt he was nothing, a nobody.

His despondency continued through his hospitalization for facial surgery. Following discharge, he would not leave his room for six weeks. He did not want anyone to see his bruises. It was during this time that he accepted his family's pressure to go to a psychiatric hospital, but only so that he could learn more about himself and reveal the great actor he was certain he had hidden deep within him.

By the time he reached the hospital, his face had healed, leaving him more handsome than ever, thanks to a surgeon's skillful revision of his nasal bones. He was no longer a hurt, worthless, despondent young man. He strutted onto the ward, bragged of his movie role, sneered at the other patients as "sickies," set out to seduce the nurses, and condescendingly humored his psychiatrist. Even empathic comments he considered an affront to his dignity—he did not need coddling. When his psychiatrist looked at him during the interview, he felt challenged and had to do battle, proving his superiority.

It was eventually decided that D.C. should begin psychoanalysis while still in the hospital. He was able to reflect on himself when not intoxicated and not indulging in grandiosity. Psychoanalysis carried enough prestige as a treatment that the patient wanted to give it a try.

He did not feel challenged or upstaged because the analyst sat out of his view. The analyst primarily listened and commented infrequently. The patient consequently did not feel discredited by attempts at help or by the offer of new insights. He did not lose his sense of himself or confuse his boundaries by projecting excessively onto the analyst. His unobtrusive analyst served as a selfobject (Kohut 1971), as another person who serves the self's function of soothing, confirming, and regulating self-esteem.

Over several months, D.C. was able to begin integrating his grandiose self with his hurt and devalued self. He slowly gained the image of himself as a talented young man who needed to work hard at his chosen profession. The realization that he needed rest, orderly living, companionship, and compassion helped him become empathic. He no longer needed to project his devalued self onto other patients. He could help them build self-esteem instead of ridiculing them.

Prior to the newer theoretical insights about narcissistic self-images, D.C.'s getting hurt before his performance may have been interpreted as an oedipal conflict (Freud 1900). His injury would have been seen as motivated by guilt over successfully displaying himself publicly for acclaim, in order to surpass his father, just as he had wished as a small boy to have his mother admire his genitals more than his father's. This understanding suggests that he undermined his own success in order to avoid guilt feelings and a fantasized castration as punishment for forbidden success. Later analysis did show some evidence for this conclusion, as demonstrated in D.C.'s dreams and fantasies, but it was not the major theme.

A traditional interpretation would not have been useful early in this analysis. An object relations approach fostered the necessary progress. An oedipal interpretation would have been insufficient, because his divided self—grandiose and devalued—determined his self-defeating behavior to a more significant extent than did whatever guilt feelings he may have had over competitive strivings. His grandiose self was so much in control that he really believed he could defeat the three thugs, or if not, that he could act despite being beaten up, as if his will could overcome the limits of physical reality. He was not primarily punishing himself, because he did not think he would fail; rather, his grandiosity led him to believe he would succeed.

This man had sufficient determination, strength, and charm that he could go to awe-inspiring lengths to make his actual person as viewed from the outside correspond to his internal grandiose self-image. These self-images needed to be delineated before analysis of guilt over competitive strivings could help. He probably would have experienced early oedipal interpretations as an attack on his perfect self-image. The analysis of oedipal conflicts could only take place after the grandiose and devalued self-images had become more integrated.

The object relations configuration of narcissistic patients places them between the rapprochement subphase and the attainment of whole object relations. It is at this time that the all-good, omnipotent, or grandiose self becomes differentiated from the all-good, omnipotent, or idealized object. The all-bad, devalued self also becomes differentiated from the all-bad, devalued object. The ego has not yet integrated the grandiose and devalued self. If these two self-experiences remain walled off from one another, the narcissist cannot become aware of weaknesses when in the grandiose state.

Normal children, 3 to 4 years of age, often display this object relations configuration. For example, children of this age today begin to play He-Man.

A 3½-year-old boy came charging into the room shouting, "He-Man," and raising his arm in triumph.
"Oh, you're pretending you're He-Man," his father said.
"No, Daddy, I *am* He-Man," he corrected and charged off into the next room.

This child could imagine himself to be identical to a grandiose object-image, He-Man, without fear of actually losing his self. He could also recognize that he was his father's little boy. He was partially able to distinguish himself from internal and external objects, but he still needed to see himself as all-powerful. During his grandiose play, he would admit to no chink in his armor unless his grandiose self was overwhelmed, perhaps by falling; then he would feel crushed, weep, and call for his father's help.

This placement of narcissistic issues in late rapprochement–early object constancy coincides with the previous psychoanalytic placement of these exhibitionistic and narcissistic behaviors at what was termed the urethral phase of psychosexual development (Tyson 1982). This phase lies between the anal and oedipal stages, approximately 3 to 4 years of age.

Kohut (1971), who based his self psychology on a study of narcissistic disorders, suggested that the roots of narcissism began much earlier than 3 to 4 years of age. He argued that failures in empathic parenting from very early life could make it difficult for children to let go of their grandiose self-images and recognize, and come to terms with, weaknesses. Tolpin (1971) described this failure of empathy as having varying implications at different developmental stages. The end result, in my view, is that such children cannot internalize their parents' empathic capacity when their self-image is ready to coalesce following rapprochement. Consequently, they cannot perform self-soothing functions, and thereby suffer a disorder of self-regulation (Grotstein 1987). Without an ability to empathize with their own troubled states of mind, these children must split off and deny weaknesses. Their grandiose self-image then becomes enhanced to defend against overwhelming feelings of helplessness and vulnerability.

Not only can previous difficulties lead to late rapprochement—early oedipal failures, but subsequent troubles can also result in a return to such problems. Tolpin (1971) clarified this issue by using Anna Freud's (1965) idea of developmental lines to point out that issues of self-esteem regulation run throughout life. Early on, during hatching and practicing, children need confirming admiration and mirroring (Kohut 1971). During rapprochement, they need empathic understanding and tolerance, as well as setting of limits. When object constancy develops and oedipal issues arise, children need to be able to identify with a parent whom they still idealize. In latency, they need the approval and admiration of their teachers and peers. Again in adolescence, children need to idealize and identify with teachers, athletes, and entertainment figures. In adult life, roles are still confirmed by others. Blatantly narcissistic behavior may be obvious in practicing-substage youngsters and again in late rapprochement and early oedipal children; but narcissistic disorders can develop with failures anywhere along the developmental line. Children must be exposed to a chronic failure of parental empathy across phases of development to acquire a full-blown narcissistic personality. Lacking a soothing and empathic parental object, they cannot acquire the ability to self-soothe through the normal process of transmuting internalization (Kohut 1971, Tolpin 1971).

Unlike Kohut, Kernberg (1974a, 1975) emphasizes the child's aggressive envy and devaluing as central to the development of narcissistic disorders. He suggests that an innate excess of aggressive drive could result in devaluation of the parental image, so that the child does not experience his parents as being as supportive as they actually may be. He admits that the aggression could be related to disappointment caused by chronic parental frustration; but he does not emphasize this possibility, and he continues to point out that the child's own aggression, regardless of its source, plays an important part in narcissistic problems. This theoretical difference between Kernberg and Kohut has not been resolved. Clinically, it seems most useful to lean toward Kohut's empathic understanding of the patient's experienced disappointment, particularly early in the therapy, regardless of how the actual, external parents may or may not have acted in the patient's early life. The therapist must at the same time keep in mind Kernberg's point, particularly later in treatment, that it is the child's own aggression and envy over which he ultimately has the most control. (The therapeutic issues will be taken up again in Chapters 13 and 14.)

A consideration of the causes of narcissistic disturbances should not ignore the possibility that poor integrative ego functions, in addition to environmental problems or increased aggressive drives, can lead to difficulty in moderating grandiose and devalued self-images. If a child cannot compare and contrast images and hold contradictory concepts in mind simultaneously, he may retain unintegrated, grandiose, and devalued self-images, despite adequate parenting and normal drive intensity. Such problems can result in a vicious circle of failure, criticism, lowered self-esteem, grandiose attempts to compensate, and failure. A child with poor integrative ego functions may have problems putting concepts together in school. Difficulty in integrating and differentiating is often global, affecting abstract thinking and problem solving, as well as development of self- and object-images. Resulting school failure and parental criticism can lead to lowered self-esteem. Attempts to compensate for feelings of shame in a child who already has difficulty comparing and contrasting self-images may result in additional grandiose fantasies, which may in turn interfere with concentration.

When failures of parental empathy are involved in the etiology of narcissistic disorders, they arise from various sources. Striving, upwardly mobile parents may be capable of empathizing with their children but may not spend sufficient time with them to communicate their understanding. They feel guilty if they do not provide well for their offspring; consequently, both parents may work long hours and place their idealized children in day-care centers. If pressures for success and financial security are not balanced with the child's needs for consistent parenting and confirmation, narcissistic problems will often arise, even in children with a good constitutional endowment and parents with empathic capacities.

Narcissistic disorders are common among all social classes. Lasch (1978) and Rinsley (1982) have both suggested that we live in an age of narcissism because of overindulgent yet simultaneously neglectful child-rearing practices. Tuchman (1978) described the prevalent exploitive and self-centered behavior accompanied by swings in self-esteem in fourteenth-century Europe. Drinka (1984) described the degenerate genius cults of nineteenth-century Europe. A study of most cultures might yield evidence of narcissism as a characteristic. It may or may not be an unusually prominent feature of post-World War II America.

Not every narcissistic issue suggests a developmental problem or personality disorder. All people have tendencies to overvalue themselves sometimes and undervalue themselves at other times. Patients with schizophrenia, mania, depression, borderline disorders, obsessive–compulsive neuroses, and hysteria all have problems with self-esteem regulation. It is only when a person has extremely and persistently poorly integrated grandiose and devalued self-images while retaining fairly clear self–other boundaries that he is considered to have a narcissistic personality. It is then that there arises a preoccupation with grandiose fantasies, an inability to empathize with others, and a dependency upon praise and admiration.

Wishes for attention, love, praise, and confirmation are not necessarily indicative of any disorder. These narcissistic longings help the individual remain open to the influence of others – unlike people with narcissistic personality disorder, who allow their grandiose fantasies to close them off from meaningful relatedness. Striving for success, recognition, and even prominence or a degree of fame, is not illness but an aspect of adaptive functioning. Not all pride is hubris. The difference between the narcissistic issues present in everyone's personality and narcissistic disorder is one of integration. People who do not have narcissistic personality disorders can recognize their strengths and accept their weaknesses simultaneously. Mature individuals can be sensitive to the needs of those around them.

People with borderline personality disorder seek the nurturance of the good object. Narcissists seek the attention and praise of the object. Normal and neurotic individuals primarily wish for the love of the object. As people mature, they increasingly wish to love and have their love accepted by another person, as much as they wish to be loved (Menninger 1942).

There are fads in diagnosis. Following Freud's work on hysteria, most patients were considered to be hysterics. More recently, borderline conditions have been ubiquitous. Now, narcissism abounds.

People with narcissistic disorders are often talented, charming, and successful. Yet their poor integration of the grandiose and devalued aspects of themselves bring about preoccupation with extravagant success fantasies and exploitive behavior accompanied by underlying feelings of meaninglessness and emptiness. Despite poorly integrated good and bad self- and object-images, they are able to retain fairly clear self-other boundaries. Because they are better differentiated and integrated than patients with borderline disorders, they are placed at a higher developmental level, that is, between rapprochement and developing whole object relations. Narcissistic disorders overlap with both borderline and neurotic disorders.

CHAPTER 12

NEUROTIC AND NORMAL
PERSONALITIES

Neurotic and normal personalities are at the whole-object relations level of the diagnostic continuum. All individuals must contend with issues of differentiating self and object, integrating good and bad, and maintaining meaningful human contact. Those with predominately normal or neurotic problems have a sense of resolving conflict within themselves and developing continuity over time.

Neurotic problems, like borderline and narcissistic difficulties, revolve around regulation of love and hate, but the symptoms less often have to do with chaotic behavior and more with guilt, depression, and sadness. When it is realized that the object one wants to hurt, punish, or destroy is one aspect of the complex, loved person, guilt and sadness arise.

People with neurotic character structures can sometimes become extraordinarily dysfunctional, although in a different way from borderline or narcissistic patients. Instead of splitting their world into good and bad, idealized and devalued, they experience positive and negative emotions at the same time, but remain unconscious of some feelings. They repress unwanted affects, manifesting them in their dreams, slips of the tongue, and symptoms, instead of splitting them off and projecting them without any simultaneous manifestation of the unwanted affect.

J.G. was a 43-year-old psychiatric social worker who had partially recovered from a severe depression with the help of antidepressant medication. At the beginning of psychotherapy, he was unemployed, and his marriage verged on collapse. He and his wife planned to live apart for several months in hopes that their mutual recriminations would stop long enough for them to rekindle a satisfactory relationship.

The patient was well versed in cognitive therapies and read about the ways he was self-defeating. He told his therapist he wanted all the help he could get exposing his self-deceptions and rationalizations. He reported how he would lie on the couch all day reading books on self-deception and depression. When his wife returned from work, he would tell her he had learned about his problem and now understood why he had not been able to get a job. His wife typically became impatient and reminded him that if he looked for a job, instead of reading about why he didn't look for one, he might find one.

The patient filled therapy sessions with similar explanations. He shifted his understanding from a cognitive framework to a psychoanalytic one. The therapist was at first heartened by the patient's progress in gaining insights into his rationalizations and defenses against success. Over the months, however, J.G.'s insights did not result in more effective functioning. The therapist became bored and disheartened, and eventually found himself wishing to directly encourage J.G. to take action. The therapy reached an impasse.

The deadlock did not change until the psychotherapist expressed his opinion that they had reached an impasse and began to review the situation. J.G. recounted his shift over five years from father of three and breadwinner to househusband and then to depressed neurotic. His account included a description of how he had been publicly humiliated by a staff confrontation at the community mental health clinic where he had worked. In the name of open communication, his co-workers put him on the "hot seat." He felt humiliated, but acquiesced politely.

This event occurred at the time his wife decided to return to work against his wishes. He became more and more controlling and demanding. She threatened divorce if he did not recognize her need for a different life-style. He then claimed he understood and apologized for his thoughtlessness. He did not negotiate some shift in roles, but agreed to all her wishes. His work performance continued to deteriorate, and he was eventually fired. At this point, he experienced recurring bouts of depression and impotence.

The therapist interrupted before the patient could begin his endless explanations. Changing from his usual nonconfrontational approach, he asked bluntly, "Why did you stand for that staff confrontation? Why did you participate in your own pillory?"

To his own surprise, J.G. burst into a torrent of angry invective about his co-workers. He was furious. As his discontent mounted, he expressed the fact that he was not happy about his therapist's confronting him. Although it might be for his own good, he felt insensitively treated and exposed to shame. He composed himself, and the session ended routinely.

J.G. apologized for his unseemly behavior at the next session. He feared he might have made his therapist feel unappreciated. Instead of allowing the patient to proceed with a series of disclaimers, the therapist pointed out that J.G. resented help because he experienced it as dominance. J.G. wanted to be the dominant one himself, but he hid his wish behind pseudo-compliance. The therapy started to move again.

When J.G. became aware of his resentment, he excessively expressed his anger to his wife. She did not try to squelch him, but was relieved that he had changed his submissive, self-defeating behavior and taken a more active role in the family. He became less angry and more assertive. He insisted that family savings be used to buy a second car so that he could drive to employment interviews. He obtained a job finding nursing home placements for hospital patients, and he hired someone to help with the housekeeping.

Before this improvement, J.G. had exhibited a pattern of submitting to the assertive behavior of others, resenting it, and then feeling ineffectual and unable to retaliate. This led to angrier feelings. He simultaneously defeated his wife by not working and punished himself for defeating her by depriving himself of an effective role in his family. In therapy, he similarly thwarted his therapist's efforts by gaining insight without acting on what he learned. That way, he appeared to take an interest in therapy but passively demonstrated that his therapist's techniques were not effective. He punished himself for this rebellion with continued depression, unemployment, and impotence. He seemed to be compliant and to try hard, yet he did not improve until this pattern was confronted and interpreted.

The conflict here was not split off. J.G. experienced anger and triumph, but he repressed these feelings. He consciously felt helpless and passive, while he sought revenge through determined inaction without being aware of it. A borderline patient would have been more likely to feel good about himself and a wife who gratified him by taking care of him. When he felt abandoned or rejected, he would have felt totally bad and despondent and might have sought other gratifications, such as drugs, alcohol, or affairs. Instead, J.G. felt both good and bad and behaved both constructively and destructively. This behavior indicated that he saw himself as worthy of success and deserving punishment.

J.G.'s behavior was as disabling as that of many borderline or narcissistic patients, even though his developmental level was higher. He had not been able to work, perform sexually, or derive pleasure from life. His symptoms demonstrated better-integrated self- and object-images than most borderline patients have acquired. Simultaneously seeking revenge on his wife, his co-workers, and eventually his therapist, and then punishing himself for his vengeance, is indicative that he saw others as both harmful and valued. He also saw himself as both victim and victimizer. One feeling was conscious and the other unconscious. When he became conscious of his anger, he felt a burden had been lifted.

This pattern of unconsciously ambivalent relationships had root in the patient's early interactions with his parents. These conflicts coincide with or follow the development of whole object relations. Because the theory of infantile neurotic conflicts is so extensively elucidated in the classical psychoanalytic literature, it will not be presented here.

Because someone has reached a whole object relations level and his problems tend to be predominately neurotic does not mean that there were no previous developmental difficulties. J.G., for example, had an underlying infantile belief that his wife, his co-workers, and his therapist should magically understand him and omnipotently meet his needs without his having to make any effort. This narcissistic attitude remained walled off and out of awareness. It was this earlier narcissistic problem that probably predisposed him to a later neurotic conflict.

While J.G. used repression to remain unaware of negative feelings, some people display the opposite tendency. Usually grief reactions do not get resolved because negative feelings about the lost object are repressed, but sometimes it is the positive feelings that are unavailable to consciousness.

T.F. was a 29-year-old law student. She came to therapy complaining of fatigue and lack of pleasure in her life. This attractive and intelligent woman, the parent of a 3-year-old boy, had been divorced shortly before the birth of her child. She did not ask for or accept child support. She worked, had an active social life, and financed her law school education. She strove to take particularly good care of her child, reading extensively about the art of single parenting.

She reported that the father of her child was a self-centered ne'er-do-well. She did not want a husband. Men did not make good parents, and she was better off by herself.

At school, she felt overworked and harassed by her teachers, most of whom were male. She would not turn to her professors for assistance, but she spent long hours debating with them about points of law and about the fairness of the grading system. Her tendency to argue with instructors began to interfere with her ability to learn. She jeopardized her class standing.

In a typical therapy session, after a series of complaints, she would turn to her male psychiatrist and say, "And I don't really see how you can help." She would then refute whatever he said. She came to sessions faithfully and paid her bills on time despite financial hardship.

Noting her ambivalence about therapy, the therapist suggested that perhaps she did not want or expect help from him or from anyone else in order to fend off awareness of how deeply she wished to have someone take care of her. Perhaps she even wished she had a marital partner, after all, to help her with her son and the bills. "Perhaps," he said, "you even loved your son's father and wanted him to care for you and your child. You must have loved him at one point."

T.F. sat silently. Her anxious arguing ceased. As she indicated later, she had been trying to keep in mind how unreliable her son's father had been to help her avoid missing him. She had lived with him for several years before she became pregnant. He had numerous faults. She could not have depended on him very much, but it was a relief for her to remember that she had loved him and longed to be dependent on him. She had apparently repressed these positive feelings for him in order not to mourn his loss. At the same time, she avoided mourning the loss of her fantasy of having an adequate mate as the father of her child. This fantasy was an internal object representation, which initially pertained to her own father. Consciously she told herself she did not have to mourn, because she had not lost anything worth missing. Unconsciously she continued to overvalue her husband–father internal object. To punish herself for betraying this idealized object, she deprived herself of helpful and gratifying relationships by denying their possibility.

Such conflicts also appear in people considered healthy.

W.B., a 55-year-old insurance executive, came to treatment to discuss his wife, who had suffered a left brain stroke two years previously. For 30 years, he and his wife had lived together in a fairly supportive fashion and had been considerate of one another, even during the hard times. They had come to care deeply for one another. They had raised two healthy children and were looking forward to retirement at a coastal home they had recently purchased.

All that changed after his wife's stroke. W.B. did not mind helping her with her walker, her dressing and undressing, and her rehabilitation efforts. However, he did not welcome the increased household chores and looked forward to his wife's resuming some of her duties as she improved. He had been helped by his wife throughout his adult life and reminded himself of her concern and of how he was now returning her thoughtfulness.

As time passed, she did regain some physical abilities, but her speech remained garbled. She also lost control of her feelings and began shouting at him. Occasionally, she even threw small household items at him. He said, "When I get angry back—I know I shouldn't take it personally, but I do sometimes—I am ashamed and get depressed."

W.B. remained conscious of his normal mixed feelings about a painful situation. He was sad rather than clinically depressed, though he used the word "depressed" to describe his feeling. He eventually learned that he needed to ask for more help from his female relatives in caring for his wife. He also began to play golf with friends more often. His mixed feelings of compassion, concern, sadness, frustration, and irritation never entirely resolved because he remained in a difficult life circumstance.

People with highly functional personalities sometimes mislead their therapists by appearing more disturbed than they really are. Out of guilt, they punish themselves by exaggerating their less fortunate qualities and portraying themselves as narcissistic, borderline, or even antisocial.

S.G. was a 30-year-old psychologist who thought she had a borderline personality. She told her psychiatrist she did well during the structure of work, but she "got in moods" after work and on the weekends. She became infuriated with her husband, acted seductively with other men, occasionally drank excessively, and did not "give much of a damn about anything." She speculated that perhaps she could not tolerate being frustrated or alone and needed constant attention.

When she worked with borderline patients, she could understand their feelings of emptiness and despair. She sometimes had such feelings. She could understand their tantrums. She had tantrums, too. Their longing for closeness was like hers. Their acting out was like hers. She, too, had used marijuana and tried LSD. During her mid-twenties, she had actually been promiscuous.

S.G. painted a rather disorganized picture of herself, although she was a fairly well-integrated woman with some hysterical and obsessive features. She did not have a specific personality disorder.

This woman had been reared in a proper, upper-middle-class, New England family. Her mother was involved with her children and the community. The patient had been a happy and energetic child with many friends. She loved and admired her father, who was a calm and self-confident man. He owned and ran the largest department store in town, as had his father before him. Until she was 7 years old, she delighted in splashing in the country club pool with him, while her mother socialized by the pool-side with family friends. S.G. felt she was Daddy's favorite.

When she was 7, her father died of a heart attack. Her mother had to go back to work outside the home. S.G. had taken pride in her treasured father and her thoughtful mother; she now felt diminished. Between the ages of 8 and 10, she began to think there was something wrong with her and her family because there was no one there to meet her when she got home from school. That was the way of lower-class families, the one's down by the creek. That was not how the better families lived.

S.G. reacted by becoming more well-behaved. If there was something wrong with her for not having a father, she would make up for it. She made herself prettier, smarter, and more polite than all the other girls. She obeyed her mother, cleaned the house, and kept her closet spotless and her clothes ironed. In high school, she was among the most popular girls and dated boys in the most popular clique. She sometimes loved and even kissed the boys she dated, but she never let things go too far. She was punctilious about arriving home on time.

In college, she drove herself to meet the highest standards academically and socially. When students began protesting the Vietnam War, she joined the movement. She also volunteered in the ghetto to help poor people. She began to doubt the appropriateness of her fastidious and slightly prudish standards.

She searched for guidance, particularly male guidance, and became infatuated with a young faculty member whom she idolized. He introduced her to a new philosophy of behavior. She began to feel it was her responsibility to express herself spiritually, sexually, and aggressively. She reacted against her overcontrolled conventionality and approval-seeking behavior, tried drugs, and experimented sexually.

She broke up with the teacher and explored her new freedom until it became compulsive in itself. She was adhering to a new standard, a morality of self-expression. She was still hoping to be a good enough girl that her lost father would return to her. No man she met was the right one. She did not feel as though she was quite right either.

In graduate school, she studied the writings of feminists, learning she could take on some of what had traditionally been masculine roles. This partial identification with her lost father allowed her to calm down, to see men more clearly, and finally to marry. She had some episodes of being irate at her husband for not being what her father would have been. She flirted with other men. Racked with guilt over these peccadilloes, she berated herself, diagnosing herself as a borderline personality.

Her psychotherapist did not share this harsh assessment. He helped her with her guilt feelings. He did not participate in her self-flagellation by overtreating her problems. Neither did he abandon her by pronouncing her healthy and sending her on her way. She needed someone to listen to her.

Clinicians often overdiagnose normal and neurotic problems as borderline or narcissistic. They frequently mistake the strength of people's feelings for the degree of their pathology. Strong feelings are not necessarily pathologic. Normal people can love fiercely. Jealous passions can verge on violence. Men and women in business struggle over power and money. Wars are waged and people are slaughtered, often by other normal people. It is not the intensity of affects that is indicative of this or that level on the developmental continuum: It is the degree of integration of those feelings which determines maturity or immaturity, health or illness.

People with whole-object relations can develop psychological troubles. Some people have deeply ambivalent relationships and repress half of their conflicted feelings. Repression differs from splitting in that the behavior, symptoms, and dreams of people who repress indicate that they experience both conflicted feelings at the same time, but strive to remain unaware of one or the other of them. In splitting, one feeling or the other is experienced consciously at one time, and then the opposite feeling, at another time, with little sense of conflict, either conscious or unconscious. People with whole object relations who are aware of their mixed feelings can suffer psychologically when they encounter difficulties for which they lack an adequate solution.

PART IV

TREATMENT

*A person begins to know that he exists
when he finds himself again in others.*

−J. W. von Goethe

INTRODUCTION

Object relations theory has not radically altered psychoanalytic therapies so much as it has subtly shifted their focus. This influence has come from an evolving theoretical framework for a variety of techniques that had previously been applied in a haphazard fashion. Insights about interpersonal and intrapsychic growth have helped provide better charts for therapeutic explorations of narcissistic, borderline, and even psychotic disorders. Additionally, they have helped explain certain aspects of the therapist–patient interaction, even with neurotic patients.

This section will not review in detail the traditional techniques of clarifying and interpreting unconscious conflicts. Although such procedures, developed for neurotic patients, remain important, and will be mentioned, it is the newer techniques, or rather, the therapeutic concepts and attitudes that will be emphasized. These approaches help particularly with disorders placed earlier on the self–other diagnostic continuum.

Although relationships alone do not suffice to help patients, I discuss this aspect of therapy first, because it is the personal element which provides the backdrop for technical intervention. Next, I describe specific techniques which foster insight and enhance differentiation and integration. In the last two chapters of this section, I mention some recent contributions to understanding the therapist's emotional reactions to patients and also discuss the influence of groups and institutions on the therapeutic situation.

Theory and techique form a reverberating and mutually enriching cycle. Theory influences clinical work. In turn, observations in the consulting room provide material for further reflections. Horner (1984) and Blanck and Blanck (1979) have provided examples of how theory and technique can be woven together.

In these chapters, various concepts from the object relations literature are defined and presented as relatively independent tools. Some clinical guidelines will be suggested as to when a particular concept or attitude might prove useful. For the most part, however, I set aside abstract theoretical debates, referring only to the therapist's growing understanding of how the self develops in relation to other people as the basis for informed intuition. This approach allows some exploration of complex ideas and attitudes without forcing premature closure on the issues of controversy.

CHAPTER 13

RELATIONSHIP

WITHIN TECHNIQUE

Psychotherapy is the talking cure. Words alone, however, will not suffice. Books, videotapes, and computer programs may benefit some who seek help; but to effect a meaningful and lasting change in self- and object-constellations, it takes an actual person interacting with another person.

A personal relationship is not in itself sufficient to change enduring patterns of thinking, feeling, and behaving. By the time a patient comes to psychotherapy, goodwill, encouragement, advice, and sometimes invective and coercion have not helped, at least, not enough.

What is needed is a therapeutic relationship, which includes both technical and personal elements within a professional context. The importance of the professional arrangement cannot be overemphasized. It reminds both parties that the therapist is working on behalf of the patient, not for his or her own personal gratification. The therapist can charge a fee, indulge his or her scientific curiosity within limits, and enjoy watching the patient grow and mature. These are the satisfactions a therapist can legitimately expect. Other gratifications, such as praise, dominance, reassurance, or confirmation of a world view, must be set aside. He can insist that interactions be predominately civil and that his own privacy and physical security are protected, just as in any professional arrangement. Within this context, however, he must be willing to listen to and try to understand whatever the patient may have to say, for the benefit of the patient.

While the therapist listens, he will learn that the patient is interested in him and will form opinions and have feelings about him. The patient's experience of the therapist will be a mixture of fantasy and perception. The fantasy part is called transference or projection, and the perception part is called the "real relationship"[1] (Greenson 1971) or the "personal relationship" (Lipton 1977, Adler 1985). At one time it was thought that the therapist remained neutral, thereby avoiding the personal relationship and freeing him to interpret fantasies. Recently, more emphasis has been placed on the interaction within therapy.

In this chapter, I focus on the relationship aspects of therapy and in the next chapter, on technique. This division is, of course, somewhat arbitrary.

HISTORY

When Freud (Breuer and Freud 1895) learned to treat hysteria by listening to his patients, he discovered that they developed strong feelings about him. They often fell in love with and had erotic fantasies about him. Sometimes they had angry or destructive impulses toward him. Rather than taking these feelings personally, Freud learned to look on them with professional detachment and discovered that such strong emotions originally pertained to parental figures. This was the beginning of psychoanalysis. He suggested that "the doctor should be opaque to his patients and, like a mirror, should show them nothing but what is shown to him" (Freud 1912a, p. 118). He should set aside his own emotions and work as a technician. He should listen quietly and unobtrusively. The less obvious he was in his own personal characteristics, the more easily his patients' fantasies about him would reveal themselves. The analyst could then interpret fantasies as arising from the patient.

---

[1]The "real" person as Greenson (1971) used the word corresponds to external object. Issues of realness versus the relativity of subjective perception will be discussed in Chapter 18. For convenience and because of tradition, the words *real* and *actual* will often be used in reference to external objects, despite the confusing philosophical connotations of these words.

This technical bent was carried further by some subsequent psychoanalysts, who suggested that interpretation is the only legitimate intervention involved in this treatment.[2] In 1961 at the Edinburgh Congress, this viewpoint led panelists to reject most of Gitelson's ideas (published in 1962) about the parent-like relationship that develops in psychoanalysis (Friedman 1978, Horowitz 1985). More recently, this technical emphasis has shifted. Many authors suggest that, although interpretation is one mainstay of treatment, other factors are involved and other interventions are sometimes appropriate (Eissler 1953, Kernberg 1984, Adler 1985, Horowitz 1985).

Neutrality no longer seems adequate to describe the analyst's emotional position vis-à-vis the patient. Terms like therapeutic alliance (Zetzel 1965), working alliance (Greenson 1965), therapeutic communion (Goldstein 1954), real relationship (Greenson 1971), and personal relationship (Adler 1985) have sprung up to describe what takes place between therapist and patient.

Freud was not strictly neutral with his patients, although he emphasized professional coolness in his papers on technique. Zetzel (1966) described him as having a personal as well as a technical relationship with his analysands. For instance, he invited the patient commonly known as Rat Man (Freud 1909) to dine with his family on one occasion, and lent him a novel, Zola's *Joie de Vivre*, on another occasion. Freud seemed to consider such interactions outside the psychoanaysis, but later analyzed the patient's reactions to them within the therapy.

Even when the therapist takes the safest route, limiting extra-therapeutic interactions with patients and remaining friendly but not familiar, technical interventions have their personal implications. We always affect our patients as an external object, not just as a blank screen on which to transfer or project internal self- and object-images. The following section provides an example of how a therapist, who mainly tried to interpret, influenced his patient as an external object, that is, as a real person.

RELATIONSHIP WITHIN TECHNIQUE: CLINICAL EXAMPLE

P.H., a 34-year-old woman, came to psychotherapy day after day appearing exhausted. She had a demanding job with a large

---

[2]In this work, I do not distinguish between psychoanalysis and psychoanalytic psychotherapy or psychoanalysts and psychotherapists. Issues related to professional politics and economics so cloud the therapeutic concerns that it seems better to set these distinctions aside for the time being.

international trading company and was a single parent who felt compelled to excessively indulge her 5-year-old son. One session, she looked particularly fatigued.

She began the hour describing how anxious, overwhelmed, and harried she was. She felt so distraught she feared she might have a psychotic episode—perhaps she needed to go into the hospital. She wanted to give up and have someone take care of her. "I am very upset, and I wish you would talk to me a little more," she said.

"You have a difficult time soothing yourself, and you would like me to soothe you by talking to you. As you have described, in your early life, you were expected to be a reasonable and responsible little girl. Perhaps this problem of not being able to soothe yourself interferes with your going to sleep. You look very tired today."

By interpreting the patient's wish for him to break with the psychotherapy procedure and gratify her desire to have him comfort her, the therapist did provide her the soothing function she could not provide herself. He talked to her as a real person. She could consequently take in the interpretation as if it were nurturance, concern, or holding rather than a professionally neutral technique. There is no way to interpret such requests without simultaneously gratifying them. Not speaking serves no purpose. It might indicate a stinginess and overconcern with rules, which the patient would eventually internalize as a part of her experience. There was no way to avoid being a real, external object in the present. The therapist could choose to gratify or frustrate the patient's wish for him to speak, either of which would have been a real action. There were more elements of the personal relationship hidden within technique as this session progressed.

P.H. went on, "Well, I have that problem, too, but last night it was my son. I couldn't help him fall asleep. He kept waking me up. I got mad and shouted at him and sent him back to bed, but he kept crying and telling me he was scared about nightmares. I felt terribly guilty. Finally, I thought it would be easier to let him sleep in my bed. I know I shouldn't do that. Everybody has told me he will get used to sleeping in his own bed in a few nights, but he doesn't. What am I supposed to do?"

"I'm not sure why you've asked for my advice when you've

just let me know you didn't heed the advice you have already gotten from others. What do you make of it?"

"I don't know. What do you make of it?" she said rather testily.

"Perhaps you would like me to demonstrate that I care about you by giving you advice. You may wish me to make a special exception for you so you won't feel so alone, the same way your son does with you. When I leave you to handle it on your own, you become irritated and protest even louder that you can't do it."

Here, the therapist declined to give his patient the advice she requested. He stayed within the therapeutic technique of interpreting her reactions to him, but gave her advice anyway. As a real, external caretaker in her life, he provided an example of how she need not give in to her son's demands. The therapist's role was to help her mature. He served this external parenting function, whether he saw it that way or not. This element of the therapeutic relationship became clearer as that session and the next one proceeded.

For the rest of the hour, P.H. talked at length about how her mother and father expected her to act more mature than her age and how she felt abandoned and full of rage about not being allowed to be dependent. When she grew up, she was determined to take care of her son the way she wished her parents had taken care of her. If her son felt deprived, she was reminded of how deprived and furious she had felt as a child. Despite these insights, she still did not know what to do. At the end of the hour, just as the therapist was about to mention that the time was up, she again said, "What should I do? I can't stand it another two days."

"Our time is up," the therapist said. "I will see you Friday."

P.H. frowned, threw up her hands, and stood. As she walked to the door, she said, "I'll see you Friday," and a slight smile crossed her face.

She was helped during this session. As it turned out, it was not the interpretations which seemed most useful to her, but instead, the therapist's personal interaction with her as an external object, as some would say, as a "real person." She made this clear during the following session.

She appeared more rested. Her son had slept through the last two nights for the first time in months. "When he came into my room saying he had had a nightmare, I got up, took him back to his room, and told him to tell me all about it. After he finished, I told him it was just a dream and he would be all right. If he had another dream, he could tell me about it at breakfast in the morning, but for now, he was a big boy and could sleep in his own bed."

P.H. may have heard the interpretive comments of the previous session, but what she internalized were the therapist's attitudes and behavior in relation to her. Just as her therapist had soothed her a bit by listening and by talking with her, she listened to and soothed her son—in his bed, not in hers. Her therapist had insisted upon ending the hour on time, and she was able to be firmer with her child. She also reminded him that she would see him in the morning, similar to her therapist's reminding her that he would see her again on Friday. Although the therapist made technically neutral comments and interpretations, it was his real attitudes and behavioral interactions with her, his personal soothing and structuring functions, which she internalized.

THE RELATIONSHIP IN TECHNICAL TERMS

The relationship aspects of this and other interactions can be understood in technical, psychoanalytic terms, even if they cannot be planned in advance according to impersonal principles of technique. It is useful to understand the personal as well as all other elements of the treatment.

Psychoanalytic technique depends on the therapist's considering everything that arises as deriving from the patient's internal life, that is, from internal self- and object-images. The personal relationship comes into play when the clinician serves as an external object in the patient's life. Transference, projection, and projective identification are technical words that are necesary in sorting out these internal and external factors.

Freud (Breuer and Freud 1895, Freud 1912b) originally discovered how patients transfer their feelings about people who were important earlier in their lives onto the analyst. In object relations terms, transference is the projection of an internal object-image onto an external person. Most therapists do not think of transference as a kind of projection. They sometimes even use the word transference when alluding to a phenomenon like projective identification. I use transference to mean externalization of an object-image, projection to mean externalization of a self-image, and projective identification to mean externalization of a self-object-image or other partial projection. These distinctions give a false impression of discrete processes, whereas actual, observed interactions are always more complex.

With this terminology, we can now reexamine the interactions between P.H. and her therapist. She saw her therapist as she had experienced her earliest important objects—her mother and father. She wanted him to comfort her, yet she expected that he would not gratify her. She was frustrated at the expected rejection. She protested that she was not angry, but helpless and in need of assistance, just as she had been with her parents. At the end of the hour, she made a plea for more reassurance and advice, even though it was time to leave. In this way, she treated her doctor as she had treated her parents when she was a child. The psychotherapist partially interpreted these attachment and abandonment aspects of the transference when he referred to her having to be prematurely independent as a child. He left the obvious sexual implications of bedtime for a later session. The transference comment was a technical intervention.

P.H. related to him as an internal object-image, but also treated her doctor as a self-image. Transference and projective identification took place at the same time, at different levels of the interaction. She not only treated him as she had treated her parents but also acted toward him as her child currently acted toward her, demanding that he spend more and more time with her. By relating to him as her child did to her, she projected aspects of her self-image onto the therapist. She placed him in her own mothering role and thereby elicited her feelings from him. The feelings she seemed to want to leave with him at the end of the hour were frustration, guilt, and worry.

As he did with the transference, the therapist interpreted aspects of this projective identification when he said, "Perhaps, like your son, you want me to make a special exception for you so you won't feel so alone?" A more complete interpretation of the projective identification would have been to add, "When you ask me for advice, you seem to be wishing, rather understandably, that I could come up with the answer to your dilemma inside of me, rather than help you find the answer within yourself." The therapist did not attempt to make all the possible interpretations at once, because, among other things, were he to do so he would have confirmed the patient's view that she needed a great deal of help, and that she could not find solutions to her problems within herself. His "real" behavior would have undercut his interpretations.

The therapist was not merely an internal object-image or self-image in the patient's mind; he was also an actual external object sitting in the room with her. When he remained calm, paying careful attention to her, but declining to meet all her demands, she introjected this aspect of his behavior, identified with it, and acted in a similar fashion. She took her therapist's actions into her internal world.

In technical terms, she transferred her object-images and projected her self-images onto the therapist. Since she also perceived him as a real, external object, these transferred and projected internal images took on aspects of her therapist as a person. Like a photographic slide projected over another figure and then rephotographed, a composite image was formed. The degree of meaningful integration this new composite had would depend on insight, that is, how thoroughly the ego had worked on the figures to integrate and differentiate them. When she reintrojected this new, altered object-image and identified with it, her internal self- and object-world changed.

It is doubtful that role modeling alone would have sufficed. Personal relationships without therapeutic techniques had not proved sufficient in the past. She must have previously met people who cared about her and could be both firm and nurturing; but she could not have allowed herself to take in these new relationships, because she feared the internal images which she projected onto them. Therefore, she had to keep her distance. Her projections and transferences needed to be at least partially interpreted before she could internalize new experiences. Her resentment of previous objects—her parents—which she transferred onto the new ones interfered with her ability to internalize new experiences. She could not have absorbed the "real" elements in therapy if this resentment had not been recognized in the form of an interpretation. Her transference feeling that the therapist, like her parents, would either abandon her entirely to her own devices or overindulge her would have distorted her perceptions of the therapist so thoroughly that she could not have experienced him as helpful. In that case, she could not have identified with her therapist's attitudes and behaviors as a new and useful aspect of herself. It can be seen, then, that the personal relationship and the technical interpretation of transferences and projections facilitate and enhance one another.

THE CONTAINER AND THE CONTAINED

The therapist provided P.H. a framework in which to contain her anxiety. Bion (1962), a British object relations theorist, developed concepts of the container and the contained in psychotherapy and child rearing. In his view, infants often become overwhelmed by extreme and unmodulated affects and communicate these feelings in their facial expressions, cries, and coos. By listening and watching, the attentive parent takes in these communicated feelings, modulates them, transforms them, gives them meaning, and returns them to the child. The child eventually internalizes this process and learns to contain his own affects.

In early life a baby may scream with discomfort. Parents become distressed upon hearing their child's cry. As if they have taken in their baby's discomfort, they feel impelled to do something. Better able to modulate affect than their infant, parents will invariably turn their distress into productive action and pick up and soothe the child, cooing and rocking him. "Oh, oh. You're so unhappy," they may coo, thereby transforming the pain into words and empathic soothing. Later, the child will be seen to coo to himself for short periods of time.

At a subsequent phase, a toddler may throw a tantrum, kicking and screaming. The parents may take in their toddler's anger, transform it to words, and comment, "Oh, you are angry. You are so disappointed." Sometimes the child cannot use even that much help. He may merely need to be held in the attention of a watchful parent while he calms down. At other times, he may verge on hurting himself or destroying valuable property. Under such circumstances, parents will need to pick up the flailing child and literally contain him and his unmodulated affects in their arms. Even if the parent is quite firm, his or her physical intervention will be much more modulated than the child's thrashing himself against the floor. In this way, the child learns to "get hold of himself." Parents not only contain a child's unpleasant affects; children also need an interested person to watch them play, enjoy their triumphs, and return pleasure and praise—a more pleasant containing function for both parent and child.

In psychotherapy, the framework of quiet listening, uninterrupted hours, and modulated and interested responses provides a containing function, which is part of the personal relationship. The therapist may have a major chore containing affects with some patients. P.H.'s psychiatrist, for example, was invited to experience her anxiety when she suggested she might become psychotic and require hospitalization. She was a business woman and understood medico-legal problems. She knew her therapist would have to consider whether or not to alter his psychotherapy procedure. Perhaps he would need to recommend hospitalization, prescribe medication, or shift from therapy to providing advice and reassurance. The therapist took in her fears, contained his own anxiety, assessed the situation from past knowledge of his patient, and decided he did not need to be as anxious as she was about the possibility of impending psychosis. Instead, he transformed her distress into a rather long and soothing interpretation and returned it to her.

Since object relations approaches to borderline disorders have been developed, therapists are more aware of being invited to contain and transform patients' all-bad feelings of rage and helplessness.

At morning report, the psychiatrist on-call described a distressing patient. "She presented problem after problem," he complained, "and no matter what comment I made or advice I gave, it always fell flat. Nothing seemed to help."

The psychiatrist was irritated at the patient's demanding dependence. "I could have wrung her neck," he said, "but we psychiatrists are supposed to be so nice."

The psychiatrist had taken in the patient's affects. He needed to contain his frustration, reflect on its source, give it meaning, and return it to the patient. Fortunately, he was able to do this and said, "How frustrated and helpless you must feel with all these problems. You must be disappointed in me that my suggestions help so little." When he made this empathic comment, his patient no longer felt so alone and misunderstood. She seemed to shift from her all-bad, abandoned self-object state, because she now felt she was with someone and he understood her. Within a few minutes, she was able to plan for how she would get through the night until she could see her therapist the next day. The on-call psychiatrist could go back to bed.

He had used the idea of the container and the contained. He assumed that his patient rendered him ineffective in order to communicate tangibly how frustrated and helpless she felt. This process took place through interpersonal projective identification. The patient, wanting to rid herself of unwanted feelings, behaved so as to elicit those feelings in her therapist. He then had an opportunity to contain and transform them into meaningful and soothing understanding. This kind of intervention is not a technical artifice, but a genuine, personal interaction.

THE HOLDING ENVIRONMENT
AND THE GOOD ENOUGH MOTHER

The idea of the container and the contained is similar to Winnicott's (1960) idea about the holding environment. Following Freud's discovery of how important oral gratification is in early life, many psychoanalysts put an undue emphasis on feeding as the primary mother–child interaction during the first year. When Winnicott coined the term *holding environment*, he put into words a growing awareness in the psychoanalytic community of how important physical holding is during the symbiotic phase of development.

The holding required evolves gradually. Children soon need to be held in their mother's attention more than in her arms. It may suffice for the parent to watch the child or talk to him rather than actually touch him. In school years it is enough for him to be aware that his mother knows he is at school or at an approved friend's house. The "good enough" mother, as Winnicott (1953) has described, provides enough holding, but not too much. She is neither neglecting nor intrusive and overcontrolling.

Winnicott's emphasizing that the degree and kind of holding did not have to be perfect, but only good enough, questions the perfectionistic trends in the parenting literature. A common focus on optimal parenting may derive from an understandable tendency to idealize children. It can cause problems when parents demand of themselves that they not make mistakes. This idealization can also devalue the child. Idealization may imply that this small organism has less capacity to adapt to the needs and errors of its parents than is actually the case. A similar tendency among therapists both to overvalue and to devalue the patient by trying to be a perfect therapist can develop. Actually, patients usually need only good enough therapists.

The object relations literature contains many analogies between the good enough mother and the good enough therapist, between the holding environment and the holding functions of therapy. Although therapists do not physically hold their patients, they do hold them in their attention. They also make their presence known to lesser or greater degrees according to how talkative, empathic, or visible they are. This concept of good enough mothering and good enough therapeutic interaction has helped therapists shift some of their attitudes, allowing them more flexibility without encouraging them to abandon their technique entirely.

Object relations theorists do not advocate that therapists should become surrogate mothers. They do not physically hold their patients, try to make up for old emotional injuries, or in other ways try to outdo the patient's original parents. Primarily, they use an understanding of development to provide a therapeutic environment conducive to the patient's utilizing the insight aspects of therapy more fully, thereby freeing natural growth processes. The personal relationship forms the context of psychotherapy.

EMPATHY

Empathy is another major component of the therapeutic context. It contributes to the holding and containing aspects of the therapeutic relationship. Empathy serves as a twofold tool for communication: it gives the therapist a means of deeply and subtly understanding the patient, and when the therapist makes an empathic comment, it performs a quietly interpretive function. A third function of empathy is its role in the personal relationship. A case vignette will illustrate these three aspects of empathy: communication from the patient, communication to the patient, and the personal relationship.

K.A. was a 17-year-old girl who was referred for therapy against her wishes by her adoptive mother. She began her first session expressing how ridiculous, worthless, and inadequate her psychotherapist seemed. "You're like all the rest," she said, "but I'll let my mother waste her money on you until I turn 18. Then I'm through."

"What would happen if you refused to see me?" he asked.

"She'd probably send me to a hospital—and I'll bet you'd go along with her. You're all pretty much the same."

The therapist listened carefully to the patient's protests. Although emotions cannot actually move across personal boundaries, he felt he was taking in her anger. More accurately, the patient's words, tone of voice, and demeanor elicited annoyance in him. She was "making him mad." He began to feel rejected as well as irritated. He was trying to help this girl; and she was rejecting him. Worse yet, she was devaluing him. Inclined to become counterrejecting and to send her on her way with no more ado, he thought, "Let her come back when she's ready for therapy, perhaps in about five years."

He did not act on his impulse, but used the concept of interpersonal projective identification to understand that the patient had unconsciously elicited his affects. The therapist put himself in his patient's position to imagine how she must feel; he empathized with her. He projected his self-image onto her, identified with this projected self-image which now became temporarily fused with the object-image of his patient, and tried to understand more deeply how she felt. Empathy is similar to projective identification, though some authors consider it to be less intense and less obligatory.

She continued her harangue. The therapist interjected, "No wonder you're furious. You have been coerced into seeing me. If you stay, you will feel defeated and dominated. If you go, you are afraid worse will happen. I am in a dilemma, too. If I take you as a patient, I participate in the coercion, and if I send you on your way, I abandon you. Perhaps you would feel rejected and abandoned."

K.A. did feel profoundly rejected. At the age of 3, she had been removed from her family because of maternal neglect. She had a stable foster home for several years until at 14, her rebellious behavior led to expulsion from public school. Her adoptive mother sent her to a "therapeutic" boarding school, where she also began psychotherapy. Two and one-half years later, she returned home. She did well in her studies, dated, and generally behaved herself properly during the next year. When her boyfriend moved with his family to another city, she again neglected her studies, abused marijuana, and refused to keep her curfew.

Empathy as a communication from the patient can be broken down into the same inductive processes as are used in scientific thinking (Hamilton 1981). It rests on the therapist's observation of the patient, his observation of his own feelings, knowledge of how other people (including infants) react emotionally, and comparing and contrasting parallels among all these observations. These parallels I term relatedness.

The therapist's empathic approach enabled him to carry out his inductive processes. He was spared a tedious intellectual process of observing the patient and himself, remembering past observations, and comparing and contrasting these observations in a conscious and deliberate fashion. Like other inductive processes, empathy as a tool of communication from the patient can generate hypotheses mainly, not facts. The patient's anger was observable. She seemed less comfortable with the hypothesized feeling of rejection than with anger, and did not express this feeling directly. Empathy gave the therapist a clue. He wondered if perhaps she was eliciting his own feelings of rejection as a way of warding off this feeling in herself.

At this point in the interaction, empathy shifted from a communication from the patient and became a communication to her. The therapist made an empathic comment. The first element of his statement was obvious. "You're furious." The second element reached deeper. "You will feel defeated and dominated." The final element reached even deeper. "Perhaps you would feel rejected and abandoned."

The therapist's empathy laid the groundwork for a later interpretation. "You are angry at me now because you are certain I will reject you and send you away just as you felt rejected and sent away by your biological mother, then by your stepmother, and now by your boyfriend." The therapist could not have made such an interpretation at this point, because he did not yet know her personal history. Had he possessed the necessary information, he still would not have made a full interpretation, because a therapeutic relationship had not been established.

This brings us to the personal relationship aspect of empathy. K.A. felt abandoned and rejected. She needed to feel attended to and understood. Her therapist provided this when he listened closely and let her know he understood. If he had given her an intellectual interpretation instead of empathic comments, she might have felt once again that her feelings were not important enough to be taken seriously. Her therapist performed an important holding and containing function when he pointed out how her predicament caused him to be in a similar dilemma and demonstrated his willingness and ability to accept her projections without abandoning her, or retaliating.

Let us reconsider now some of Kohut's ideas described in Chapter 11, this time focusing on their implications for treatment. Kohut (1971) postulated that narcissistic disorders arise from a failure of maternal empathy. The child needs a mature and responsive parent who can empathize with his needs. One moment, the parent can delight in his child's grandiose display. A few moments later, when exhibitionism overstimulates the toddler, his empathically attuned parent can curb the display by adopting realistic attitudes (Greene 1984). Through a process that Kohut calls transmuting internalization

(Kohut and Wolf 1978), the child takes in this empathic responsiveness and makes it a part of himself in terms of a healthy self-image and an ability to empathize with himself and self-soothe (Tolpin 1971).

Chronic failure in parental empathy contributes to narcissistic vulnerabilities, which the therapist must later help the patient ovecome by providing empathic responses. The possibility that patients may have a congenital deficit of autonomous integrative ego functions leading to an inability to perform transmuting internalizations is not thoroughly discussed in the self psychology literature, nor is the possibility that the patient may defensively need to reject the therapist's empathic comments fully considered.

Numerous clinicians have found Kohut's ideas concerning empathy useful with narcissistic patients, as well as with some obsessive or hysterical patients with narcissistic vulnerabilities. Classical borderline patients frequently experience empathic comments as a seduction designed to avoid hostility, or they fear it as a kind of fusion; they often do poorly without fairly direct confrontations. The empathic therapist under such circumstances will utilize his abilities to understand the patient without prematurely conveying this understanding directly. Unlike borderline patients, narcissistic patients seem to flourish with empathy. They often need long periods of empathic paraphrasing before they can accept even gentle confrontations and interpretations.

TITRATING THE CLOSENESS
AND THE NEED-FEAR DILEMMA

Paying close attention to the relationship aspects of technique has also helped with the adaptation of psychotherapy to the treatment of patients with psychoses. I have described how psychotic patients tend to blur self–other boundaries. Their longing for symbiotic unity can be so great that they easily experience fusion. As the self–image sinks into or becomes swallowed up by the object-image, they can feel themselves literally disappearing into the object. This loss of self is often catastrophic—a ceasing to exist, a disintegration. Consequently, while psychotic patients seek fusion, they also fear it and avoid it. Burnham and colleagues (1969) described this tendency among schizophrenic patients as the need–fear dilemma.

Psychotherapists find themselves perplexed by this "ambitendency" (Mahler et al. 1975, p. 107) among schizophrenics. On the one hand, such patients demand help, medications, and reassurance. On the other hand, they miss appointments, refuse to take medications, and retreat into aloof isolation. If the therapist does not respond to demands, the patient may feel abandoned, helpless, and worthless. If the therapist does respond, the patient may feel invaded and controlled. Since there is no "right" answer, the therapist cannot find an appropriate emotional stance or attitude. Neutrality certainly does not help, objectivity cannot fill the bill, and evenly suspended attention is too uninvolved. Advice is overinvolved and is experienced as demanding. Empathy feels like fusion. In such circumstances, the therapist must constantly be on the move with respect to the patient's emotional position. This process I term titrating the closeness.

When the therapist begins with a psychotic patient, he can move interpersonally closer by asking questions, making empathic comments, and translating metaphors into abstract language. As he becomes more engaged with the patient, he will notice signs of anxiety—a louder voice, loss of eye contact, turning away, or silence. At this point, the patient is indicating that the need for closeness has turned to fear of fusion or loss of self. The attuned therapist will notice this shift and retreat until the patient is optimally involved. This to-and-fro process must occur over and over again if the patient is to maintain object relatedness so that therapy can proceed.

Titrating the closeness can be done in actual physical terms. The therapist can move closer and closer to the patient until the patient shows anxiety. Then, he should retreat. Therapists do this by leaning forward or back in their chairs. Many psychotic patients need therapists who are warmer and actually sit closer to them than is customary for psychotherapy. Unfortunately, therapists are often somewhat frightened of their psychotic patients and mistake their own anxiety for the patient's; they never establish the optimal distance. Therapists must respect their own need for distance—which is all right—as long as they do not attribute this need to the patient's "aloof psychosis."

Optimal physical closeness may not be practical for all psychotic patients because some feel a need to be physically held. Hospital patients are sometimes held in restraints or in sheet packs; nurses occasionally hold their hands or pat them. For psychotherapists, it is generally preferable to sit close to such patients, to interact with them warmly, and to hold them metaphorically in close attention, but not actually to touch them, other than with a brief pat or handshake.

It is not the purpose of titrating the closeness to make up for hypothetical, inadequate maternal holding. Rather, it is to enter into the psychotic patient's object world sufficiently to establish meaningful contact. Once such contact is achieved, the therapist can set to work gently helping the patient to clarify self–other confusions and develop a better idea of who he is in relation to other people.

POSITIVE PROJECTIVE IDENTIFICATION

Projective identification has most commonly been described in reference to patients projecting their hostility onto therapists (Spillius 1983). Less often, it has been described in reference to patients projecting loving or creative feelings onto their therapists (Klein 1946, Grotstein 1981a, Ogden 1982, Hamilton 1986). If we go to the next step and consider that therapists, as well as patients, utilize positive projective identification, we see that it can play an important role in the therapeutic relationship.

I begin with an example of this process in supportive psychotherapy. In some circles, this treatment would be called case management.

> The receptionist of a public clinic took the new director aside. "R.J. is hanging around again," she said. "He's been here for years, and he's nobody's patient. He won't keep appointments or take any medicine or anything. He's smelly, and he keeps leering at us, making lewd comments. We're frightened of him. Someone usually tells him to leave or calls the police."
>
> There in the waiting room sat an edentulous, bearded and bedraggled, middle-aged man with no shoes and crusty feet. He apparently lived on the street.
>
> The administrator sat down next to him. "Mr. J.," he said, "we would like to help you, and I think we have some therapists in the clinic who can help you; but I'm afraid you will need to come to appointments if we are going to do you much good. I'll give you an appointment with a nurse practitioner, named Ms. C.M. It's at ten o'clock tomorrow morning. The receptionist will write it down for you. Now, you be sure to come back at ten tomorrow morning."
>
> Within two months, C.M. had the patient back in shoes, wearing clean clothes, hair combed, and sporting a new set of dentures. He was polite and friendly to the receptionists, and many of the staff members who had thought he was untreatable

enjoyed chatting with him in the hall. The nurse's colleagues were most impressed. She became rather a star in the clinic. She felt proud and pleased and almost magical in her abilities.

One day, the director took her aside and asked her how she had done it. She told him she had merely assumed that this obviously filthy wretch, whom everyone had wanted to throw out of the clinic, was a worthwhile human being who could be helped, despite all evidence to the contrary. She then treated him according to her expectations; and he responded.

In object relations terms, she had described projecting her own self- and object-images of a valuable human being onto this man who presented himself as somewhat less than human. She tried to influence him with her attitude, by treating him as if he really were that valuable person she wanted him to be. She was engaging in positive projective identification. He responded accordingly.

R.J., however, was far from being as well integrated as was his therapist. He eventually projected his omnipotent, grandiose internal fantasies back onto Ms. M. The more he saw her as omnipotent, the less he did to help himself. He began to deteriorate. At this point, the therapist had to remind the patient that there were limits to her abilities and that it was really his effort, not her magic, which helped him. She had only helped him feel better about himself so he could improve his own situation. He would need to keep exerting himself if he was to maintain his improvement.

One of the problems with positive projective identification on the part of the therapist is that it appears magical. Both therapist and patient have at times been led into the belief that feeling mutually positive about one another is enough, and that effort and conflict can be entirely avoided. This problem can be surmounted, however. Patients could not be treated at all if it were not for the therapist's ability to maintain an irrational conviction that the patient is really a fine human being despite his feeling and sometimes acting as if he were a thing.

The psychoanalytic literature contains examples of therapists whose attitude displays elements of positive projective identification. Giovacchini (1975) made the following comment about a difficult patient:

"He described himself as a 'perfect jerk'; silently, I was inclined to agree with him, and yet I knew that I was, at the same time, dealing with an intriguing and complex person who had something within him that was both fascinating and worthwhile" (p. 23).

Surely, such an attitude contains elements of positive projective identification, of seeing one's own value as a human being in the patient and identifying with it. Giovacchini indicated he had little perceptual evidence that his patient was other than "a jerk." He relied on an internal conviction, an internal image of an intriguing and complex person, and projected that image onto his patient.

Kernberg (1977) described a similar attitude: "The therapist needs to maintain faith in the patient's capacity to work on his problems, faith that some area of humanity which is still potentially available does exist" (p. 295).

Kernberg made an important qualification, however, which must be remembered when utilizing positive projective identification. He went on to say that when the therapist is confident enough to trust the patient's potential for growth, without denying the patient's capacity for destructiveness, he can more effectively deal with negative aspects of the transference. The therapist who defensively denies aggression, attempting to maintain an image of a friendly or nice patient, will have difficulty. That is, when using an ability to project good qualities onto the patient and thereby eliciting those qualities from him, the therapist must take care to simultaneously utilize his integrative ego functions and avoid denying the patient's more unfortunate attributes.

Some authors—perhaps Kernberg and Giovacchini themselves—might argue that the phenomenon these two psychoanalysts described is not projective identification at all, but good ego functioning. They might maintain that the therapist is reminding himself of a reality factor, rather than creating a reality through projective identification. My reply would be that questions of general human value and faith are always projections in that we are considering our own internal beliefs to be characteristics of the external world. They might also argue that the analyst was not trying to induce his feeling in the patient or to control him. I would suggest that the analyst's technique may have been neutral and his demeanor unobtrusive, but his goal was to influence the patient, as the goal of all therapists is to influence their patients in a useful way. I suspect that, among other things, they had intended to help the patient gain improved self-esteem, the very attribute of the therapist's self that was projected. If we are to study the real or personal aspects of the therapeutic relationship, we must be willing to consider the therapist's own irrational functioning as well as that of the patient. We must also maintain a healthy respect for the beneficial aspects of our own less logical psychological functioning.

ATTITUDE AND TECHNIQUE

Providing a holding environment, containing and transforming affects, empathizing, titrating the closeness, and focusing on the patient's value as a human being are all aspects of the personal relationship within the psychotherapeutic interaction. Yet, when one tries to teach these "real" aspects of treatment, they suddenly seem insubstantial. Primarily, attitudes are under discussion, not behaviors.

Freud and subsequent classical analysts focused on interpretation as the behavior that changed patients. Neutrality and free-floating attention were the attitudinal components that helped the therapist to arrive at interpretations and communicate them clearly, that is, to behave in the technically correct fashion. Soon, however, various authors noticed that patients experienced interpretations as nurturing, felt held by the analyst's concern, and were encouraged by his steadfast therapeutic work in the face of apparent chaos and anxiety. Without these elements, patients did not improve. One can hardly help but wonder if perhaps the therapists' attitudes, even those of classical analysts, fairly directly influenced their patients.

At times psychotherapists go too far in focusing on these attitudes, and develop a quasi-mystical view of therapy. Some believe the patient and therapist enter an empathic communication which involves the direct transfer of emotions across personal boundaries. Others focus on projective identification as the vehicle for transfer of emotions. Along these lines, I have heard a respected and senior psychoanalyst say to his residents, "She introjected my good mother. You see, I introjected my mother so my patient could introject that same good mother which was inside me." It sounds as if the psychoanalyst thought his mother was actually inside him and that his internal objects could directly cross personal boundaries. We can only assume that he was using a therapeutic shorthand rather than promoting a magical belief system—from the phrasing, we cannot be sure. It sounds similarly mystical when beginning psychotherapists return to their supervisor the week after gaining a new insight about their patient, and say, "You know, I didn't do anything different. I just thought about it differently, and the patient improved. It's like magic."

The magical idea that emotions, internal object representations, and attitudes are capable of crossing personal boundaries cannot be entirely disproven, but it is more likely that subtle communication between therapist and patient conveys the therapist's emotional position with regard to the patient. This communication takes place through tone of voice, the frequency and length of utterances, metaphoric speech, subtle connotations of word choices, dress, facial expression, posture, even muscle tone and the brightness or dullness of the eyes. In therapeutic work, we cannot consciously control all these aspects of our behavior in a purely technical fashion, any more than a baseball player can consciously calculate the timing and vectors involved in flexing and relaxing various muscle groups while swinging the bat. Even if we could theoretically deduce how we should act and play the part, we would only succeed in conveying a facade. What we do is listen closely to our patients and come to new understandings and attitudes, which are conveyed in our behavior.

Neutrality on the part of the psychoanalyst has always been mixed with warmth and a genuine human concern for the patient. Neutrality in itself is an attitude that is part of the relationship. It suggests safety, interest, lack of condemnation, and a certain faith in the patient's spontaneous curative capacities.

The technical and personal aspects of therapy overlie one another. Technically, the therapist provides a background onto which the patient projects his fantasies of internal self- and object-images. Transference is the word traditionally used for the projection of object-images. It is the therapist's job to interpret these transferences and projections as elements of the patient's internal life.

The therapist cannot perform this task without taking into account that he is seen by the patient not only as a fantasy but also as an external object in the patient's life. No matter how unobtrusive he may be, the therapist remains a real person, and his action or inaction has implications for the patient. The patient takes in these personal characteristics of the therapist through introjection and identification. Some of the concepts used to describe these relationship aspects of therapy are the container and the contained, the holding environment, good enough mothering, empathy, titrating the closeness, and positive projective identification.

These relationship aspects of treatment must be combined with techniques for promoting insight and growth, which will be discussed in the next chapter.

CHAPTER 14

TECHNIQUE WITHIN RELATIONSHIP

Although object relations theory has provided new concepts with which to understand therapeutic interaction, technical interventions remain essentially the same as those previously used. These techniques are clarification, confrontation, and interpretation within the structure of a therapeutic setting. They are used for the same purpose: to promote insight and growth.

INSIGHT AND GROWTH

Far more than intellectual understanding, insight represents a conscious and unconscious advance in self and object integration and differentiation. I have shown how these are the processes that constitute psychological growth, as well as other kinds. Integration through insight is demonstrated in the following case examples.

A 60-year-old depressed woman whose husband had died the previous year talked about her despondency. She slowly realized she was whipping herself with remorse because she had been annoyed with her husband and had not treated him well the year before his death. Eventually, she understood that she punished herself not only because she had been harsh toward her husband, but also because she had loved him. If she had not cared for him, she would not have thought her inconsiderate behavior deserved punishment. With this insight, different aspects of herself came together. Regret replaced depression.

A 35-year-old narcissistic man came to experience his grandiose feelings as overlying profound sadness and pain. He started to value the small, hurt aspect of himself; his need for constant attention and praise lessened. He no longer had to use people's admiration to ward off awareness of feeling inadequate. His internal self-representations shifted, resulting in psychological growth.

A 28-year-old, drug-abusing, and promiscuous borderline woman slowly learned in therapy that other people could sustain concern for her, despite her shortcomings and their own. She began to understand that her male companion continued caring for her even when he needed to go to work or attend to other tasks. He remained fond of her through her periods of withdrawal or times when she felt bad. This view of herself in relation to other people became more established; her constant need to seek immediate pleasure and excitement abated. She developed a sense of security and improved frustration tolerance.

Insight has little to do with applying an intellectual theory to thoughts and actions. It is the bringing together of different feeling aspects of the self in relation to others in new and meaningful ways.

CLARIFICATION, CONFRONTATION, AND INTERPRETATION

The principal techniques used in achieving insight and growth are clarification, confrontation, and interpretation.

Clarification denotes asking for more information. The therapist may do so by posing a direct question. For example, he may say, "Could you tell me precisely what your boss says when he criticizes you?" Less directly, he could say, "Tell me more," "Go on," "Yes," or any number of indications that he wishes to hear more about a subject. A psychoanalyst presenting a case remarked repeatedly, "I'm not clear." In this way, he asked the patient to clarify things to him.

Confrontation as a technical word means making an observation to a patient about himself. Unfortunately, it has an aggressive connotation which is not part of its technical purpose. Confrontations can sometimes be forceful, or, at other times, they can be gentle. A therapist might say to a weeping patient, "Yes, that has been a great loss for you." This empathic comment confronts the patient with her loss in that it brings it back before her from an outside viewpoint, although she is already conscious of it. Clearly, she would not be likely to experience such a confrontation as hostile. A patient describing how she got an "A" on a test may elicit the empathic confrontation, "Yes, you're proud of your new success." By providing external confirmation, such readily accepted confrontations promote self-reflection at times of high emotion. This helps the patient overcome the tendency to experience strong feelings at one time and forget them later. These interventions do not necessarily break down resistance or otherwise assail the patient.

Other confrontations can be experienced by the patient as critical or hostile, despite the therapist's intention to be nonjudgmental. Pointing out contradictory statements often seems critical. One therapist said to his patient, "On the one hand you think that your colleagues will support your position; yet, a few moments ago, you mentioned that you don't trust any of them. What do you make of that?" Some patients would be interested in such an observation, and would explore its implications. Others would feel criticized and challenged to explain or defend their logic. Either way, the confrontation is not aggressive or critical in and of itself—it is the patient's reaction which makes it so.

There are a few confrontations that must be made that do imply criticism or make a demand, no matter how they are phrased. A therapist might comment, "I've noticed you have not paid your bill in two months." The implication is that the bill must be paid.

Adler (1985) suggests that therapists sometimes need to confront their patients with vigor. Since many patients exaggerate any hint of aggression on the clinician's part, I prefer to deemphasize this aspect of the intervention. I define confrontation as any comment that points out something about a patient, whether gently or forcefully. It literally means to bring two things face-to-face, in this case the patient and an aspect of himself.

An interpretation is a comment that indicates that a present feeling, attitude, or behavior is a repetition of a former one. Interpretations are often thought of as explaining causation, but they are also effective if they indicate parallels. One therapist had occasion to comment, "You fear I will reject you if you are annoyed with me, just as you feared your mother would send you to your room for disrespectful behavior. Evidently, she did in fact do just that." Such an interpretation does not assert causation, which is a theoretical rather than a technical issue. It does juxtapose two aspects of the patient's life. Thus, it invites integration.

When most effective, interpretations delineate parallels between the infantile life, the present-day life, and the transference. To be more complete, the above-mentioned interpretation may at some point include the statement "You are similarly afraid that your husband will leave you if you bring up your dissatisfaction with him."

At one time interpretation connoted making conscious something that was unconscious. For patients who split off aspects of their experiential world instead of repressing them, the issue of consciousness is not germane. Psychotherapists still make interpretations. When a therapist interprets splitting, a link or association between two events is being created. When he interprets repression, he is facilitating the memory of a previously existing association. By defining interpretation as pointing out parallels between current and past thoughts, feelings, and behaviors, this term becomes freed from old, unresolved issues concerning causation and conscious versus unconscious. Sometimes, I use words like "drawing parallels" in place of the word interpretation.

In this chapter, I do not illustrate the use of clarification, confrontation, and interpretation to promote insight and growth in primarily neurotic patients; these subjects have been extensively discussed prior to the development of modern object relations theory. Here, I concentrate on some of the ways ideas from this theory have helped in the application of therapeutic techniques to patients with narcissistic, borderline, and psychotic disorders.

CONFRONTING STRUCTURE BREAKS

Structure is the arrangement of psychotherapy which provides a framework for clarification, confrontation, and interpretation. It is a set of expectations that the therapist holds for the patient and himself. The frequency and timing of appointments is part of the structure. The expectation to end on time is part of the structure. Other elements include arrangements concerning payment, vacations, missed appointments, and even seating or use of the couch. More obvious aspects of structure are the often unspoken agreement that neither the patient nor the therapist will act in harmful or abusive ways toward one another or engage in sexual relations with one another, and that patients will refrain from suicidal or dangerous actions, and will not take drugs or alcohol before appointments.

A therapist may initially discuss or negotiate the arrangements with a patient and also remain responsible for his own expectations. It may be useful with some neurotic patients to discuss the arrangements and renegotiate them from time to time. With borderline or psychotic patients, their self–object differentiation is so tenuous that they often cannot tolerate such flexibility. Then, the therapist must accept responsibility for setting the structure to provide stability in the therapeutic relationship. This helps the patient experience interaction with a predictable person.

Confronting behaviors that go outside the structure is vital with borderline patients (Kernberg 1975, Masterson 1976, Rinsley 1982, Adler 1985). The therapist brings up such behavior as a reminder of his steadfast attitude. This approach serves to clarify self–other boundaries and enhance object constancy. A common form of breaking structure early in the treatment of borderline patients is missing appointments, often without calling to cancel.

L.B. was a 25-year-old homosexual man who complained of his inability to hold a job and of shifting sexual partners. In the first two sessions he explained how much he needed help. He missed his third appointment. He arrived the following week and began talking of how he had been seeking work. He talked for 20 minutes about his determination to find a job. He did not mention the missed appointment and his apparent difficulty remaining in therapy. His therapist confronted the structure break by saying, "I noted you missed your appointment last Tuesday. You haven't said anything about that."

"Oh, you see, I thought the job would be more important," the patient said, continuing his topic of employment possibilities.

His therapist gently interrupted and reminded him of his neglect of the treatment arrangements. "Perhaps we should take a closer look at your difficulty keeping appointments. What do you make of it?"

"Nothing really. I was just too busy. I didn't think you would care. Is that a problem for you?"

The therapist learned that his patient did not think the

therapist was any more committed to working within the arrangements than he was. "I didn't think you would care," he said. This statement also ambiguously implies that he may have thought the therapist would not care about him as a person. Confronting the break in structure called attention to attitudes about the therapist in relation to himself. He saw the therapist as uncommitted and uncaring. The patient was the one who actually felt that way. "I was just too busy."

The therapist could then bring up another aspect of disregarding the arrangements. He mentioned the patient's apparent difficulty remembering the possibility of good experiences.

"Evidently," he said, "you don't expect me or anyone else to care enough about you to really expect you to meet, or to wonder where you are. That must be very lonely for you."

Such a statement confronts the negative transference (Kernberg 1975), as well as the break in structure, while maintaining an empathic attitude (Kohut 1971). When a patient goes against the therapist's expectations, he is displaying negative regard for his expectations and, consequently, for at least the structuring aspect of the therapist, too. Insofar as his feelings are transferential, he is displaying negative transference when he is breaking the structure. Thus, confronting breaks in structure often also confronts negative transference. The therapist hypothesized that L.B. broke the structure, at least partially, because he did not feel cared about in the transference.

At this point in L.B.'s treatment, his early experiences with his parents were not known to the therapist. He could hypothesize that the patient experienced his parents as disinterested and uncommitted. This is how he experienced the therapist, who as an external person was actually primarily interested, committed, and acceptant. When he mentioned the patient's going outside the framework, he defined himself as a real person. He added the comment about how lonely it must have been for L.B. to experience him as uncaring. This further defined himself as empathic.

Therapists sometimes have to work at confronting breaks in structure and other negative material without seeming aggressive or cold. One way to do so is by empathizing with the patient while confronting him. To maintain an empathic attitude under such circumstances, however, therapists need to remind themselves of their concern for the patient, no matter how the patient may see them at the moment. As part of this process, their confrontations serve the purpose of revealing the patient's distorted perceptions, rather than serving as vehicles for covert demands or criticisms. This effort helps the therapist refrain from being drawn into the all-bad self–other state, especially when the patient is condescending or devaluing. Such devaluing in L.B.'s case was implied when he said, "Is that a problem for you?" using a condescending tone of voice. The therapist needed to seek out the split-off all-good self–other state, wonder about its absence, and empathize with how the patient must feel in his abandoned state.

Empathically confronting breaks in structure is an important technique. It is one way the therapist maintains his existence as a predictable and dependable person for the patient, while, at the same time, pointing out the patient's difficulty experiencing other people as dependable. The therapist's integrated frustrating and nurturing aspects remain constant in the structure, as if to say, "Yes, therapy can be frustrating, and you must put effort into coming to sessions; but it is also gratifying to have a dependable person to listen to you and try to understand you." The therapist need not make this claim directly. His attention to structure provides the message in the context of his behavior.

SETTING LIMITS

Sometimes confronting breaks in structure does not suffice to change a patient's behavior, and his inconsistency continues to threaten the usefulness of treatment. The therapist may need to set limits; this constitutes a kind of ultimatum. It is explaining a consequence of continued breaks in structure. Such an intervention is not a clarification, confrontation, or interpretation,[1] but is sometimes necessary as part of providing a context in which treatment can proceed.

Like ultimatums in any area of discussion, limit setting should be saved for last. First, the therapist should make sure he had adequately explained the arrangements and, sometimes, the reasoning behind them. Second, he should call the patient's attention to exceeding the bounds. Next, an interpretation may be in order. Often such techniques can be used over and over before setting limits.

---

[1]Eissler (1953) called techniques outside the interpretive mode "parameters" of treatment. He suggested that they must later be subjected to interpretation themselves if the treatment is to be maximally effective.

With most patients, limits are implied rather than explicit. The therapist usually does not have to say, "If you don't pay your bill, we can't continue." Most patients pay their bill, and the issue never arises. With borderline patients, limit setting should be held to a minimum because it threatens them with abandonment.

The only consequences that a therapist can effectively impose are the discontinuance of therapy and the breaking of confidentiality. If a patient threatens suicide, the therapist can recommend hospitalization, but cannot impose it. He could call the patient's family to help protect him. This breaks confidentiality and changes the nature of the treatment relationship. In more extreme circumstances, he might need to initiate commitment proceedings. Here, it is not the psychotherapist's power that holds the patient—it is the court's power. The therapist provides privileged information. As often as not, the court will release a patient over a doctor's conviction that the patient is suicidal. Under such circumstances, the therapist must decide whether or not to continue with a compromised and possibly dangerous treatment.

The limits of confidentiality and continued treatment are usually practical matters. If a patient is dangerous to himself or other people, it would be foolhardy to value privacy over life and limb.[2] If a patient does not keep half the appointments, therapy will have little influence. If a patient arrives at appointments intoxicated, his integrative ego functions are impaired, and he cannot gain insight; there is seldom use in continuing. If the patient habitually intimidates his therapist, how can the care provider help? If the therapist is not being reimbursed for his professional services, it is not practical to continue.

> B.G.—described in Chapter 2 as a man with severely shifting identities—responded favorably to limit setting. He came to the first few appointments and then missed two. As a part of structuring before setting limits, his psychotherapist said, "For therapy to help you, it is necessary that you come to appointments regularly."
>
> The patient responded with regular attendance for two weeks,

---

[2]Dangerousness is a complicated issue and cannot be thoroughly addressed in this work. There are some cases, for example, when a patient becomes more suicidal the more intensively he is treated, possibly because when other people take responsibility for his life, it increases self–other confusion and enhances omnipotent rescue fantasies. In such cases, it may sometimes be best to seek a consultation and to consider the possibility of not setting limits on dangerous behavior. Under such circumstances, new limits must be arranged. Usually, however, one must set limits on dangerous behavior.

but then his chaotic ways returned. His therapist gently confronted the break in structure, to little avail.

A few weeks later, B.G. continued to be sporadic in attendance. The psychiatrist offered an interpretation. "Perhaps you
are ambivalent about therapy. On the one hand, you may wish to
come to appointments, but on the other hand you may not be so
sure. This could repeat a previous pattern. How was it when you
took your troubles to other people earlier in your life?"

"My parents were very strict," he responded dutifully. "If I
went to my mother with problems, she would punish me or
ridicule me, which was worse. But I don't see what that has to do
with this. I just forget sometimes."

"You want me to help you with your troubles, but perhaps you
are afraid that, like your mother, I will ridicule or criticize you.
Such feelings could make it easier to forget appointments."

The patient changed the subject and went on with something
else. He ignored his therapist during the remainder of the
session, very much in the way he sometimes entirely ignored
sessions by not going to them at all.

A few weeks later, the therapist tried a different approach,
commenting on the patient's poor object constancy rather than
his ambivalence in the transference. "It seems that you entirely
forget how you value therapy sometimes. Therapy isn't there for
you, so you don't come or even call."

B.G. listened politely and then went on describing how he had
become interested in listening to some music with a new acquain-
tance last time he missed a session. He seemed to forget the topic
under discussion and became enthusiastic about the style of
music he had heard. He wanted to tell all about it.

His psychiatrist could have listened quietly, but because forgetting about treatment threatened its efficacy, he decided to
persist with the subject. He could have done so by commenting
about how the patient seemed to forget him right in the session
itself. Such a remark would have again focused on poor object
constancy in the here-and-now of the transference. He decided,
however, that this patient might hear a self-comment better than
an object-comment.

"Yes, you have an aspect of yourself which values therapy. For
instance, you seem to like telling me about the music right now;
but you sometimes forget the part of yourself that values
therapy, when you have to stop whatever you are doing to come
to sessions."

B.G. appreciated this observation and discussed it for several minutes. He also began arriving on time for the next few weeks. Not long afterwards, he returned to his old ways. It was at this point that the psychiatrist began setting limits. Clarifying the structure, confronting, and interpreting had not changed a pattern which made psychological work impossible. It was time to focus on the issue.

He said, "I'm afraid I won't be able to help you with your difficulty with shifting relationships, jobs, and religions if you can't somehow get here regularly."

"What do you mean?" the patient said. "Is this the last session?"

The patient was sensitive to abandonment and inconstant in his view of self and others. He expected this relationship to end any minute.

The patient had invited his doctor to clarify his limit setting. The therapist became more specific. "No, this isn't the last session. I still think therapy can help you if you get to appointments regularly; but if you miss more sessions without calling, we should spend a month winding things up. Then you should take six months off to consider what you want to do about treatment. If you stop missing appointments now, we can continue without interruption.

This method of setting limits by offering to interrupt therapy, instead of entirely discontinuing it, avoids the problem of repeating old abandonments. Rodman (1967) has reviewed the literature and provided several case examples of this method of setting limits.

B.G. became indignant. "I have trouble remembering things. That's why I came for help. That's the whole reason I'm here."

"It's unfortunate that you need to change some of the very behavior you need treatment for before you can get help, but I'm afraid that is the way it is. Our knowledge is not so great in this field that we have learned to help in any other way."

"Well, I guess I'd better come then," the patient said. He now seemed compliant, almost submissive. "I'll get here. I can do that, but may I ask, what does therapy do for me if I can change my behavior on my own? I'm not challenging you, just asking."

The psychiatrist resisted the temptation to change from limit setting to interpreting at this point. He was tempted to comment on how B.G. became submissive when threatened with abandonment, as he had with his mother. Instead, he provided the requested explanation: "You may want someone to help you find out why it is so difficult for you to stick with things. It might also be helpful for you to have someone remind you that you can, and must, do the persisting yourself, because that power resides within you, not outside."

In this example, limit setting did not involve the application of force by the therapist. Actually, it overtly recognized the therapist's acceptance of limits to his own omnipotence and entailed no aggression whatsoever. When setting limits, it is important for the therapist to acknowledge his own limitations. That way, the patient does not feel an omnipotent care giver is withholding perfect and effortless treatment out of malice or stinginess, and it does not imply that the patient has done anything wrong. It is quite natural for patients to have omnipotent fantasies about healers, but it is not useful to indulge those fantasies to the point that growth becomes impossible, nor does acknowledging limitations imply that therapists are without any ability to help, as some patients would have us believe. If therapists go to the confusing extreme of telling patients that all responsibility for their improvement lies with them, it can be abandoning via therapeutic nihilism. The therapist must set limits without accepting either the patient's idealized or devalued projections as his own.

After the psychiatrist told him that therapy would have to be interrupted if he missed more sessions, the patient went to the opposite extreme for months. He did not miss a session, and often arrived a half-hour to an hour early. He began to describe his doctor in glowing terms and seemed to idealize him thoroughly. B.G. acted as if he had to be a perfect patient, or he would be instantly dismissed. Months later, he came back to this issue and remembered that his mother had threatened to send him out into the street if he did or said things which hurt her pride. He felt as though he constantly needed to gratify the narcissism of anyone who was in a caretaker role. He attempted to do so by idealizing the therapist.

Setting limits is not a clarification, confrontation, or interpretation, but a real action on the part of the therapist, which often repeats previous parental actions. It always has a profound effect on the patient. This effect is sometimes unpredictable. Later in therapy, such an intervention must be further explored, often at the initiative of the therapist (Eissler 1953). Patients seldom bring up real actions of the therapist.

Setting limits does not always suffice. Some patients are not able to stay within the bounds. If limit setting is done clearly and carefully, treatment with a subsequent therapist may benefit. This is possible if the new therapist does not join the patient in devaluing his previous treater. Many patients, especially those who are seriously ill, go through a series of treatments before they settle into a helpful relationship (Katz et al. 1983).

Describing limits brings patient and therapist face-to-face with their relatedness. This intervention reminds both parties of their individuality and the framework in which they relate to each other. It helps both patient and therapist resist the temptation to give in to omnipotent expectations and reminds them of the limits of what is possible in any human interaction, including psychotherapy.

CONFRONTING NEGATIVE TRANSFERENCE

Since Freud (1905b) reviewed his unsuccessful treatment of Dora, psychoanalysts have maintained a keen awareness of how important it is to recognize and interpret transference if therapy is to proceed past the early stages. Therapists must sometimes address these issues within the first few sessions in the case of severely disordered patients. Kernberg (1975), influenced by Klein, who interpreted transference early in the treatment, emphasized that this technique is especially important with borderline patients.

Negative transference is the projection of a bad, devalued, abandoning, or at least disappointing or rejecting internal object onto the therapist. This "bad" object-image is usually associated with angry, hostile, or frightened feelings, which must be brought into the discussion so that they can be modulated and integrated. If they are left unattended, anger or disappointment may lead to premature interruption of the treatment.

> W.J.—the 29-year-old receptionist described in Chapter 6—displayed negative transference when she began a session with the statement, "I feel horrible and alone. No one understands me anyway. What's the use? I don't even know why I come here."
> The therapist could have focused on her demoralization (Frank 1974) or emphasized the stress factors in her external life leading to discouragement. Instead, he chose to work within the transference.

"You must be disappointed in me," he said. "You hired me to try to understand you and help you, but you still feel like no one understands you."

This confrontation does not add new information. It is little more than a paraphrase. Nevertheless, it does highlight negative feelings about the therapist and also serves as an empathic communication. Since tactful, well-timed confrontations have an empathic element, the current debate over whether therapists should confront (Kernberg 1975) or empathize (Kohut 1971) is often a needless dispute.

Confrontation of negative transference with borderline patients seldom heightens hostile feelings. In fact, it usually diminishes them. In W.J.'s case, she had felt all alone and misunderstood by everyone, including her therapist. When he confronted and empathized with her disappointment in him, she no longer experienced herself in an abandoned self–other state, because she was now understood by him. This intervention—the therapist understanding how misunderstood the patient felt so that the patient was no longer misunderstood—seems paradoxical and a bit clever. If it is genuine, however, it can be helpful, particularly with angry and abandoned patients.

When W.J. felt that her therapist was in empathic contact with her, she shifted to an all-good, self–other state. "No, no," she said. "It's not you. You are the only one who cares. I feel so much better when I'm here. It's that bastard husband of mine—and my mother."

She had just a moment before indicated she did feel misunderstood, but she seemed to experience no contradiction in expressing how cared about she now felt. This obliviousness to contradiction indicates a shift in self–object state. At this point, if the therapist accepted his new, idealized role and allowed all the unpleasant feeling to be split off and projected onto her husband and her mother, the therapy would have temporarily calmed. Meanwhile, the patient's home life would have deteriorated because of her exaggerated, all-bad view of her family. Since the goal of therapy was to help the patient with her relationships outside treatment—not necessarily to make a comfortable situation for the therapist—it was necessary for him again to confront the negative transference.

"Yes," he said. "I realize you feel understood by me right now, and that is important. A moment ago, however, I think you did feel misunderstood, as you told me. Sometimes, I'm not there for you."

Gently confronting the negative transference in this way—while the patient saw the therapist as a good object—helped her use her ego functioning to integrate good and bad aspects of the object. I term this element of confronting negative transference juxtaposing good and bad object relations units. This technique for promoting insight and growth will be discussed further in a subsequent section of this chapter.

Although early confrontation of negative transference can be vital with borderline patients, emphasis on this technique can sometimes prove detrimental to the treatment of obsessive, narcissistic, or schizophrenic patients—all for slightly different reasons. Patients with prominent obsessive features are too critical of any tendency they may have to defy authority. They underestimate their capacity for warm, dependent relationships. Early confrontation of negative transference confirms their worst fears that they are defiant and recalcitrant individuals who deserve punishment and must be further controlled. They react by defending themselves with self-justifying rationalizations. It is preferable early in the treatment of obsessive patients to focus on their high standards and their wishes to please and help. They will point out their own hostility soon enough.

Narcissistic patients feel injured if they are confronted early in treatment. Kohut (1971) has demonstrated how important it is for narcissistic patients to idealize the therapist for long periods of time. If the therapist searches for signs of hostility hidden behind idealization and confronts it, narcissistic patients can feel profoundly misunderstood and hurt. Indeed, they suffer yet another narcissistic injury, because they cannot see themselves as the ideal patient of an ideal therapist. Empathic comments, apparently, are as much confrontation as they can initially tolerate. Kernberg (1974b), however, is probably correct when he suggests that their grandiosity and devaluing must be explored at some point. Patience and tact, not early confrontation of negative transference, become the key to success with these individuals.

Schizophrenic patients are sometimes reassured by gentle speculation about negative feelings early in treatment. Usually, clarifications should be used instead of confrontations to address negative transference or projections. When a schizophrenic woman mentioned her fear of being poisoned, her psychiatrist asked, "Have you had such worries about me?" She denied paranoia about him. He wisely accepted her word on the subject.

Schizophrenic patients generally have low self-esteem and a tenuous connection with other human beings. They experience any comment about their negative feelings as further proof of their social unacceptability. It is usually preferable to look for the positive in what they have to say (Hamilton 1986) and return to hostility later. This approach allows them to enter into an all-good or symbiotic self–other state. Searles (1961) has described them as needing to experience closeness with their therapist before they can begin to differentiate. Confrontation disrupts their symbiotic fantasies. This intervention usually must wait until they develop a more solid sense of self.

One must take care not to apply advances in the treatment of borderline patients to the treatment of psychotic patients. The psychotherapies of borderline and psychotic states involve distinct levels of self–object differentiation and integration, and each requires a different approach. Confronting negative transference is a good tool, but not for all purposes.

CONFRONTING ACTING OUT

Acting out has acquired various meanings in the psychoanalytic literature. It generally refers to a patient's doing things to dramatize conflict instead of talking about it in the sessions (Freud 1914b). It can also refer to chaotic or mischievous behavior of any kind. Some therapists call such impulsiveness acting up and reserve the term acting out exclusively for symbolic representations of unconscious material that has arisen in treatment. I believe that once a patient asks a clinician for help, all acting out outside the sessions has symbolic reference to the therapy and that acting up is always acting out. The therapist must confront these behaviors to bring them under therapeutic influence.

J.G., a 24-year-old college student, felt disappointed in her therapist when he yawned in a session. Instead of telling him how she felt, she indulged in drug abuse and promiscuity over the weekend. She minimized the importance of her escapade and reported she had been bored and wanted to have some fun.

"You haven't done that kind of thing for a long time," her therapist said.

"Once every 6 months isn't very often," she replied.

Her therapist confronted her inconsistency once again. "You'd mentioned you were trying to stop that sort of thing, because you end up feeling poor about yourself afterward. Have you changed your mind?"

"No," she said, "I just wanted to have some fun. My boyfriend is such a bore. He called, but I told him I was too tired to go out. Then I went to a bar."

For the past 8 months, she had been dating a fairly stable man who was genuinely interested in her. Now, she was throwing him over and returning to previous, more chaotic behavior. Her therapist confronted the acting out again. "You have been saying you liked him and felt he was fond of you. Now you are saying that isn't important to you."

"Let's change the subject. That is boring," she said, and yawned.

The yawn reminded the therapist of his lack of tact the previous session after he had been up much of the night helping in the emergency room. He was now in a position to interpret the acting out. Earlier, he had not been sure how the acting out had pertinence to the therapy. After repeated confrontation about her inconsistent behavior, he could interpret the relationship between acting out and therapy.

"When I was tired last session and yawned," he said, "I must have hurt your feelings. Just as I seemed too tired to pay attention to you, you told your friend you were too tired for him; but you were still lonely, so you turned to drugs and casual relationships to make you feel better."

The information for this interpretation would not have been available if the therapist had not first confronted the acting out. As the connection between such behavior and therapy was revealed, the negative transference became obvious.

Acting out is usually related to negative transference. A patient seeking gratification in self-defeating ways suggests that he does not feel the therapist is providing adequate care, just as he felt his parents did not provide adequate nurturance, attention, or guidance. In this example, the patient had a negative reaction to the therapist as a real, external object—her feelings were hurt when he yawned. These understandable feelings were augmented by transferential feelings about her parents, who were generally disinterested and superior in relation to their daughter. As a child, she had had to turn wherever she could for emotional involvement. These issues could only be discussed further after what had been acted out was brought into the therapy.

B.G., who has been discussed previously, in his second year of thrice weekly sessions, canceled two appointments in succession following his therapist's vacation. These were his first missed hours in a year. In the next session, he announced he had visited a religious community and intended to sell all his belongings and move to the commune. There, he said, he would get the guidance he needed while he continued treatment.

His psychotherapist confronted the acting out by saying, "While I have been gone for two weeks, you have found a new group to take care of you." Like many confrontations, this statement is little more than a paraphrase of what the patient had said.

"It doesn't have anything to do with you," B.G. said. "I just want to go to the commune. I know you have to go on vacation."

The therapist again confronted the acting out, this time adding a comment about the implied negative transference.

"Remember how it wasn't long ago when you would get suicidal during my vacations, and we'd put you in the hospital so you wouldn't feel too abandoned. It would certainly be understandable for you to feel a bit neglected when I leave you in such straits—and this time, I didn't even put you in the hospital. It must be disappointing that I would leave you that way."

"At least I don't get suicidal anymore; but you know how I get enthusiastic about these groups; and it does seem like a nice place."

"I'll bet. Did you meet any interesting people?"

Here, the therapist avoided the error of seeing the rival all-good object as entirely bad. By exploring the merits of the patient's plan, he did not participate in his tendency to see things in all-good or all-bad terms. He had succeeded in bring up the negative transference as an item for discussion. Serious acting out was now much less likely, and the possibility of joining the commune could be discussed more objectively.

"I did," B.G. said. "They're trying to live up to the old Christian ideal. No personal property. No greed. Everyone working for the good of the other; but there are always troubles.

You know how vain the deacons in the Messiah Group got—and greedy! They wanted everybody to contribute half their income."

This other element of acting out required a further confrontation. "And you are thinking about giving away all your property to these new people?"

"Well, not really. I get these ideas, but I won't do it. I just need to make sure you care about me."

His therapist could then choose whether or not to comment on the possibility that the patient felt devalued when he left on vacation. B.G. could have been symbolically dramatizing this feeling by literally devaluing himself, that is, giving all his property away. Confrontation had brought this issue to the patient's mind when he said, "I just need to make sure you care about me." Further comment was not necessary at this point.

Confrontation of acting out brings split-off self–object states into here-and-now interaction within the therapy, where they can be influenced. It is not used as often to make unconscious feelings conscious. Because these acted out feelings are experienced consciously in a different setting, they are not mentally brought together by the patient and cannot be integrated, consciously or unconsciously. Confronting acting out allows for consideration of new aspects of the self in relation to one another, and thereby promotes further differentiation and integration.

JUXTAPOSING GOOD AND BAD OBJECT RELATIONS UNITS

When patients split the self- and object-world into chaotically shifting all-good and all-bad units, it sometimes proves so disconcerting to therapists that they become immobilized. Since the patient's experience of them shifts dramatically, therapists have difficulty finding a stable point from which to start. Their interpretations become split by the patient. When the therapist interprets how the patient divides up his life outside the therapy, the patient often feels accused of being sick. The clinician thereby becomes an accusatory part of the all-bad unit in the patient's internal world. If the therapist does nothing, the patient may feel neglected and again see his potential helper as part of the all-bad unit. Sympathy, encouragement, and advice lead to inclusion of the therapist in the all-good unit, until such efforts fall short, as they eventually must. Then, the polarity changes and the therapist is again relegated to the worthless, powerless, and devalued all-bad object-world. How can the therapist provide a moderating influence if the patient sees him in extreme ways?

One approach to this problem is to pay close attention to transferences and to begin juxtaposing positive and negative affects in the therapy. In the example of W.J. (the 29-year-old receptionist with borderline personality), the patient began the session feeling alone and misunderstood. When the therapist empathized with her feeling neglected by him, she shifted to an all-good, self–other state: she and the therapist were symbiotic partners. She idealized her relationship with him and attributed her all-bad feelings to her husband and her mother, who represented the all-bad objects in her internal life. Thus, she maintained a split, all-good, all-bad experiential world. Rather than basking in this idealization, the therapist juxtaposed his patient's positive and negative affects by reminding her that even though she felt understood by him now, she had previously felt he was "not there for her." This juxtaposition allowed her integrative ego functions to work on her growing awareness that she had both positive and negative feelings concerning the same person.

This example illustrates that it is easier to juxtapose good and bad object-images in the transference when the patient is feeling good about the therapist. If the patient is feeling misunderstood when the therapist tries to point out how the patient valued him a few moments ago, it sounds as if he is arguing on his own behalf. The patient then feels more misunderstood. Juxtaposing positive and negative object-images when the patient is feeling good about the therapist is related to what Pine (1984) calls "striking while the iron is cold" (p. 60). In the heat of a negative transference or some other emotional turmoil, there is little use encouraging the patient to examine his feelings. It is better merely to empathize and wait.

One can work by juxtaposing positive and negative object-images outside the therapy. The therapist could have commented that W.J. sometimes saw her mother and her husband in alternating extreme ways, depending on whether they were gratifying or frustrating her. It becomes necessary at some point to comment on similar splits within the transference. As Freud (1912b) put it, one cannot defeat an enemy "in absentia or in effigie" (p. 108). To alter a patient's relationship patterns, those patterns must arise in the therapy relationship.

Kernberg (1975) reemphasized the importance of working in the here-and-now transference with borderline patients. If splits within the transference are not addressed with such patients, any comment the therapist makes attempting to juxtapose all-good and all-bad object-images becomes embroiled in the patient's alternating good–bad experience, and it cannot be effective.

Juxtaposing positive and negative self-images functions similarly to commenting on object-images. The therapist must be careful not to point out positive or negative attributes of the patient as if they were objective facts or the therapist's personal assessment. Learning of the therapist's tastes in human character traits is of little use to the patient, and comments along such lines can hurt the patient's self-esteem. Instead, he must refer to aspects of the self which the patient values or disparages himself. It is the patient's own contradictory values which he must integrate.

P.H., the 34-year-old businesswoman described in Chapter 13, had difficulty helping her son sleep in his own bed. During the session, she complained that when she became anxious and irritable, she felt she hated her son. In turn, she loathed herself for being such a "bad mother" as to hate her own child. She wanted to give up and die. She could not understand how psychotherapy would help her. She was in an all-bad self–other state.

P.H. was not borderline in her personality structure, but she had a poorly integrated, bad-mother self-image. When she was in such states of mind, she could not take in anything good—least of all, helpful comments from her therapist.

"When you feel so bad about yourself," he said, "you forget your capacity to care about your son; and you value that trait in yourself, the ability to care for others; but you forget that responsible, concerned, and valuable aspect of yourself when you become so discouraged."

She seemed not to hear this statement, which was designed to juxtapose her good self-images with her bad self-images. She was a bad mother, and that was all there was to it. Nevertheless, she could reassure the therapist she was not so despondent as to be suicidal.

The next session, she felt much better. Several friends had called her over the weekend. They invited her to dinner, helped her with child care, and told her they had been worried about her. She had looked unhappy recently, they said. As she described her weekend, she appeared much more relaxed than at the previous session.

"But," she said, "I feel guilty about Carla. Here I was complaining about my troubles and she was about to lose her job, but

I couldn't hear it. I was too preoccupied, and I really care about her."

Now that she was no longer in an all-bad, self–other state, her therapist could juxtapose the positive and negative self-images more effectively. He said, "So today you are more aware of your capacity for concern. When you get into those states of feeling like a bad mother, and everything is hopeless, you have a hard time reminding yourself of the qualities you value in yourself. At other times, you are aware of both qualities—your caring and your selfishness."

"I hope I can get so I remember them both," she said. "I get so tired of this up-and-down."

When she was in a more integrated state of mind, she could juxtapose those aspects of herself she valued and those she found less useful. Realizing she cared for others but had let them down, she could feel guilt instead of despair. The therapist took this opportunity to remind her of her recent all-bad, self–other state. When she was in these moods, she forgot her good integrative functions and felt like a bad mother, sometimes even calling herself a witch or a monster. Discussing this issue when she felt better gave her the opportunity to integrate her bad-mother self-image with her more mature identity. Once again, the therapist "struck while the iron was cold" (Pine 1984).

CLARIFYING SELF AND OBJECT
IN PROJECTIVE IDENTIFICATION

Handling projective identification requires special adaptations of psychotherapeutic techniques, as does splitting.

Intrapsychically, projective identification refers to attributing aspects of the self and associated feelings to the object and then attempting to control those feelings in the object. This element of controlling the self in other people entails a partial boundary blurring. Interpersonally, projective identification refers to behaving in such a way as to elicit unwanted feelings in the therapist and then trying to manipulate the therapist's feelings. Intrapsychic and interpersonal projective identification usually occur simultaneously.

Since projective identification involves at least partial self–object boundary blurring, techniques for dealing with it require clarifying boundaries, without abandoning the patient. These technical interventions must be made in the context of a containing or "holding" relationship, as described in Chapter 13.

An example of clarifying boundaries can be seen in this case:

L.R., a 32-year-old woman, had severely beaten her 3-year-old boy. She sought therapy and regained custody after having both her children temporarily removed from the home.

She became increasingly isolated from her friends and neighbors. In the treatment, she similarly withdrew. She presented a facade of being a perfect mother. Her therapist found herself increasingly critical in her thoughts about the patient. "How could this withdawn, unresponsive woman adequately mother her children?" she thought. "Surely she will explode again." The therapist felt mounting pressure to treat L.R. with perfect tact to prevent another episode of child abuse.

With some thought she was able to overcome her timidity and say, "I can't help but wonder about your not having any trouble with your children? A 3-year-old and a 1-year-old can be quite a handful."

"Oh, sure, but everything's under control."

"I wouldn't be surprised if you were a bit afraid that I might criticize you if you complain, or perhaps you may even fear I will report you to the court."

L.R. then launched into a long description of how her husband, her neighbors, and her social worker had not forgiven her.

"Perhaps you fear I will condemn you also," her therapist commented.

"Well, do you?" L.R. challenged.

The therapist assumed that both intrapsychic and interpersonal projective identification held sway. The patient had projected her own self-condemnation onto the therapist and tried to control potential criticism by presenting a picture of the perfect mother. Interpersonally, her sultry withdrawal had evoked feelings of condemnation in the therapist. As is frequently the case with projective identification, feelings the patient projected onto her corresponded to some degree with the therapist's own feelings, independent of the projection. The therapist, herself a mother, did not condone child abuse, or withdrawal and social isolation as coping mechanisms.

If the therapist had tried to deny her feelings of repugnance to claim, "I don't condemn you," she would have been colluding with the patient's view that her own conflicts could be solved outside herself. She told her, "I think you have not forgiven yourself for harming your children in this way, aside from what I or anyone else might think."

In this intervention, the therapist pointed out that the patient saw her own self-condemnation in the therapist. She did not claim to forgive or approve of her abusive behavior. She suggested that the therapy issue was the patient's self-condemnation. She clarified self–other boundaries, which helped the patient differentiate. She also fostered integration when she juxtaposed the patient's self-image as someone who could love and forgive with this condemnation. In addressing projective identification, the therapist provided her patient with an enhanced opportunity to reintegrate projected bad aspects of the self with good aspects of the self and to differentiate herself from others.

Using traditional psychoanalytic therapy techniques alone, the therapist would have been more likely to interpret transference than projective identification. She may have commented that the patient expected harsh condemnation and punishment from her therapist, as she had from her own mother. This would not have addressed the fact that it was no longer her mother condemning her—it was the patient herself. She had introjected her abusive mother's harsh attitudes and identified with this critical parental introject, making it a part of herself. The first step in addressing these issues was to help her recognize her own harshness and self-condemnation as her own, not the therapist's. The boundary clarification helped interrupt projective identification so that subsequent comments could be heard as noncritical and helpful. If such an intervention had not been made early, the patient's experience of being criticized and condemned by the therapist may have grown to be unmanageable.

A child psychoanalyst (Boverman 1983) sent a note with the following vignette from his practice:

> "A very difficult, borderline, anorexic, mischievous, young lady calmed down immediately when I met her for the first time in consultation and commented, 'I think I now understand you. You are feeling so much pain and disorganization and confusion inside that you would like to give it all to me.' "

The psychoanalyst interpreted interpersonal projective identification by clarifying boundaries. When he said, "You would like to give it all to me," he implied that the patient's distress was within her despite her wish to put it in him. He made this self–other distinction without rejecting or abandoning the patient, in that he said, "I think I now understand you," and explained that he did understand how much pain and disorganization she felt. In this way, he contained her affects, modulated them, and gave them words.

Projective identification can involve projection of good aspects of the self as well as less valued aspects. Psychotic patients are prone to project their grandiose and omnipotent self-images onto the therapist and then attempt to elicit perfect care.

R.J., the disheveled man who had responded so well to his nurse's expectations (Chapter 13), provides an example.

"You're wonderful," he told her. "You have helped me more than anyone. Why, I'm even ready for a job." He projected his own good attributes onto his therapist, giving her all the credit for his improvement, when he deserved some credit for his own efforts.

"But Vocational Rehabilitation won't cooperate," he went on. "They trained me to be a computer programmer and I want to own a gasoline station. They aren't with the program. I don't know what's the matter with them. I guess you'll have to straighten them out."

He indicated that he projected not only his effective functioning onto his therapist but also his unintegrated view of himself as omnipotent. He seemed fully convinced that she could get this agency to do whatever he wanted.

She responded by clarifying boundaries and ignoring the grandiosity for the moment. "I don't think you give yourself enough credit for how much you've helped yourself, through your own efforts. You think Vocational Rehabilitation or I can make you more productive, but really it is primarily your own effort."

He went on, "They won't listen to me. I'm starting to be annoyed with you. You can talk to them, but you won't do it. I need that gas station." He seemed to believe that she, or a training program she could get him into, would not only train him as a gas station attendant, but actually provide him with a station of his own. He was still projecting his omnipotent self-image onto his therapist and then trying to manipulate her to get the impossible.

His therapist said, "I think you'd like to magically have a gas station; and when you realize you can't do magic, you hope maybe I can; but I can't do magic either." Here she clarified

self–other boundaries and simultaneously confronted his omnipotent fantasies. By saying, "I can't do magic either," she maintained her relatedness and refrained from abandoning the patient; patient and therapist were separate, but similar.

"Well, I guess I'm just stuck, then." He now seemed able to
accept his situation, but he reverted to a helpless stance, which
again put his therapist in the position to accept the omnipotent
helper role.

She said, "Yes, you're kind of stuck, but there are some things
you can do to get a little more money." She once again modulated his helplessness and pointed out that he had his own
sources of power. She was still trying to show him that the ability
to take effective action which he had projected was inside him.

"Like what?" he asked.

He again invited her to accept the projection of his own
effective planning function.

She again attempted to return his projected effectiveness to
him by clarifying self–other boundaries. "I'll bet you can think of
several things you could do without my telling you."

"You're so damned stubborn. Sometimes I don't know what
I'm going to do with you." He shook his head. "You're really
something. You're really something." Then, he laughed.

R.J.'s attempts to project omnipotent fantasies onto his therapist
and then to get unlimited help from her required continual clarifying
of self–other boundaries. It was tedious, repetitive work. His staying
with it and chuckling indicated he had to some extent reintegrated his
projected capabilities by the end of the session. The fact that he shook
his head and said, "I don't know what I'm going to do with you,"
indicated that he felt he was capable of doing something and that he
felt equal, if not somewhat superior, to his therapist. He no longer
saw her as an omnipotent self-object.

"It must be frustrating that I can only help so much," she said.

She did not leave her vulnerable patient alone with his frustration
at not being able to control the world magically through her. She
empathized with his loss of a projected omnipotent self-image.

When clarifying self–other boundaries to deal with either positive
or negative projective identification, the therapist must take care not
to overreact and abandon the patient. The therapist needs to maintain

meaningful relatedness to prevent the patient from feeling abandonment rage and a need to project it into the therapist.

SUPPORTING SELF-ESTEEM WHILE CONFRONTING THE GRANDIOSE SELF

Promoting differentiation through boundary clarification and integration through juxtaposition of affects runs into special problems in the
case of grandiosity. Most patients with borderline or narcissistic
personality have prominent grandiose self-representations, which are
poorly integrated. This grandiose self alternates with a poorly integrated, devalued, or worthless self. When grandiosity is confronted
or challenged, the patient may suddenly be faced with feelings of
worthlessness and hopelessness. He may become enraged at a
sudden loss of self-esteem and decide that the therapist has betrayed
him. Patients often defend themselves by becoming even more
grandiose, perhaps leaving therapy. On the other hand, if therapists
never confront their patients' grandiosity, they do them an equal
disservice. Patients continue to face failure upon failure, because they
repeatedly expect the world—especially the people close to them—to
accommodate their unreasonable and grandiose expectations. Consequently, therapists must eventually help patients recognize their
exaggerated self-expectations while supporting their self-esteem.

One way to accomplish this delicate task is to explore the adaptive
and socially valued aspects of grandiose thinking while simultaneously indicating the drawbacks of this approach to life.

> D.C.—the 23-year-old actor who was beaten up before his
> performance—repeated a similar behavior in the hospital. On an
> outing with other patients, a group of local ruffians ridiculed one
> of the group. Incensed at this humiliation, D.C. attacked the
> heckler, knocking him to the ground. A restaurant owner inter-
> vened before the other youths could join in the fray, and D.C.
> escaped without injury.
>
> When he returned to the hospital, he instantly became a ward
> hero. Filled with pride, he refused to follow unit rules. He
> adopted a superior and condescending attitude with the nurses.
> His treatment was jeopardized, because he felt it was an affront
> that he should have to meet the least expectations.
>
> "Okay, you had a success," his ward psychiatrist said. "That
> must feel pretty good."

"Sure it does."

"You helped your wardmate by defending him and that's valued by our society, though you went a bit too far. You like to help."

The psychiatrist was supporting self-esteem and pointing out the beneficial aspects of grandiosity. The patient also sensed a less welcome comment on its way.

"Come on. Come on," he said. "Let's hear it."

"Your courage and energy are qualities which allow you to use your talents more fully than some other people can. So you value these qualities in yourself."

The psychiatrist did not give in to the patient's demand that he be treated bluntly and untactfully. It was a part of D.C.'s grandiosity that he thought he did not need to be handled gently.

"I'm waiting," he said, still sounding a bit superior.

He evidently expected to have his self-esteem attacked. Narcissistic patients often have a prominent devaluing, internal object-image from which they must defend themselves. D.C. projected this critical and harsh internal image onto his therapist and attempted to control it by identifying with it and adopting a superior manner. It is easy for therapists and other caretakers to slip into taking on the attributes which such patients project onto them; they must consciously resist the temptation.

"Once you have one success, you evidently forget the more sad, dependent aspects of yourself, and you demand that you do more than one person could possibly do."

"Like what?"

"Like taking on the whole world by yourself and not letting anyone help you even a little."

"I let people help me when I need it."

"Right now you aren't letting the nurses help you. That's really what the ward rules are for, you know. The nurses make rules to help people get along with one another; and you need to get along with these people so you can stay here and not get so lonely that you have to start using cocaine and getting drunk and ruining your promising career. You need to let the nurses help you follow the rules."

"Okay, okay, boss. I'll settle down."

The psychiatrist pointed out aspects of the patient's grandiosity that are congruent with society's values. He also discussed his underlying dependency needs without threatening the admirable aspects of his grandiosity. More work remained. At the end of the interchange, the patient still related to his psychiatrist as a boss, rather than as someone he could turn to for help with his more sensitive self. His feelings of humiliation remained barely approachable at this point in treatment; they required further work in psychoanalysis.

Psychotherapists often present a challenging, narcissistic facade to their own therapists, whether they have a personality disorder or not.

S.W., a psychologist, presented herself as a competent, cheerful patient, who immediately understood every comment her therapist made. She was a bit superior and sometimes elaborated interpretations before her therapist could. She was the daughter of a schizophrenic mother and a depressed father who could not care for her. She had been reared by foster parents after the age of 5. She felt insecure and was certain she would be rejected at any moment. In adulthood, she dealt with this difficulty by moving from one relationship to another, discarding the man before he could leave her.

Eventually, her therapist felt he needed to touch on S.W.'s grandiosity, which interfered with her acceptance of help. At that session the patient said, "Tuesday, at the end of the hour, I felt like I should stay and help you with that big stack of papers you had. I don't see why I always feel like I have to help everyone else. I know, I know, you are going to say it is transference of my feeling . . ."

"I wonder," her therapist interrupted, "about your anticipating my comments. Apparently, this talent has helped you overcome many obstacles. There were times in your life when you would not have gotten the help you needed if you had waited for it, so you created it yourself. Yet, you are still left alone that way, because you don't get to hear what I would really have said, only what you think I might say."

S.W. quieted down. She became sad remembering the many times she had desperately needed help and it had not been there.

S.W.'s grandiosity was not especially obvious. The therapist did not comment on it directly. Nevertheless, the patient did have the grandiose self-image of a self-made professional who had overcome a background of disadvantage. When the therapist indicated the adaptive aspect of this capacity, it allowed him to point out how this approach to relationships can be excessive and unnecessary.

A related way to support self-esteem while confronting grandiosity is to interpret its origins. The patient does not feel accused or blamed.

> B.G. (the patient with shifting identities and religious interests) frequently became haughty with his friends. "Frank picks out these awful paisley ties. I mean, paisley is grotesque, and I told him so."
>
> "You don't approve of his taste?" his therapist said.
>
> "Well, everyone is entitled to his own tastes, but . . . well really, it's ludicrous. It's embarrassing to be around him. I always try to keep myself up. You should see my apartment. It's gorgeous."
>
> His therapist said, "As a child, you were expected to want only the best, and your parents ridiculed you if you didn't maintain the highest standards. So you and the people you value must keep up high standards or you feel you will be humiliated."
>
> B.G. went on to describe how, as a child, if he listened to rock-and-roll instead of Mozart, his mother would sit him in a chair while she berated him. She used to tell him he would die poor, filthy, degraded, and alone.

B.G.'s haughty behavior, which led to the loss of many valuable friends, was not directly confronted, except perhaps by his therapist, commenting, "You don't approve of his taste." Instead, the therapist pointed to the origin of the patient's superior attitudes in his parents. That way, the patient could understand and accept his perfectionism without feeling humiliated.

When psychotherapists are tactful, patients feel valued and do not suffer a severe narcissistic blow when facing difficult issues. Patients will soon enough become open about their own shortcomings, including grandiosity, if they feel the therapist values them.

I have described the techniques of clarification, confrontation, and interpretation. The focus has been on variations of these interventions, which have made treatment of the more severe disorders possible and have added new dimensions to the treatment of neuroses. These variations include confronting breaks in structure and acting out, setting limits, juxtaposing positive and negative affects, clarifying self–object boundaries, and supporting self-esteem while confronting grandiosity.

All these techniques for promoting insight are used within the context of a viable treatment relationship. Given an adequate psychotherapeutic environment, these interventions promote differentiation and integration. They facilitate the patient's growing awareness of self as having a coherent identity, with strengths and weaknesses. They can assist development of a fuller and more consistent appreciation of others.

CHAPTER 15

COUNTERTRANSFERENCE

In recent years, countertransference has been recognized as an increasingly useful therapeutic tool. Freud (1910) originally defined this term as the analyst's unconscious, infantile reaction to a patient. He considered it something to be eliminated. Subsequently, countertransference also came to mean the therapist's conscious and appropriate emotional response to a patient (Kernberg 1965). As such, it became a valuable clue about how a patient typically interacts with others.

The therapist will be affected by a patient the way other people are. His emotional impressions provide a sample of feelings the patient tends to bring out in those around him. If the therapist is not too intrusive, this sampling will derive more from what the patient brings to therapy than from what the therapist brings to it.

Dr. H. J. had countertransference in the former, more narrow sense. He presented a session with G.R., a middle-aged accountant, to his supervisor.

"Mr. R. started out telling me all his troubles with his boss and his wife, as usual. Then, he told me . . . well . . . I was really surprised, flabbergastered, you might say. He just sort of out-

235

and-out told me that with his last boss he had had a . . . I guess, a homosexual affair. I mean here was this virile man telling me he had had this, this relationship. I know DSM-III says homosexuality isn't necessarily a sickness, but . . . I think this man is sicker than I thought. I guess I'm a bit old-fashioned."

"Whether it's a sickness or not, we would need to know how this episode worked out for Mr. R.," his supervisor commented, "but hearing about it surprised and disturbed you."

"I should say so; and he . . . well, I really don't approve. I guess it's part of my conventional upbringing."

The psychotherapist displayed anxiety, which interfered with understanding his patient and inhibited his communication with his supervisor, as indicated by his halting speech. It is common for men to display anxiety about homosexuality, especially when talking with a male authority figure, upon whom they may feel dependent. This anxiety reflects residual infantile conflicts about dependent and submissive longings, which need to come to light if the therapist is to remain effective. These feelings or attitudes also reflect learned societal attitudes about homosexuality and must be discussed and put in a broader context. Dr. H. J.'s anxiety about the therapy content arose independently of his patient's interactional style—the anxiety derived more from him than from his patient.

Fortunately, the therapist was able to use this opportunity to become more aware of his own ambivalent feelings about closeness to males. In turn, he could use his improved self-awareness to understand his patient better.

The following is an example of countertransference in the broader meaning of the concept.

Dr. D. M. described her reaction to F. B. This 63-year-old man's wife had suffered an incapacitating stroke 5 years previously. Thereafter, he had become increasingly depressed, eventually leading to loss of his job, which increased his feelings of worthlessness.

"The guy drives me nuts," Dr. M. candidly told her supervisor. "Every week it's the same thing—whining and complaining. I don't know what to do. We aren't getting anywhere, and I'm left with this hopeless feeling. I don't know if I can help this guy. Maybe I should transfer him."

"How frustrating," her supervisor said. "It must be very hard to listen to him week after week only to see him spin his wheels."

"And I come in here and you just emphasize. Come on, tell me what to do," she chided.

"So you feel helpless and hopeless about him, as he feels helpless and hopeless about his wife. Perhaps that is his way of communicating with you, arranging things so you will feel as stuck as he does."

Further discussion led Dr. M. to decide she could use her feelings of being stymied to empathize with her patient. She reestablished constructive communication. She could now say, "How discouraging it must be to visit your wife in the nursing home each day and find yourself unable to help; and worse yet, you must feel that no one can understand your despair."

In this case, the therapist's frustration did not represent an unresolved unconscious issue on her part as much as it did an appropriate reaction to her patient's characteristic relationship style. Attempts to help F.B. evoked feelings of hopelessness and helplessness, because he complained bitterly but did not improve with help. The therapist's feeling had more to do with the patient's characteristics and less to do with her own personal issues. This was countertransference in the broader sense. The two kinds of countertransference usually overlap.

PROJECTIVE IDENTIFICATION
AND COUNTERTRANSFERENCE

The concept of projective identification has been used to help sort out countertransference issues in the broader sense. Patients can behave in such a way as to elicit unwanted affects in the people around them, including clinicians. The less modulated and integrated a patient is, the more stereotyped and powerful these projections will be. Psychotic patients arouse stronger feelings than do borderline patients (Colson et al. 1985, Hamilton et al. 1986), and the latter, stronger feelings than neurotics. When working with more disturbed patients, clinicians can expect to have intense emotional reactions, which can override whatever personal issues the therapist may bring to the sessions.

Because projective identification can determine countertransference, Grinberg (1965, 1979) has labeled this phenomenon projective counteridentification. Kernberg (1965) has noted that countertransference can derive from the normal empathic capacity of therapists whose patients employ projective identification. Therapists who are sensitively attuned to their patients are bound to feel chaotic emotions which are projected onto them. He emphasized that clinicians who allow themselves to become consciously aware of their reactions gain important information about the patient's internal world.

Dr. D.M. provided an example of empathically using countertransference as Kernberg suggested. She learned how helpless and hopeless her patient felt when she realized he had elicited similar emotions in her. She could then shift from unmodulated projective counteridentification, which she did not understand, to empathic awareness of her patient's plight, which she did understand.

Psychiatry residents often report to their supervisors that they are confused, even when they have adequate information from the patient and knowledge of diagnostic criteria with which to make a diagnosis.

Dr. D.D. said, "This is the most confusing patient I have had yet. I don't know whether she has schizophrenia or bipolar disorder, or whether she's borderline with some psychotic features or psychotic with some borderline features. I'm perplexed."

"Perhaps," his supervisor suggested, "she is as perplexed as she is perplexing. If we look at the chaos within her and set aside, for the moment, the confusion she causes around her, perhaps we can make some sense out of this."

Dr. D.D. then described how his patient had been a graduate student with a circumscribed but conventional life-style until a month previously, when she began having feelings of not being herself. Her school functioning deteriorated and her manner of dress became disorderly. After discussing the situation further, he hypothesized that she might be having a first psychotic episode.

When Dr. D.D. returned to his patient, he could let her know that he understood how perplexed she was about what was going on within her. He could then help her stop avoiding her frightening experiences, which she had been doing by jumping from subject to subject. As they systematically explored her symptoms, she mentioned that she had begun hearing strange voices. Her doctor concluded that she was in the confusional stage of a first psychotic episode. He knew that approximately half these patients recover without having a subsequent episode and half go on to develop a chronic mental illness. He had further diagnostic work to do but could begin helping the patient come to terms with her problem. His own confusion had been the key to understanding how perplexed his patient was. It helped him make a diagnosis.

THE CONTAINER AND THE CONTAINED

One method by which countertransference can be advantageously managed is by using Bion's (1962) concept of the container and the contained. He suggested that children have strong affects, which threaten to overwhelm them. They externalize their distress and elicit similar feelings in their parents. This process is interpersonal projective identification—the parent internalizes the projected feeling, contains it, modulates and alters it, and then gives the transformed affect back to the child in the form of holding behavior or a comment such as, "Oh, I know. It really hurts when you skin your knee. Ouch!" The child can reintroject the transformed affect and thereby alter his internal experience.

When therapists listen closely to their patients, they similarly take in their strong feelings as countertransference. By remaining calm and finding meaning in their patient's distress, they perform a containing function. Dr. D.D. did this when he used the confusion his patient had communicated to him to understand her better. He could then help her cope with her distress.

In the emergency room, consultants are expected to remain calm in the midst of turmoil. Sometimes patients with a seemingly insoluble dilemma only need to convey their sense of urgency to the consultant and have it taken seriously. Many a crisis has been averted when the psychiatrist says something like Dr. B. said to his patient. "That is quite a problem," he said. "I can see why you are upset, and it's particularly difficult for you, because you feel that you have to take care of it tonight. It's hard for you to wait until tomorrow."

To make such a statement effectively, the consultant must take in the patient's sense of urgency. If he does not allow himself to be open to the patient, he will not be able to empathize and will sound contrived. When he feels countertransference urgency, he must resist the temptation to take immediate action or he will become part of the turmoil. By acting, he would implicitly validate the patient's feeling that the anxiety cannot be tolerated and must be dispelled. If he contains these feelings and returns them to the patient in modulated form, it reassures the patient. When he calms himself, he calms those around him, communicating by demeanor and words that most problems can wait.

Using countertransference effectively depends on the therapist's ability to be aware of his emotions without defending too vigorously against whatever unpleasantness might arise. Clinicians repress and distort their feelings for their own, nontherapeutic purpose. Anger can turn to guilt or boredom. Fear can become nonchalance. Sexual arousal can appear to be disdain or the wish to help. Sadness can be masked with optimism. Displacements can also interfere. It is common for anger or demanding behavior felt toward a patient to be manifested as righteous indignation about a disruptive family or a neglectful institution. For therapy to proceed, these countertransference distortions and displacements must be sorted out. The result will not be a completely neutral interest—as was once thought—but the ability to be more directly aware of strong feelings that patients bring to the session and elicit from the therapist.

Using these ideas, let us look at some typical countertransferences.

BOREDOM

Kulick (1985) reviewed the literature on boredom in the therapist. This feeling can derive from a mutual avoidance by both patient and therapist of aggressive or competitive strivings. An attempt to keep such feelings at a distance may lead to an absence of all emotional contact. A similar reaction may also arise from discomfort with affectionate or sexual longings on the part of the patient, the therapist, or, more often, both.

Another cause of countertransference boredom is the experience of being treated like a self-object (Adler 1984) or a part-object for long periods of time. With patients who have poor differentiation and integration of their self- and object-images and see the therapist as a thing, a fantasy, or even a hallucination, the feeling of involvement in a human relationship may falter.

B.G. spent months relating to his therapist as if he were his fantasy. While the psychiatrist was an American of mixed heritage, with farmers and woodsmen as forebears, the patient fancied him as deriving from noble English stock. The therapist lived in a small, wood-frame house in a middle-class neighborhood, whereas the patient fancied him in a Tudor mansion with stained glass windows. He drove an inexpensive domestic car, but the patient had him racing about in a black Porsche. B.G. imagined his therapist wearing elegant evening clothes when he went to the opera. He related to him as if he actually were this elegant person. Instead of a somewhat awkward and talkative psychiatrist, he saw a British psychoanalyst who made sparse and well-timed interpretations. As a result of the patient's relating to him as a fantasy figure, the therapist often had trouble maintaining interest. It seemed that B.G. was not talking to him but to his own daydream of his ideal self. Fortunately, once the therapist realized the patient was not relating to him as an external object, but as a self-object, the task of elucidating self-images and idealizing transferences (Kohut 1971) took on an interest of its own.

DEVALUING

Devaluing is another common countertransference. Therapists sometimes make disparaging comments about their patients to colleagues. This tendency is more common early in their careers, but usually persists to some degree. Contemptuous or derogatory remarks often suggest that the patient has projected a devalued self-image onto the therapist, and the therapist has reacted by devaluing the patient in return. The clinician is acting upon projective counteridentification rather than understanding it and using it productively in the treatment.

Emergency rooms and large, impersonal clinics foster these interactions. Here, the patient and the clinician have little opportunity to experience each other as real people. Their insignificance in relation to a large institution provides fertile ground for devaluing.

A senior psychiatrist took call for his junior colleagues one Friday afternoon so that they could have a long weekend. After meeting with a persistent heroin addict, he stopped by the office of another psychiatrist. "I just did something I haven't had the opportunity to do in years. I told a junkie I wouldn't give him any drugs."

His friend chuckled. "They can be quite a handful."

"The little weasel told me if I didn't give him any sedatives, he would go back on heroin and it would be my fault. His children would suffer because of his continued addiction, and that would be my fault, too."

"What did you do?"

"I called the drug treatment program and found out he hadn't kept his appointments there. Then I told him it causes problems to give addictive medications to people with drug problems. I had decided not to give him anything and referred him to the drug treatment program on Monday. He said he thought it was a terrible program."

Although the psychiatrist had been polite and had acted appropriately with the patient, afterward he called him "a junkie" and "a weasel." He was involved in countertransference devaluing. A few moments later, he said to his colleague, "I don't know why these guys annoy me so, even now when I don't have to see them very often."

As may be discerned from the conversation, most people devalue drug addicts—it was not this psychiatrist's idiosyncratic response. The patient had been devaluing him, trying to make him feel inhumane if he didn't hand over the desired prescription. The patient claimed he was not only causing him to get worse, but was also harming innocent children. He could be conceptualized as projecting his feeling of failing himself and his children onto the psychiatrist and trying to manipulate the doctor to control his own feelings and to get the drug he sought. He was also devaluing in that he treated this physician as if he were merely an avenue to a desired substance, a thing. He did not treat him as a whole person who had expert knowledge and compassion and could help, but as a part-object.

In infantile terms, the drug-seeker did not treat the psychiatrist like a nurturing figure, but like a disembodied nipple, an avenue to the good milk, the drug, and nothing else. Rather than gaining insight into the projective identification of devalued self linked with depriving part-object, the psychiatrist displayed his projective counteridentification by devaluing the patient in return. It was only later, when he discussed his reaction with a colleague, that he gained insight into his feelings. His familiarity with protocols for handling spur-of-the-moment drug requests and his well-established professional demeanor helped him treat the patient politely and give him a clear message, despite his devaluing. In a more intimate setting, such as psychotherapy, his attitude would have undoubtedly been communicated to the patient.

THERAPEUTIC ZEAL

Therapeutic zeal is another possible derivative of unrecognized countertransference. Patients may induce therapists to repeat old traumas in the guise of heroic treatment. This interaction has been described in relation to schizophrenic patients (Searles 1967a). It is common with many serious illnesses.

One of the ways to treat posttraumatic stress disorders in soldiers is to encourage them to talk about their war experience. Many of them are terrified of returning, even in memory, to what had been painful. Most therapists or discussion group leaders gradually reconstruct the experience. At times, therapists find themselves pushing their patients to abreact their trauma all at once by an implosion technique. The idea is that the patient will be continually confronted and brought back to the worst of his memories until he breaks down and lets out his emotions with a rush, this time in a safe consulting room rather than on the battlefield of a foreign country. Unfortunately, the consulting room is not always safe from an emotional standpoint.

Although implosive techniques can be beneficial, they are high-risk endeavors. Many patients fall by the wayside. Both patients and therapists have made the analogy that the clinician was like an infantry group leader, inducing his men to move into enemy fire while ignoring their fears and their good judgment. Once again, the patient must set aside his individual judgment and follow a leader into an inhumane circumstance. They can feel more harmed than helped by this zealous approach.

Some soldiers are able to carry out their duties as tasks to be accomplished for laudable goals, in the face of dreadful aspects of war. Many, however, have to rely upon their grandiose self and their harsh and high self-expectations to carry them through. They may split off and project their dependency, fear, tenderness, and doubts in the reasonableness of their action, seeing that aspect of themselves in the enemy or in politicians and officers, in noncombat soldiers and civilians, or in any other group they consider cowards or bumblers. The grandiose, harsh self is projected onto comrades, and, particularly, the leader. If projective identification is involved, they will partially reidentify with the projected grandiose self-object.

In group therapy, these soldiers may again project their harsh, demanding, and grandiose self-expectations onto the group leader and then reidentify with these attitudes. Under the influence of such powerful projections, inexperienced leaders can become grandiose in the countertransference. Whether experienced or not, they can sometimes act on their feelings by leading the men into a sudden onslaught of unmanageable emotions. The leaders must refrain from acting on their heroic impulses and become aware of their countertransference grandiosity in order to empathize with how the soldiers felt called upon to do frightening and dangerous things.

The countertransference of psychotherapists of Vietnam-era soldiers with posttraumatic stress disorder has been described by Frick and Bogart (1982) and by Newberry (1985).

VICTIM-VICTIMIZER ROLES

Victims have a special place in our society. They elicit strong feelings in the people around them. The innocent victim fascinates people.

Because self-other boundaries are permeable, even if a victim is innocent of complicity in his own downfall before the trauma, he is no longer innocent of it afterwards. He internalizes the victimizer, and that role becomes a part of himself. This common phenomenon will be discussed in relation to countertransference.

Sexual abuse of children is a topic of great concern. Women therapists in particular have many female patients who were sexually molested as children. It is common for these therapists to seek consultation about them. At first, these women can be gratifying patients. Their phobias, depressive episodes, and dissociations clear rather quickly when they gain awareness of the forgotten trauma, and this discovery phase can be exciting. Then things may bog down.

One therapist expressed her frustration this way:

E.W. keeps hitting me with the same stuff over and over. She tells me all these stories, but she doesn't improve. It's like she's shoving all the unpleasantness into me and then just walking out the door, calm as a clam; but I find myself thinking about it all evening."

The therapist was feeling penetrated and victimized, somewhat the way her patient had been treated sexually and then abandoned as a child. The victim had introjected her victimizer and identified with him. She was now victimizing her therapist in the transference.[1]

Perhaps even more commonly, sexually abused patients tantalize their therapists with bits and pieces of information and then retreat into vagueness. They thereby invite an intrusive therapeutic assault.

---

[1]This is an instance where the word transference also refers to projective identification, because what is externalized is sometimes an object-image and sometimes a self-image, depending on whether the patient is experiencing herself as victim or is identifying with the victimizer at the moment. I have retained the word transference because it is common to use this word to indicate the "as-if" quality of such interactions as well as their infantile origin.

Clinicians find themselves tempted to force the patient to "open up." Such behavior in patients does not suggest that they originally invited seduction, but that once they had been abused, they attempt to reproject the introjected victimizer and gain control over the situation. By projecting or transferring the abuser onto others, they hope to control the unwanted internal object outside themselves. Unfortunately, they cannot master the situation this way, but are more likely to invite further abuse. In therapy, the same pattern occurs even with a supportive female therapist. The transference–countertransference paradigm of therapist as rapist and patient as victim, or vice versa, is equally common with adult victims (Rose 1986).

One psychologist told her supervisor, "It's like she's forcing me to treat her roughly. She lets me know there's something to talk about, but then she gets coy. I feel like shaking her."

"You don't want to feel like shaking her," her consultant said. "You are having that role forced on you. You really want to feel kind and helpful."

After further discussion, this psychotherapist, who specialized in women's issues, was able to return to her patient and say, "You mention these 'things' your stepfather did to you. Then you get vague and evasive. Sometime we will need to discuss these 'things' in some detail, if you are to continue improving. If I push you, however, you might feel I am forcing my way into something private. So I will listen and wait and you will talk more about these things when you are ready."

Her patient wept with relief.

This therapist sought help in mastering her countertransference. She harnessed the genie and turned it into a powerful tool. She could now understand her patient with more immediacy and depth.

Countertransference is not always handled productively. Therapists may try to avoid the patient's projection of victimized self-images or transference of victimizing object-images. One way to do so is to identify with the patient and to project the victimizer further onto current people in the patient's life—their family members, the medical or legal system, or, not uncommonly, men in general. While such therapies can be supportive and helpful, they cannot allow the patient to overcome her victim role. The projections with which such therapists collude merely calm things down while allowing the patients to victimize themselves over and over again. These patients cannot relinquish their identities as wronged. They remain victims forever.

ANGER AND GUILT

Anger in the countertransference is commonly displaced onto other people: family, colleagues, or institutions. It may also be turned to countertransference guilt, which immobilizes the therapist.

In a study of five outpatient therapists observed during 26 sessions (Hamilton et al. 1986), clinicians had strongest feelings about psychotic patients with a questionable diagnosis and a potential for violence to themselves or others. These aggressive and impulsive patients could not be managed by their families, the police, or institutions. Many of them had been asked to leave psychiatric hospitals. They demanded care, yet refused to cooperate with diagnostic procedures, no less with difficult therapeutic regimens. These patients implied, or actually stated, that the therapist would be responsible for any disruptive or dangerous activity they might undertake. One would expect clinicians faced with such patients to find them frustrating. Some authors have discussed them in terms of countertransference hate (Winnicott 1949, Poggi and Ganzarain 1983). The therapists in this clinic, however, expressed virtually no irritation with them. Their predominate feeling was guilt. One psychiatrist said, "I might be negligent." An experienced nurse practitioner commented, "I should try harder." A psychiatry resident described treatment as "a kind of psychological rape," when he knew that it was the patient, not the therapist, who was sexually aggressive. One clinician said, "The patient is becoming more like me, and I'm not sure that's good." Any annoyance was displaced from the patient to the institution or family. A typical remark was, "My frustration is with the system, not the patient."

Many therapists, as helpers, feel they must care about their patients and not find them annoying, much less, infuriating. They often believe they must be able to help everyone and maintain objectivity. When patients elicit strong negative feelings in them, therapists may become immobilized with guilt, which interferes with their setting appropriate limits. They become inactive; nothing they do can help. At other times, they displace their annoyance onto their colleagues and see them as hostile or critical when they are not.

Kernberg (1965), among others, has indicated how useful it can be for therapists to allow themselves direct awareness of countertransference anger, thereby freeing themselves from immobilizing guilt. When therapists in this study began to experience their frustration more directly and noted that it derived from unmodulated, primitive aggression in their patients, they became much more effective. They could then better contain their countertransference anger and help their patients similarly contain their own feelings. They began expecting patients to keep appointments. They insisted on a thorough diagnostic evaluation before prescribing medications. They required patients to treat them in a civil fashion. In other words, they used their energy to hold their patients within a reasonable and potentially helpful treatment environment. Having become aware of their countertransference anger, they could more easily keep these troublesome patients in their attention, accept their projections, and empathically confront the rage these patients felt.

POSITIVE COUNTERTRANSFERENCE

In recent years, positive countertransference has not received nearly the attention that negative transference has. Originally, however, countertransference referred primarily to erotic fantasies a therapist might have about his patients (Freud 1915). These feelings can be very strong. In the transference, it is only natural that patients who talk about the intimate details of their emotional and sexual lives in private will have some erotic feelings about the person with whom they are talking. In the countertransference, it is likewise understandable that clinicians will have some loving and erotic feelings when their patients fall in love with them.

It is usually easy enough for clinicians to consider whatever arousal they may feel as being primarily elicited by the patient and to understand what it means in terms of transference. Problems arise when self–other boundary problems, aggression, or grandiosity in either the patient or the therapist interferes. Patients who have a symbiotic attachment to the therapist can experience this closeness in terms of sexual longing. The complete love and adoration these patients have for their therapists can be most compelling. If the clinician is lonely, insecure, and needing to be idealized, it can be tempting to accept the patient's erotic feelings as his or her due, instead of using countertransference to empathize with how deeply attached the patient wishes to be and with how frustrating it must be not to have such desires totally gratified. Other therapists become so threatened by these feelings that they become unempathic and distant. It is most useful for therapists faced with such feelings to consult with a colleague who can help them stay therapeutically engaged and refrain from acting on erotic desires and grandiose longings to be idealized.

Some patients use seduction to hide hostility. They may covertly wish to achieve dominance through flirtation. Clinicians may be tempted to regain dominance by sexually exploiting them. A more common problem is for the therapist under such circumstances to retreat into apparently neutral aloofness. This may be an attempt to defend against seduction. The therapist may continue to engage in a private battle for dominance, a battle of wills. This situation can provide gratification for the therapist—the patient continues to use seductive ploys, and the therapist sanctimoniously refrains from involvement. A better course is to reflect on whatever feelings may be aroused, try to understand the patient's behavior, and bring the behavior up for discussion. Patients are often relieved when therapists comment on their seductiveness, because it relieves them of guilt feelings or fears of excessive closeness.

My female colleagues have mentioned positive countertransference responses to aggressive male sexuality in therapy.

Dr. M.W. said she became immobilized when a male patient spent session after session detailing sadistic sexual fantasies. She attempted to explore his feelings and ideas, wondered about their childhood roots, and speculated on their dynamics.

At first, she found all this exciting. She told her supervisor she had never had such a fascinating patient. He had interesting fantasies and was unusually willing to talk about them. He appeared cooperative, and he was polite and likeable.

Over several months, he had more and more fantasies and gained little insight. He soon began to assail her with menacing imaginings. He became increasingly hostile in sessions. She felt confused and trapped, but did not know why, because she liked the patient so much. After several months, he left treatment in a huff.

Upon reflection, Dr. M.W. decided she had at first been excited by being privy to this male patient's intimate fantasies. That was part of the reason she found him so interesting and likeable. When he began to act out those fantasies symbolically by subjecting her to repeated sadistic stories, she became infuriated by his assault. Perhaps, she speculated, she had defended herself from awareness of this attack by reaffirming her belief that she liked him. She became therapeutically immobilized.

Soon after, she had a similar patient. This time she could use her insight to confront his acting out. She could now say, "As much as you protest that you would like to get over having these ideas, you seem to derive pleasure from telling them to me. You even smile a bit, as if you have me at your mercy. Perhaps you have felt as though you were at someone else's mercy at another time in your life." She was thus able to use her countertransference feeling of being both excited and victimized to begin exploring how the patient had felt when his mother would obsessively scrub his genitals until they were raw.

Another female therapist mentioned generally positive feelings about an angry male patient. She felt sorry for him, felt he was wronged, and wanted to help him.

T.E. was a 36-year-old man who complained to his woman psychiatrist for months about how angry he was at his ex-wife. He carried himself in an upright posture and spoke in a commanding voice. When he also complained of his psychiatrist's not helping him more, she felt a bit intimidated, but primarily wanted to help him. She wished for his approval and wanted to be a good therapist for him.

The psychiatrist mentioned to a colleague that her patient was apparently feeling hostile, while she was feeling a generally positive countertransference, wishing to help. She was not sure at first if her positive feelings might be a defense against her anger or if she was empathically sensing a projected aspect of her patient's self-image. She speculated that he might have very much wanted approval and warmth from his ex-wife, and now wanted them from her in the therapy. He may have been attempting to elicit those feelings in her through interpersonal projective identification. She decided to explore the issue by speculating on the patient's positive feelings in the therapy.

She told the patient, "I think you are most comfortable talking about your anger. It is much harder for you to become aware of how much you want me to understand you and care about you."

This comment resulted in renewed progress. The therapist had used her awareness of positive countertransference to better understand the patient.

In this chapter countertranference has been defined, in the broad sense, as a clinician's emotional response to a patient. It includes the therapist's normal emotional reaction to a patient's social cues, which reflects how other people also respond. A related phenomenon is the clinician's projective counteridentifications, feelings that the patient disowns and elicits from the therapist through interpersonal projective identification. Countertransference is no longer considered something to be eliminated; it has become a useful tool in understanding patients.

Countertransference as the experience of a patient's projected emotions may be interfered with by the clinician's conflicts and biases. Countertransference in the broader sense of providing subtle information about the patient can be distorted by countertransference in the older, more narrow sense, in which it derives from the therapist's unconscious conflicts.

Like any powerful tool, countertransference is a difficult instrument to master. When using an understanding of how people confuse self–other boundaries through projective identification, therapists must be certain always to recover their own secure boundaries; simply to attribute their feelings to the patient, invoking the idea of projective identification, will not do. Therapists need to know themselves well enough to identify their own characteristic ways of reacting to people and their own psychological defense mechanisms.

Feelings may give the therapist clues about a patient's internal life. They may be elicited by a patient's behavior. The patient may have fantasies of projecting feelings into the therapist. Despite all this, whatever the therapist feels is his own human emotion, similar to but separate from the patient's feelings. Awareness of countertransference can help therapists generate hypotheses about how patients may be feeling and what feelings they may spilt off. Other evidence must confirm or deny the hunches. In the absence of evidence outside countertransference, therapists can become lost in a muddle of fantasies and wonderings about wonderings.

Countertransference can be explored in supervision with a colleague. In such difficult work, the therapist needs a reminder from time to time that "he has no great secrets to conceal and that his experiences, as well as those of his patient, are not more or less than simply human" (Will 1975, p. 954).

CHAPTER 16

GROUPS, SYSTEMS, AND PARALLEL PROCESSES

Object relations theory concerns itself with internal versus external, self versus other, and the processes by which these boundaries are maintained at times and crossed or blurred at other times. These concepts can be applied to systems larger than the individual person, such as families, groups, and institutions. In this chapter, I emphasize the application of object relations theory to work groups concerned with helping other people; families will be mentioned too.

From theoretical considerations, certain predictions about work group functioning can be made. Chapter 5 described how projection and introjection are used psychologically to cross self–other boundaries in individuals. Loved and hated, good and bad self- and object-representations are projected and introjected. Identification can be used to attribute an aspect of an object-image to a self-representation. Projective identification can be used to attribute aspects of the self to objects and to elicit those qualities from them.

If these principles are applied to groups of people, we can predict that groups will externalize unwanted or bad qualities onto other groups. They may even attempt to control the projected evil in others, in a way similar to projective identification in individuals. They may

251

divide the world into all-good and all-bad camps, as in splitting. They may take in qualities from the outside, as in introjection.

GENERAL SYSTEMS THEORY

General systems theory (Bertalanffy 1950, Menninger et al. 1963) describes the establishment and crossing of boundaries as characteristic of all living systems. Biological or psychological systems are defined by their boundaries. The function of systems is to maintain those boundaries while transporting energy and wastes across them. Kernberg (1980) used systems theory combined with the object relations theory of boundaries to examine organizational functioning.

Nutrients must be internalized and wastes externalized in living systems. Internal or external excesses of energy threaten to disrupt boundaries and must be avoided, repelled, or expelled. On a mountain trail, a hiker needed to ward off a blow from a 50-pound fir branch after a gust of wind dislodged a massive bough from an 80-foot-high old-growth fir. He heard it crashing toward him, raised his arm, and violently thrust the limb aside. He received only a scratch rather than a severe blow on the head. In systems terms— which can at times sound ludicrously abstract—he deflected the energy of the falling wood so it would not disrupt his boundaries, with the potential of causing his death. He maintained himself as differentiated from his surroundings.

Excess energy from inside also needs to be expelled. As the hiker climbed higher on the trail, winding back and forth up the side of the Columbia River Gorge, he began to perspire. He removed his blue stocking cap and tucked it in his belt. By removing his cap, he allowed excess energy, in the form of body heat, to escape. He had removed a boundary layer when he took off his cap. For systems to function, boundaries must be maintained at an optimum degree of permeability and impermeability.

BOUNDARY CLARIFICATION

These same principles can be applied to work groups.

> Dr. R.W. took a temporary assignment at a psychiatric clinic. His job was to improve the organization, which had become so chaotic that there was violence in the halls. Patients made threats

to clinicians; one patient had attacked a social worker, requiring several people to intervene. Morale was very low, and staff members were immobilized.

Dr. R.W. observed the clinic for several weeks. He noticed that the reception desk was placed in the middle of the offices. Patients were well into the work space before anyone greeted them. Intoxicated wanderers from the street intruded into the clinic. His first intervention was deceptively simple; he clarified boundaries by moving the reception desk near the elevator and building a door separating offices from the waiting room. This new, internal-external boundary was symbolic, because the door was not locked. Nevertheless, chaos in the clinic decreased noticeably. Morale improved, and the professionals regained their accustomed self-assurance.

Just as an individual binds anxiety and turmoil when he becomes more certain of his self–other distinction, this group of clinicians became more stable when they clarified their boundaries. Other changes, such as clarifying referral procedures, also clarified boundaries, but not so tangibly.

If established boundaries change, even for the better, a period of potentially maladaptive disorganization can temporarily ensue.

New computers had been installed in one well-functioning psychiatric clinic, which was part of a larger organization. These machines improved the speed and accuracy of scheduling.

Everyone was pleased with the change until middle-level administrative personnel visited the clinic for the first time. Several made comments about productivity. Staff members gossiped in the halls, voicing their fear that the business administrators, armed with misleading computerized data, might make ill-informed decisions which would adversely affect clinical work. Perhaps clinicians would be fired and clinic space converted to administrative use. Time and emotional energy were spent rumbling about lack of administrative support; they had difficulty paying attention to and being supportive of their patients. Perhaps R.S., one of the business people, should be dismissed, they said.

Carrying computer printouts about productivity, R.S. went to the clinical director, who was a psychiatrist. Previously, only the clinical director had had access to these data; he used to discuss it with the larger institutional management as he released it.

Now, the information was available directly to all levels of management. A boundary crisis had arisen. It was not until this encounter that anyone understood the problem.

With the boundary shift—which no one had recognized—clinical and administrative groups had slipped into the kinds of primitive mechanisms to which individuals resort when their boundaries become unclear. Projections were rampant. Clinicians tried to protect themselves and their clinical space by attributing problems to R.S. and calling for his dismissal. They were trying to eject him from their group, as they feared he was trying to eject them from their jobs and their clinical space. R.S. and other management personnel became suspicious of clinicians and felt they must control them to secure their own jobs and the good functioning of the organization. This in-fighting is similar to projective identification in individuals, whereby each attempts to see his own anxieties in the other person and thereby control his feelings through someone else. When both parties participate in projective identification, a vicious circle ensues.

The solution came with a boundary clarification. Management needed to decide whether or not they still needed a clinical director, now that they had a machine to gather information about productivity. Once the decision was made in favor of retaining a clinical director, management and the psychiatrist-director were able to discuss actual workload. R.S. and the psychiatrist learned that productivity was above standard. Management found a way to enhance that already good record by improving the accuracy of recording work load and billing. The computer could also help with some clerical work that clinicians had been doing themselves, and therapists could increase their actual productivity without working harder. With this solution, anxiety and gossip in the hallways decreased. Staff members once again focused on patient care in their characteristically attentive fashion. This process of clarifying boundaries in groups to decrease projective identification is similar to the procedure in psychotherapy with individuals (see Chapter 14).

BASIC ASSUMPTION GROUPS

Parallels between individual self–other boundaries and group boundary issues may not be the only application of object relations theory to group dynamics. What about attachment, aggression, and love? Can these important drives or needs be applied to groups?

Child development and individual therapy have shown that people require closeness to other people (see Chapter 5). When these dependency needs are not met, they experience frustration and longing, that is, aggressive and loving feelings in relation to the lost object. Groups display the equivalents of dependency, frustration, and longing. We shall not confine our exploration of these issues to theoretical speculation, inasmuch as they have been demonstrated in some detail.

During World War II, Bion, a British psychoanalyst and object relations theorist, investigated group functioning at Northfield Military Hospital. He developed a method of reestablishing group morale by focusing on a common task (Grotstein 1981b). After the war, he continued his work at the Tavistock Clinic in London. He found that when the task of a group is not clear or meaningful, group members spontaneously act as if they have an assumed purpose. Bion (1961) called these the basic assumptions of dependency, fight-flight, and pairing (see Rioch 1970). These assumptions roughly correspond to attachment, aggression, and love in individuals.

At the Menninger Foundation, Dr. Ramon Ganzarain, a South American psychoanalyst, organized and conducted groups modeled after those developed at the Tavistock Clinic. Psychiatry, psychology, social work, nursing, and pastoral counseling trainees gathered in eight groups of seven, with one leader each. They met once weekly for six 90-minute sessions.

The seven men and women in Group A greeted the leader, who said nothing. Group members asked the leader how they should proceed. When he did not respond, they talked with one another about what to do. Perhaps one of them should be the leader? For 2 weeks, they discussed who should lead, why each person might like such a role, and why each person did not want to assume the responsibility. How could they learn about groups if they did not have a leader?

The basic assumption of the group was that the members were to be dependent upon a leader who would give them knowledge. This sort of group is termed a dependency basic assumption group. There is a similarity to the longing of young children who are taken care of by a parent; they want to incorporate or introject what is needed from the caregiver. When this basic assumption was frustrated, the group considered potential conflict.

"I'll bet as soon as we elect a leader," said Mel, one of the group members, "this guy will wake up and take over. Then we'll have a struggle. It's just like these guys."

"When I won't give you guidance," the leader finally said, "you want to create a new leader to give you direction; but the group is afraid there might be conflict."

After chuckling about this oracular statement—the only one the leader made in 3 weeks—group discussion of potential conflict widened. Group members shifted to speculation about the other seven groups.

Mel commented, "I'll bet they're as frustrated as we are."

"I wonder what they're learning," Mary said.

"We need to organize ourselves," Gary suggested. "They probably already have a structure and leaders and are making lists of group roles. We're just obsessed about why we can't do it."

"What are we supposed to do, anyway?" Mary asked. "Are we supposed to make a structure?"

"We're supposed to observe our own functioning and learn about groups," Gary said, "but I don't think we are doing very well. The others are probably way ahead of us."

"Our leader's no good," Mike chimed in. "We need a new one."

"Oh, forget it," Mel said. "Let's go have a beer."

At this point, the basic assumption had shifted from dependency to fight-flight. Internally, conflict was expressed in terms of competition among leaders, sometimes taken even to the extreme of human sacrifice. Externally, the group tried to define itself by comparing and contrasting itself with other groups. It tended to do so in competitive or aggressive terms. This process is similar to the way small children become aggressive when their dependency is frustrated and attempt to avoid conflict by projecting it outside the dyadic boundaries. They may then try to escape the projected aggression by shunning the bad object.

The combination of fighting and flight can also be seen in the scapegoating common in many groups. Frustration of dependency needs can lead to aggression and conflict within the group. This group "evil" may be assigned by the fight–flight group to the scapegoat who is extruded. The analogy to projection is clear.

At the next session, Mel and Mike renewed the call to leave the group and have a party. Gary wanted to stick with the task of trying to organize, learn about human behavior, and catch up with the other groups. Juan, Linda, and Bob commented occasionally, but remained less involved.

"Let's you and I go," Mel said to Mike, "and we'll take Mary along."

Mary smiled, and everyone laughed. A previously subtle flirtation between Mary and Mel, which had also been shared with Gary, now became focused. All the group members were excited about the prospect of Mary and Mel having a tryst.

Mary saved the situation when she commented, "Well, as Gary has remined us, the task is to learn about human interactions in this group." Her smile and coyness indicated she enjoyed the attention within the group. Everyone encouraged her.

The basic assumption had shifted from fight-flight to pairing. The group now acted as if its task were to foster loving relations. In more primitive terms, the hope of such groups is to foster a pair who will have a baby as a new savior. The prospect of such an offspring adds excitement, hope, and meaning to the group. The creative effort is usually metaphoric, but is sometimes literal. This process is similar to positive projective identification in children and individual patients. The group has a longing for dependent and loving relationships and attempts to create the good object by externalizing it and reintrojecting it. The messiah is born out of the group and provides it with hoped-for nurturance and guidance, which the group merely incorporates or introjects.

These artificial groups were formed within a larger social order. All the participants were students of the professions within an academic and clinical context. The groups were small and manageable. When large groups are involved, basic assumption functioning becomes even more obvious.

As a part of the previous exercise, small groups were melded into two large groups of 28 members each. Their task was to meet toward the end of a daylong session and discuss what they had learned. Dependency basic assumptions again occupied the early part of the meetings.

Group A discussed the need for a leader and used their common political heritage to settle on a process of nominations and elections. They assigned a leader and two ambassadors who were empowered to represent the group only if they checked back for a majority opinion on each statement. They were required to report everything said by Group B.

Soon, an ambassador from Group B arrived in Group A to observe their process. She said, "I have come to sit in on your group for 5 minutes, if that is agreeable; but I have been asked not to talk."

Group A members joked in an excited way about the "spy." They also expressed fantasies about spying on the other group. There was much tension and anxiety in both groups. After the "spy" left, Group A sent an observer to the other group.

Group B relied upon a different cultural tradition, that of an informal gathering or party. Group members were free to do and say as they saw fit within certain unspoken social conventions. The exception was the emissary, who did and said what she pleased, except in her role as observer, when she could say nothing. They had a minimum of organization.

Members of both groups joked about fantasies of gang warfare. They disparaged the other group, developing hurt feelings about how they were perceived. They reminded themselves it was only an exercise and hoped the experience would not have lasting repercussions on their collegial relationships. Each group felt they were managing the experience in a more mature fashion than the other.

At the plenary session, Group B allowed each member to speak individually. They had evolved no structure of leadership and communication. They had, however, developed a collective opinion that Group A had grown in a distorted, sick, and dangerous fashion. Their organization and highly structured communication earned Group A the nickname the Gestapo Group.

The designated spokesperson for Group A said that they experienced Group B as hostile and dangerous, just as Group B seemed to experience them. The spokesperson added that Group B seemed to be attacking Group A's structure in a provocative fashion. The nickname for Group B was the Mob.

One of the exercise leaders interjected, "Perhaps we have learned that both groups in an unstructured situation define themselves in terms of contrast to and conflict with the other group. In that way, they create boundaries and externalize conflict."

Members of both groups agreed with this view. The faculty leaders encouraged members to explore the advantages and disadvantages of highly structured versus informal groups. They helped participants accomplish their task of learning about group functioning. As a part of this process, they reviewed the basic assumptions, and how fight-flight had predominated in this daylong session, with each group defining itself in contrast to the other one. The process involved an externalization of aggression to the other group, similar to projection in children.

All groups, like individuals, function differently. A pairing basic assumption predominated in the large group exercise of the following year. Both groups agreed to abandon the task and meet elsewhere for the purposes of having a party. The following week, faculty leaders pointed out how group members had acted out a pairing basic assumption, bringing the two groups together to form an offspring in the form of a party and lasting relationships. Members were not chastised for this choice; and they were able to learn in retrospect. An additional benefit of their behavior, which was not task related, was that many people struck up new acquaintances and enjoyed themselves at the party.

Groups rely more on basic assumptions when the task is not clear or meaningful. When the task is meaningful, basic assumption functioning diminishes. This observation has been borne out on psychiatric wards. During the late 1960s and early 1970s many psychiatric hospitals experimented with focusing on staff interactions in meetings. Staff members often lost sight of their task of patient care and were preoccupied with how they interacted with one another. Emphasis on principles of treatment receded into the background. Such groups of otherwise experienced professionals often became dependent on charismatic leaders, fragmented into factions, or developed a "loving" group spirit to the detriment of productive, clinical discussion. They forgot their goal and acted on dependency, fight-flight, and pairing basic assumptions. These wards were dysfunctional when it came to difficult decisions concerning disruptive patients. Violent behavior and suicide rates sometimes increased without any effective action being taken.

By the late 1970s, many administrators had noticed that focusing excessively on intrastaff issues had interfered with task performance and led to indulgence of basic assumptions at the expense of work. Administrators from differing theoretical persuasions set out to remedy the situation. They focused meetings on the task of patient care. They clarified roles and boundaries. They made reference to intrastaff issues only when they could directly relate it to a specific effect on patient care. This clear task orientation helped mobilize the creative energies of staff members, and hospital wards became more functional and also congenial places in which to work.

SPLITTING IN GROUPS

Bion's study of basic assumption groups is not the only object relations contribution to group functioning. The concept of splitting has been productively applied to ward staffs, as well as to individuals. Patients with split internal object relations have been found to stimulate fragmentation of staff groups who work with them (Burnham 1966, Adler 1985).

W.R. was a 25-year-old college graduate who had not been able to support herself, because repetitive self-induced vomiting and laxative abuse interfered with her ability to teach. She was fiercely independent, refusing to seek help or accept guidance; but she needed to live in her parents' home because she could not keep a job or have any steady relationships, and her physical health was deteriorating.

In an attempt to control her binging and vomiting from outside herself, she insisted her parents put locks on the kitchen cupboards. After an argument about this issue of locked cupboards, her parents consented, only to learn that she binged at the corner store and vomited in secret. The locks inconvenienced her parents and did not help the patient.

When W.R. was admitted to a private Boston hospital, staff members wanted to help her. She became a special patient. Some staff members were her confidants and expressed conviction that gentle nurturing and removal from family conflicts would cure her. Others felt she needed to be put on a strict regimen of nutrition and exercise. These staff members argued that she should be watched 24 hours a day and not let off the ward if found vomiting. If she did not gain weight, she should be fed by nasogastric tube. The first group insisted that she would eat better if permitted to go to the dining room by herself, allowing her autonomy she had never had.

Staff members accused one another of being excessively coddling or rigid. One nurse threatened to report patient abuse if the patient was not granted a pass to go to the corner store. Another nurse threatened to request a transfer if the patient was allowed to coerce and manipulate the treatment team. The psychiatrist was pulled in both directions and had trouble settling on an even course which would be agreeable to most staff members. Stymied, he asked for consultation.

The consultant listened to the clinicians at length. He interpreted that the patient had split internal object relations. She projected internal representations of all-good, nurturing figures onto some staff members. Other staff members she treated as all-bad, depriving figures. The staff group split reflected the patient's own split internal object relations. They needed to discuss the patient until they healed their own split. Perhaps then they could help their patient integrate her extreme feelings about nurturance and deprivation.

Ward staff members found this interpretation reassuring and set about developing an integrated treatment plan. Working together on this task, their strong feelings abated and productive work resumed.

The consultant had explained that the patient used projective identification to engender nurturing and depriving feelings in different staff members who may have had proclivities in one direction or another. She recreated her split internal object world around her. It can often be observed that patients with extreme split internal object relations engender strong disagreements in those around them. Adler (1985) explained that splitting and projective identification in the patient can lead to a situation where

> staff members who are the recipients of cruel, punishing parts of the patient will tend to react to the patient in a cruel, sadistic, and punishing manner. Staff members who have received loving, idealized projected parts of the patient will tend to respond to him with a protective, parental love. Obviously a clash can occur between these two groups of staff members. [p. 204]

In addition to the tendency of some patients to set staff members against one another, clinicians must be alert to covert staff dissension (Stanton and Schwartz 1954), which might lead to split treatment groups independent of the patient. Patients can be vehicles to express group problems. In W.R.'s case, the treatment impasse could be conceptualized as a fight–flight basic assumption, resulting from the psychiatrist's indecisiveness and failure to keep the treatment team task oriented. These kinds of complications must always be considered in treatment teams, because group conflicts can manifest themselves in individual patients and individual conflicts can manifest themselves in groups.

W.R. had split internal object relations and created turmoil around her before hospitalization. Additionally, the treatment team was usually well functioning and task oriented. We can assume that the patient's contribution to the splitting was greater than inherent staff differences in this instance.

PARALLEL PROCESSES IN SUPERVISION

Parallels similar to those between internal patient dynamics and treatment team functioning have been observed in the supervisory relationship. Supervisors who are rigid and critical with their subordinates will often find that a subordinate acts in a similar manner toward his patients (Doehrman 1976). This phenomenon may be a variation on what Anna Freud (1936) has described as identification with the aggressor. Reciprocally, subordinates often act toward their supervisors as their patients act toward them (Searles 1955, Sachs and Shapiro 1976).

Dr. J.N., a generally confident and resourceful psychiatry resident, repeatedly said, "I don't know what's going on. She doesn't have any early memories. There's nothing there. I don't know how I can help her resolve conflicts if after 2 years of therapy she still doesn't remember a thing. Nothing. Nothing at all." Session after session, he could not come up with an insight into the patient's amnesia for childhood experiences.

His supervisor felt a curious lack of resolve and indecisiveness. He tried to recall what his supervisors would have said in such a circumstance, but he too drew a blank. As he mused, he remembered his supervisor explaining parallel processes to him years earlier, and he decided to emulate her.

"Well," he said, "I am drawing a blank too. That may help me understand how hard it must be for you to work in the dark with this patient."

"So you think I am acting toward you the way my patient is acting toward me?"

"What better way to let me know what you are going through—and perhaps she is helping you feel how she must have felt with her mother. She drew a blank."

This comment helped Dr. J.N. establish empathic contact with his patient. The therapy began to move once again. He could now say to his patient, "You sometimes act and say you feel emotionally absent in here with me. That way you let me know how it feels to be with someone who is emotionally absent. That way, I can experience firsthand how abandoned and at a loss you sometimes feel. Perhaps the nothingness you describe is actually a memory of your mother's not being there for you emotionally when you needed her."

This interpretation of parallel processes is based on the idea that the patient internalized a maternal absence, an emptiness. Through projective identification she elicited that feeling from her therapist. He elicited a similar feeling from his supervisor. This inferential process is complex and a bit subtle, so the therapist had to be tentative in his conjecture. The patient could correct him if he was off the mark. If he was accurate, the patient would feel deeply understood.

Although parallels are easily observable, it can be difficult to determine the mechanism and direction of causation in any specific case. Using an awareness of this partially understood phenomenon need not await complete theoretical elaboration. Not only therapists can use the concept—administrators can, too. They can encourage therapists to be understanding, empathic, and appropriately structuring with patients if they treat the therapists in a manner that creates a nurturing and structuring environment.

FAMILIES AND BORDERLINE PERSONALITY DISORDER

Clinicians have described family splits as similar to borderline patients' internal splits. Shapiro and colleagues (1977) have found that "families demonstrate a tendency toward splitting which parallels that of their borderline adolescent. Within the family group, attributes of 'goodness' (providing, gratifying, loving) and 'badness' (depriving, punishing, hating) are separated one from the other and reinvested in different family members so that each family member appears relatively preambivalent and single-minded . . ." (p. 79). They further suggested that the family system used splitting and projective identification in such a way as to "contribute" to the child's poor self-integration. Masterson and Rinsley (1975) reached a related conclusion when they learned that mothers of patients with borderline disorders are often poorly integrated themselves and behave toward their children in extreme ways, which parallel such patients' feelings and behavior patterns.

Gunderson et al. (1980) reported a second, perhaps larger group of families, in which the parents clung so tightly to one another as to exclude the child from "attention, support, and protection." In these families, the borderline patient's feelings of internal emptiness and aloneness (Adler 1985) would reflect an actual absence of meaningful parental involvement. The possibility remains that factors within the child, such as an inability to attach to parents or to take in nurturing relationships, resulted in the disturbed family relationships. Causation is difficult to determine, although parallels between the patient's external relationships and his internal object world are observable. These parallels can be explained in terms of projective identification.

FAMILIES AND SCHIZOPHRENIA

There are parallels between the fragmentation and distorted thinking of patients with schizophrenia and the disorganization of their families. Bateson et al. (1956) noted that family members made mutually contradictory demands upon patients. These "double binds" are similar to the mutually contradictory behaviors and statements which patients themselves produce. Bowen (1960) commented on the discontinuity between the emotional and conventional aspects of the relationships of parents of schizophrenics. Lidz (1964) observed "marital skews" in such families. Many experts have thought that the family system causes the schizophrenia. As Wynne and Singer (1963) formulated the case, "The fragmentation of experience, the identity diffusion, the disturbed modes of perception and communication, and certain other characteristics of the acute reactive schizophrenic's personality structure are to a significant extent derived, by processes of internalization, from characteristics of the family organization . . ." (p. 192).

Despite these parallels in patient and family system, more and more investigators now believe that most cases of schizophrenia derive from a biological brain disease, along lines described by Torrey (1983) in his book for families of schizophrenics. They argue that families are distressed by the chaotic communications and behavior of the schizophrenic person and tend to make odd statements in an attempt to make sense out of the incomprehensible.

I endorse the practical approach of suspending a search for an interpersonal causation of the problem. Atheoretical studies have been conducted by researchers in England and the United States (Brown et al. 1962, Vaughn and Leff 1976, Goldstein et al. 1978, Falloon et al. 1982) demonstrating that patients who suffer from schizophrenia, of whatever origin, need more hospitalizations and do much more poorly in general if they have excessive contact with families who have high "expressed emotion," or E.E. This finding does not necessarily imply that high-E.E. families cause illness—many normal families may have high E.E. It does imply that such patients cannot tolerate emotional intensity.

Training to help families decrease expressed emotion has been demonstrated by the same researchers to help the schizophrenic patient remain stable. Lowering expressed emotion in the family may serve a containing or integrative ego function which the patient introjects, thereby helping him modulate his own emotions. Perhaps it is the result of decreasing environmental stimulation and thereby providing less about which to become upset. Regardless of the mechanism, training in lowering expressed emotion is another example of a constructive use of parallel processes between system and individual: decrease expressed emotion in the system, and thereby help the individual modulate his own emotional life.

Extrapolating from the family to the community, researchers are investigating similar parallels between the schizophrenic individual's symptoms and characteristics of their social network (Cutler and Tatum 1983, Hamilton et al. 1987).

In this chapter, some ways in which object relations theory can be applied to systems other than the individual patient have been explored. The ideas of internal and external boundaries, splitting, and projective identification have relevance to groups. Feelings of attachment, aggression, and love correspond to the group phenomena of dependency, fight-flight, and pairing.

There are parallels between internal, individual psychodynamics and how groups function around a patient. Splitting within a patient can lead to development of divisions in treatment teams. Conflict within groups can elicit conflicts within individuals. These parallels may be thought of as being mediated by projective identification.

PART V
BROADER CONTEXTS

We have never prided ourselves on the completeness and finality of our knowledge and capacity. We are just as ready now as we were earlier to admit the imperfections of our understanding, to learn new things, and to alter our methods in any way that can improve them.

—Sigmund Freud, "Lines of Advance in Psycho-Analytic Therapy"

INTRODUCTION

Object relations theory has supplied the major advances in psycho-analytic theory over the past 30 years. The American study of this subject has retained its grounding in ego psychology. Psychoanalysis has remained open to influence, sometimes with struggle, sometimes readily. These factors have helped to make object relations theory an influential psychology.

The first two chapters of this section will describe some broader applications of object relations concepts. Folklore and mythology will be presented in terms of developing object relations in Chapter 17. Chapter 18 will treat ideas concerning the sense of reality.

When psychoanalysis is used to explore related fields, it yields a rich return. Ideas and images from literature, folklore, mythology, religion, and philosophy enhance psychologic concepts. Object relations theory can gain more than it can give to these related subjects of study.

The final chapter will describe how object relations theory developed within psychoanalysis.

CHAPTER 17

FOLKLORE, MYTHS, AND TRANSFORMATIONS OF THE SELF

In the beginning God created the heaven and the earth. And the earth was without form, and void.

Genesis 1:1–2

In this way, the Bible begins describing an undifferentiated and unintegrated mass—the stuff out of which humankind was molded.

The Greeks, and later the Romans, according to Bulfinch's (1855) account, portrayed it this way:

Before earth and sea and heaven were created, all things wore one aspect, to which we give the name Chaos—a confused and shapeless mass, nothing but dead weight, in which, however, slumbered the seeds of things. Earth, sea, and air were all mixed up together; so the earth was not solid, the sea was not fluid, and the air was not transparent. [p. 12]

In ancient India, the Vedic myths also described a dark and watery chaos before there was being and not-being (Masson-Oursel and Morin 1959). Much later, the Japanese, with their composite mythology, described the young world as similar to floating oil or a jellyfish

271

before Izanagi and his sister, Izanami, consolidated and fertilized the moving earth to create the island of Onokora (Bruhl 1959).

These stories about the world's birth have striking similarities to that of our discipline, particularly Mahler's description of the human infant's psychological birth. Object relations theory indicates that we all begin in an undifferentiated state, without form, and void. Slowly, we take shape, separating and individuating. Splitting, dividing things up into good and bad, light and dark, is one of the first steps in this process.

What accounts for these similarities? Are the mythical descriptions evidence of an unconscious memory of preverbal experience? Are our psychological theories determined by an early exposure to traditional tales? Are myths and scientific theories both reflections of archetypal thinking patterns? Are the apparent similarities merely an artifact of metaphoric language – a false analogy?

Although it is not entirely explanatory, my understanding is that early storytellers were concerned with the same problems of human life as are modern scientists, clinicians, and artists. They noted that all life begins with undifferentiated germ plasm, a seed or egg, which grows more complex and organizes itself into a functional, living organism. They constructed their cosmogony accordingly.

Schafer (1978) pointed out that there is a difference between psychoanalytic meaning and causation. Speculating on what conscious and unconscious factors impel an author to create a story, or a group of people to retell a story, is a slightly different question from what meaning the tale may have for a listener or a group of listeners, or even for the storyteller himself. Function is yet another issue.

In this chapter, I briefly review the history of psychoanalytic interest in mythology and folklore, and look at some themes to see what meaning they may have in terms of developing object relations. I suspect that the function of these stories is related to their meaning in that they bind societies together and help individuals with their aloneness by depicting universal problems and potential solutions in terms that are meaningful to all members of a society. They touch on issues at the core of our existence. It is the meaning alone, not the function of that meaning or the cause of that meaning, which I emphasize.

HISTORY

Psychoanalysts have had a long-standing interest in folklore and mythology. Freud (1913b), and earlier, Freud and Oppenheim (1911),

Jung (1912, 1945), and Rank (1914) were among the early analysts who compared individual fantasies with mythology and folk themes, searching out their meaning. Freud derived his name for the Oedipus complex by comparing dream themes with a Greek myth.

More recently, in *The Uses of Enchantment*, Bettelheim (1977) described the importance and meaningfulness of reading fairy tales to our children. This child analyst, influenced by existentialist thinking, suggested that all fairy tales begin with a developmental problem and indicate possible solutions to that problem. The hero or heroine of the story moves toward acquiring a more integrated self and must come to terms with what is often a life-and-death dilemma. Fairy tales provide an avenue for understanding, communicating, and coping with developmental tasks.

Beyond Bettelheim's suggestions, the direct use of myth and folk stories in treatment has a long and controversial history. Referring to Slochower's (1970) concept of mythopoesis, Pruyser and Luke (1982) discussed the Gilgamesh epic as a "liturgical drama," which assists man in dealing with the narcissistic trauma of an increasing awareness of the inevitability of death. Simon (1978), in his study *Mind and Madness in Ancient Greece*, pointed out how poets were once the primary agents of healing. Levi-Strauss (1963) demonstrated the remarkable similarity between shamanistic practices and psychoanalysis. Jung (1945) explained how knowledge of universal themes in folklore, mythology, and religion assisted therapists in their work. Heuscher (1974, 1980), an existentialist-Jungian psychiatrist, described the direct use of folklore in psychotherapy. Ekstein (1983), along more traditional lines, described how interpreting the metaphor, which often has a mythical quality, can help in the treatment of severely disturbed children. I discussed the application of empirical folklore techniques to the understanding and treatment of an adolescent child with residual practicing-subphase dilemmas (Hamilton 1980).

Psychoanalytic thinkers have focused on both the meaning and the function of traditional stories and have created new functions. Perhaps it is better said that they revived old applications for these tales in the arena of therapy. They have dealt less thoroughly and satisfactorily with causation. Let us look at a few stories and themes to see what they may mean in terms of developing object relations.

DIFFERENTIATION

Returning to Genesis, it begins with an earth which is "without form, and void." The account goes on, "And darkness was upon the face of the deep. And the Spirit of God moved upon the face of the waters."

Apparently, God was not satisfied with this shapeless, dark, watery mass. So He began the process of dividing one thing from another and assigning each a place within the scheme of things.

> And God said, "Let there be light"; and there was light.
> And God saw the light, that it was good;
> And God divided the light from the darkness.
>
> Genesis 1:3–4

God also divided the waters above the firmament from the waters below, and the land from the sea, and the day from the night—each with its own great light; He created the creatures, which multiplied, each after its own kind.

This Judeo-Christian account of our very beginnings has to do with differentiation out of an amorphous matrix. First comes the division of light and dark, wet and dry. Integration, too, is indicated by consolidation of the waters and by each creature reproducing after its own kind.

In the Greco-Roman account, a nearly identical evolution takes place. Bulfinch's opening lines are taken from Ovid's account, which was written during the first century, in exile in Tomi on the Black Sea. Ovid's work, reflecting Rome's wholesale incorporation of earlier Greek mythology, recounts the metamorphoses or transformations which are the stuff of life. Ovid's tales begin:

> Forever at war: within a single body
> Heat fought with cold, wet fought with dry, the hard
> Fought with the soft, things having weight contended
> With weightless things.
>   Till God, or kindlier Nature,
> Settled all argument, and separated
> Heaven from earth, water from land, our air
> From the high stratosphere, a liberation
> So things evolved, and out of blind confusion
> Found each its place . . .
>
> [In *Metamorphoses*, translated by R. Humphries, 1955]

This account of early differentiation includes a motivation beyond God's creative urge suggested in Genesis. The amorphous mass inherently contains the seeds of destruction—warring opposites. This mythical account of origins parallels Klein's (Segal 1964) conception of the death instinct. In her view, infants, like all living matter, have an inborn tendency toward self-dissolution. This inherent self-destructiveness must be split off and projected outward to preserve the child's life. According to this conceptualization, the earliest psychological differentiation arises from a need to manage aggression from within, just as Greco-Roman mythology suggests the earth must be divided up to separate internally warring factions.

Along with most American object relations theorists, Kernberg (1969) does not find the concept of a death instinct useful. He suggests that early splitting occurs because the symbiotic child cannot yet integrate pleasant and unpleasant affects. Only later, during differentiation from the mother, does the child actively and defensively split the good and bad self- and object-images to protect what is wanted from being overwhelmed by what is not wanted. Before differentiation, splitting is a passive inability to integrate experience.

The Judeo-Christian and Greco-Roman cosmogonies provide interesting parallels to object relations theory in that they begin with an undifferentiated mass which must be divided into polar opposites. The Judeo-Christian account indicates that a creative urge led to differentiation, and the Greco-Roman account suggests that the need to manage aggression led to this division. Major theoretical debates continue today concerning the impulse to grow versus the need to manage conflicting instinctual urges as determinants of differentiation. These differences are reflected in the Kernberg–Kohut debate (see Chapter 19), as well as in many other controversies regarding the place of drive theory in object relations theory (Greenberg and Mitchell 1983).

Numerous other parallels to earliest development exist in Western, as well as other, traditions. The sexual implications of the story of Adam and Eve have been well described. It can also be discussed in terms of more infantile issues. It was greed, eating from the tree of knowledge of good and evil, which resulted in expulsion. In an attempt to get even more than paradise had to offer and more than God chose to give, Adam and Eve acquired knowledge of their separateness, their anatomical distinctness, and lost their paradisaical symbiotic existence. In object relations terms, the child's hunger and wish to have what the mother has, to devour the mother's good nurturing quality and have it for itself, can result in a feeling of object loss and vulnerability. If the child greedily wishes to devour the essence of the breast, and not just receive milk which is given, it can suddenly find itself alone. If it steals from the container and loses its goodwill, who will take care of it? Similarly, Adam and Eve wished to have God's innermost secrets, his knowledge of good and evil, his capacity to give and withhold. This excess on their part led to their awareness of their aloneness.

I will speculate on another analogy concerning the Garden of Eden story. Originally, a child is in a symbiotic unity. As if it is in the presence of God, all its needs are met; it is not even aware of its separateness. As ego functions develop, the child can soon differentiate between frustration and pleasure, good and bad, and self and other. This knowledge leads to loss of symbiotic unity. Wishing to retain a sense of omnipotence, the child may feel that he has stolen the knowledge of good and bad and of separateness from the provider of all things, the parent, when in fact he had it developmentally bestowed upon him. Perhaps this biblical story of earliest beginnings is still meaningful because it represents a gain in knowledge of good and bad which accompanies the loss of symbiosis—a loss we have all suffered.

PRACTICING

After the child learns to differentiate himself from his mother, and as he develops upward locomotion, he becomes taken with practicing his own power and independence. He now compensates for whatever insecurity he may feel in the face of his smallness and separateness with grandiose elation. He flees mother's embrace, only to seek her and flee again. He throws open the cupboards and ransacks the pots and pans. If still breast-fed, he yanks at the nipple. He coos and laughs and upends his plate of carrots. This prankster lives in a world of magic, surrounded by his own narcissistic sparkle and sense of omnipotence. Yet he is vulnerable, seeking and needing attention, admiration, and confirmation.

These psychological issues of practicing-subphase youngsters may be likened to trickster themes in folklore (Hamilton 1980). One of the most elaborate trickster cycles is the Polynesian version (Luomala 1949).

Maui-tikitiki-a-Taranga was a "happy-go-lucky young culture hero, transformer and trickster" (p. 28). He was described as a "precocious nuisance" (p. 3), "a wonder-worker, a miracle man, a sorcerer, who altered the original form of the world and vanquished the gods" (p. 11). Maui-of-a-thousand-tricks was the "eight-headed super-super-man of the south seas" (p. 12). Yet his origins were humble.

Maui was an abortion, a miscarriage of his mother, Taranga. She swaddled him in hair cut from her topknot ("tiki-tiki" in Polynesian) and laid him in the arms of the ocean waves. Wrapped in seaweed, he was nourished by the foaming bubbles of the surf until he was washed up on the sands, surrounded and protected by jellyfish. Flies alighted on him to lay their eggs so that maggots might eat him. Seabirds flocked to peck him to pieces. In this plight an ancestor god, Tama-nui-ki-te-Rangi found the boy. Maui was thus raised in the home of the gods.

Normally, the spirit of a blood clot or miscarriage is shunned by Polynesians. It is said to brood over its lack of affection and indulge in mischief to annoy villagers and their gods. Maui was partially saved from the "warped independence of a castaway" (p. 32) by the prayers of his parents and the ministrations of the deities. Still, he belonged nowhere. His divine foster parents taught him contempt for men. Yet, he rebelled against the gods and was "inevitably and irresistibly drawn back to the fireside of his human relatives" (p. 32). Even when he found his mother and was brought into her bed and received her lavish affection, he was still not satisfied. This prodigal left once again, always restless, always seeking.

When his brothers would not take him to fish with them, he turned into a bird and flew out to their boat at sea. Another time, he turned himself into an insect and hid in the planks at the bottom of the outrigger in order to accompany them. These tricks, like many of his pranks, were for the purpose of seeking objects, searching for reunion with his family. This regressive tendency, turned creative, led to his providing humankind with fire, new inventions, new islands, and even a social order.

Object seeking had its dangers for young Maui. He was threatened by cannibalistic monsters, whom he killed outright or beguiled to their death. Repeatedly, he dived into huge, man-eating clams only to slaughter them and return with pearls for his mother. In one story, he approached an ancestress, Muri-ranga-whenua, whom all the people appeased with gifts of food. He hid these offerings and lured her out of her dark cave. Her stomach distended itself, ready to incorporate him. By chance, the western breeze wafted his scent toward her. Recognizing her descendant, she gave him her magic jawbone, instead of eating him. Once again, Maui escaped, more powerful than ever with his new instrument of enchantment.

In another story, he was not so lucky. He attempted to murder his cannibalistic ancestress, Hine-nui-te-po. This dark mother had eyes of jasper and a barracoutalike mouth. Maui entered her sleeping body, through what portal we are not told. If he succeeded in leaving through her mouth before she woke, she would die. She woke early and squeezed Maui to death.

These stories of seeking and avoiding the lost mother are reminiscent of Mahler's (Mahler et al. 1975) description of the practicing toddler. To and fro he goes denying his helpless dependency, his smallness, his aloneness. Omnipotent and magical in his wishes, he is forever exploring. He regressively seeks a return to merger or fusion with his mother, as represented by Maui's entering her bed, her body, the man-eating clams, or the cave of his ancestress, only to escape again, triumphant.

These stories show how grandiose and omnipotent fantasies betray a simultaneous feeling of inadequacy and aloneness, as does Mahler's account of development. Maui was a castaway, exquisitely vulnerable; but the gods gave him protection. Just so, the toddler newly aware of his aloneness and helplessness seems both vulnerable and elevated. His omnipotent fantasies are his gods, which protect him. At times, he projects these images onto his parents, who must seem godlike—giving bounty and grace. Alternately, the parents must sometimes seem like giants or monsters, consumed with rage, perhaps devouring. Because he is oral and incorporative in both his pleasure and his anger, he experiences his parents as devouring when they are only scolding.

There are similarities between the problems of adult patients with various difficulties and those of children at different developmental stages. The patients who have these developmental problems also have similarities to the corresponding folk themes. Children who are not provided enough parental support often indulge in grandiose fantasies of gods and evils and deceptions. Many of them retain elements of this practicing-subphase mentality. The resemblance to Maui is clear: they feel like outcasts. Attempting to overcome their vulnerability, they constantly seek confirming objects. Grandiosity and impetuous activity thinly veil their pseudoindependence.

Fortunately for some of them, the creative and constructive aspects of their fantasies can protect and nurture them, as the gods did Maui, so that they can survive without succumbing to an overwhelming depression. The price they pay is a certain alienation from other people, the appearance of involvement without a true feeling of belonging. They trust everyone and no one. Like the trickster, they are the searchers, the wanderers, the explorers. Only under certain circumstances can they develop a relationship in which they feel understood by, and in turn, can understand another person, deeply and over time. Only then can they give up their practicing-substage grandiosity, which compensates for their envy of those who belong.

RAPPROCHEMENT

The precarious elation of practicing lasts only a few months. Soon, an increased cognitive ability to see himself in relation to the larger world tames the child's pseudoindependence. He returns to mother, ready to come to terms with her various aspects in a new way. He must also come to terms with his many conflicting feelings and strivings.

"Little Red Riding Hood" illustrates many rapprochement themes. The Grimms' (1812) version, called "Little Red-Cap," begins by describing a small girl who was loved by everyone. Her grandmother, who loved her most of all, would have given her darling anything she wished. Thus the story begins with an all-good self—Red Riding Hood—whom everyone loves, and an all-good object, the bountiful grandmother, who is totally gratifying. Self–object identity is suggested by the little girl insisting upon always wearing the red cap her grandmother had given her.

Red Riding Hood had to become aware of her good object's shortcomings, as does the rapprochement child. Both maternal figures, her mother and her grandmother, had their less satisfying aspects. Her grandmother became ill and weak; and her mother wished the child to deliver a basket of food and a bottle of wine to the old woman. Her mother instructed her, "Set out before it gets hot, and when you are going, walk nicely and quietly and do not run off the path, or you may fall and break the bottle, and then your grandmother will get nothing." Here, the concern was for the grandmother's nurturance, not the little girl's welfare. Whether or not Red Riding Hood would fall and hurt herself was not mentioned—the concern was for the bottle. Clearly, it was a long trip; otherwise, the girl would not have had to begin early in the morning. Furthermore, the mother was concerned about her own problems and was asking her daughter to do something which she was not quite capable of doing. Both maternal figures were depriving. As rapprochement-subphase children must learn, Red Riding Hood was about to learn that mothers are not only gratifying, but also demanding of gratification, and they provide prohibitions which require self-restraint.

The good little girl set out with her goodwill, her mother's good advice, and her basket of good food. Away from her mother, she fell in with the greedy wolf, who eventually devoured her. At first, he seemed benign enough. He pointed out the pretty flowers, and Red Riding Hood forgot her mother's advice not to stray off the path. She picked flower after flower, deeper and deeper into the woods. She ostensibly intended to give them to her beloved grandmother, yet she neglected her duty. Her inability to forgo immediate pleasures for the sake of her maternal figure—aided by her self-deception that she was doing it for her grandmother's benefit—gave the wolf ample time to speed to the unsuspecting old woman's house. In short order, the bad wolf devoured the good grandmother with Red Riding Hood's complicity.

How did this good little girl get off the track, leading to the destruction of her beloved parent-figure? Actually, her neglect of her caretakers was stimulated by their neglect of her. Her grandmother became ill and needed care and nurturance before Red Riding Hood was old enough to provide it. Her mother sent the little girl out with advice only, when she still needed an adult to accompany her. Abandoned, she turned to whatever gratifying object might be available. The wolf at first seemed pleasant enough, but instead of taking care of and gratifying her, he intended to eat her for his own satisfaction. Thus, the wolf represents exaggerated characteristics of the mother and the grandmother, who at first seem all-giving, but who then allow their own needs to take precedence. The fact that the wolf and the grandmother are two aspects of the same object is supported by Red Riding Hood finding the rapacious animal in grandmother's home, in her bed, wearing her clothes. In object relations terms, abandoned by the mother-grandmother, Red Riding Hood did not yet have a sufficient ability to remember the good object in its absence. Her longings and rage at abandonment led to the good internal object-image being swallowed up by the bad object-image.

The wolf represents not only the bad object but also Red Riding Hood's aggressive and greedy self, as Fairbairn (1940) commented. Red Riding Hood empowered the wolf to devour her grandmother by giving him explicit directions to her home. She also took his suggestion to pick flowers. At first she was full of goodwill toward her grandmother. Her selfishness soon revealed itself. She forgot all about the person to whom she intended to give the flowers. The wolf was eating her mother-figure while she was also getting her fill, running about picking flowers (Bettelheim 1977). In the Grimms' (1812) tale, only "when she had gathered so many she could carry no more, did she remember her grandmother" (p. 141–142). The story directly indicates the identity between an aspect of the little girl and the wolf. When the grandmother asked who was at the door, the wolf identified himself as "Little Red-Cap." Thus, the wolf can be conceptualized as a combined bad self- and object-representation, filled with aggressive hunger.

When Red Riding Hood entered grandmother's house, she felt strange. Something was wrong. She longed for her good mother-figure, but everything about her was too much—the ears that listened to her were too big; the eyes that looked at her were too big; the mouth that kissed her and spoke with her had teeth which were too big. All the sources of attention and comfort, the organs by which her grandmother recognized her and held her in her attention and communicated with her, were exaggerated by devouring need or greed. Finally, the "terrible big mouth" swallowed her in one gulp.

Now, the identity of little girl and mother-figure was complete. Grandmother and Red Riding Hood were in one skin, consumed by their primitive and aggressive oral wishes. They represented the bad object relations unit.

Fortunately, an outsider passed by to extricate the dyad from their enmeshment. The hunter, a good father figure, at first intended to shoot the bad wolf. Luckily, he sensed some good inside and put down his gun. Carefully snipping the wolf's belly, as in a cesarean section (Bettelheim 1977), he delivered Red Riding Hood and her once-again good grandmother from their peril. As was mentioned in Chapter 5, fathers or father figures often serve to facilitate the disentanglement of regressive symbiotic bonds between mother and child during rapprochement.

Red Riding Hood learned that while the good self and object may temporarily disappear, they will reappear. The arrival of the hunter symbolizes not only an external father figure, but it also represents the arrival or return of the little girl's own integrative ego functioning. She could now recognize that good exists within the appearance of temporary badness. Despite the devouring and selfish aspects of herself and her mother, the capacity for good intentions and love and nurturance still existed. They were the same as they had been previously, before the frustrating experience which led to such rapacious longings, as represented by the wolf's devouring them. Splitting of early rapprochement gave way to object constancy. From this experience of temporary loss of the good object and good self, Red Riding Hood learned to carry her mother's wise counsel more firmly within her and to remember it always.

The ending line reads, "Red-Cap thought to herself: 'As long as I live, I will never by myself leave the path, to run into the wood, when my mother has forbidden me to do so.' " So Little Red Riding Hood had learned that even mother's frustrating prohibitions could be protective and caring in their own right, and she could now carry them with her as a part of her self. She had been swallowed up by her longings and reborn to a higher level of self-and-other integration. This is the task of the rapprochement subphase of development.

OEDIPAL DEVELOPMENT

This rich and complex story can be understood to have many different meanings. Like a palimpsest, the next layer reveals an oedipal interpretation, emphasizing the efforts of a developing girl to come to terms with her budding sexuality. While acknowledging other issues, Bettelheim (1977) focused primarily on the sexual themes in the story. I draw heavily from his discussion in the following account.

Bettelheim and other psychoanalytic authors before him pointed out that the wolf seduced Little Red Riding Hood into leaving the path to grandmother's house in order to pick flowers—a symbol of love and reproduction both by tradition and by the fact that flowers are the reproductive organs of plants. Consistent with the oedipal theme of wishing to dispose of the mother-figure, as well as to conceive a baby with father, Red Riding Hood gave the wolf explicit directions to grandmother's, thereby making her demise possible. The grandmother is a thinly disguised mother figure. Such displacements and substitutions are common in stories. The wolf represents Red Riding Hood's destructive, rivalrous oedipal longings and her sexual appetite, as well as masculine sexuality. Condensations of this sort appear in stories, as they do in dreams (Freud 1900). Too immature as yet to deal with such powerful internal feelings or with the real external world of men, she was overwhelmed and devoured by the wolf. Fortunately, a good and restrained father figure, the hunter, saved both her and her (grand)mother. He restored order and harmony. Little Red Riding Hood learned to follow her mother's directions and refrain from venturing into the forest of mature relationships until she was ready and had parental permission and guidance.

These sexual and aggressive themes of the oedipal period first clearly manifest themselves when the child is 3 or 4 years old, as the rapprochement crisis resolves itself. Classical psychoanalysis once focused almost entirely on such strivings. The little girl shifts her primary affection from her mother to her father. She wishes to have her father's exclusive attention and love. Like mother, she wishes father to impregnate her so that she can give him a baby; but her mother stands in her way, and she imagines eliminating her. Fearful that her mother will retaliate for such secret wishes, the little girl settles on achieving gratification by being a good little girl and identifying with her mother. Someday, she tells herself, when she grows up, she can have her own husband and her own baby, just as mother does. The oedipal conflict thus resolves itself, to rearise at puberty and again during the late adolescent departure from the parental home. Bettelheim is correct: there are striking similarities between the story of "Little Red Riding Hood" and the unfolding of the oedipal conflict in children.

It is not surprising that this complex story should have both oedipal and rapprochement themes. Whenever maturing sexuality manifests itself, more fundamental issues of separation and abandonment must be reworked. The most obvious problem is that, if the daughter is going to have sexual relations, the incest taboo requires that she leave home to find a mate. Old feelings of abandonment arise. Can she really leave her beloved mother? Can she survive without the good, external object? Is her own sense of goodness secure enough within her that she can take it with her? Can she accept the fact that her mother is more attached to her husband than to her daughter—that the mother will stay with him when her daughter leaves? Can she accept that in order to be truly like mother in her most creative aspects she must leave her? Will her mother allow her departure? Will her mother turn vengefully on her if the daughter abandons her for a life of her own? Will she have her mother's blessing to carry with her into the larger world? Can she come back home again from time to time if need be? These are but some of the separation issues occasioned by oedipal conflicts. They cannot be well answered unless the girl has established an adequate object constancy at the end of rapprochement. It seems appropriate, then, that the story of "Little Red Riding Hood" should have both oedipal and rapprochement themes, one superimposed upon the other. Like the fantasies and developmental issues of individuals, this fairy tale has layer upon layer of rich meaning, each pertinent to some aspect of self and object relationships.

In this chapter, I have examined several stories in terms of developing object relations. The function of traditional tales is related to their meaning. People may tell and retell, read and reread these stories because they are meaningful, that is, because they externally represent powerful, internal self- and object-constellations. Such stories bind social groups together and help individuals overcome feelings of isolation by serving as reminders that our deepest concerns are shared by our fellow humans. Functions, however, like meanings, may be multiple. Within limits, they may change with our viewpoint.

Although folklore and mythology have been widely examined in terms of Freud's ideas about psychosexual development and Jung's ideas about archetypes, their study in terms of object relations theory has just begun.

CHAPTER 18

REALITY IS RELATEDNESS

In this chapter I examine some ideas about reality in object relations terms. This theory does not answer the age-old questions about what is true or what is real. It does, however, have implications about how and when people develop a sense of what is real and how they lose and regain this sense.

Object relations theory suggests that our conventional sense of day-to-day events depends first upon a dyadic relationship—self and object. A third element is added for contrast and confirmation—something that is outside the dyad.

PSYCHOSIS AND UNREALITY

It always seems rather presumptuous when mental health profession-als define psychosis in terms of "losing touch with reality," as if psychiatrists or psychologists or anyone else had an inside track on the nature of existence. Philosophers, artists, poets, mystics, theolo-gians, physicists, chemists, and a host of scholars have grappled with this question of what is and what is not. To trace the different ways the word *reality* is used in psychoanalysis alone would be excessive for this work.[1] Yet, we are all too ready to pass judgment upon our patients' beliefs, until one of them humbles us, declaring, "You are nothing but a hallucination yourself. It is the other voices which are real."

People suffering from psychoses have probably taught us more about the sense of reality than any other group, including children, primitives, poets, and mystics—from whom we have also learned.

F.Y., the 32-year-old woman who confused her purse with her self, lost and recovered her sense of reality quickly. A closer look at the relationship aspects of the session described in Chapter 4 will reveal a connection between her external relationships and her sense of reality.

F.Y. had come to the therapist for immediate help. She felt desperate. Her mother had died recently, and she feared she was on the verge of losing her marriage and her job. She had had a psychotic episode 10 years earlier and feared she was "losing it" again. She wanted help.

Her psychiatrist had a different agenda. His case load was rather full. He was preparing for a 2-week vacation and needed to teach a class on psychiatric diagnosis before he left. He had accepted the referral as a favor to a friend and because he would have room for another case after he returned from vacation.

F.Y. began to communicate to him how desperate she felt. The psychiatrist listened but did not convey his interest in an overt fashion. His preparation for the class he would teach influenced him to keep the session unstructured longer than might have otherwise been his custom. He wanted to see how she would do.

The patient talked faster and faster. She seemed to be grasping for something. The psychiatrist did not respond to her need. "A woman's purse is a part of her," she said, clutching her handbag. "I mean it really is her. I don't know if you understand. It's not like a man's wallet. Men carry wallets and they may care about the wallet, but a woman's purse is actually her. My purse is messing me up. I try to get it straightened up. I spend all day dumping things; but the more I work on it, the more mixed up things get."

The patient had lost her sense of reality at this point. Her self–other boundaries were confused. Her internal self-image and her thought

[1]One of the best-known and most useful psychoanalytic discussions of reality concepts is found in Frosch (1970).

about an external object, her purse, had become intermingled. There is always a shifting of self–other boundaries when the sense of reality is lost.

The psychiatrist intervened at this point. He reminded her that the purse was a symbol for her self, but was not actually a part of her. He also commented on her most recent losses. He said, "It sounds like you need someone to talk with so you can sort things out." The patient felt less alone and calmed.

What the psychiatrist said may have helped F.Y., but the fact of his communicating with her in an understanding fashion was equally important. She had been desperately searching for someone or something. Her mother, husband, and work were not there for her, and neither was the psychiatrist at first. "I don't know if you understand," she had said. She focused on the closest thing to her, her purse, and began to fuse with it. She was no longer alone. She and the purse were one thing; but as she sank into this symbiotic closeness, she lost her sense of self as a distinct entity and became frightened. She lost her sense of reality.

She regained her everyday sense of reality when the psychiatrist intervened. There was now F.Y., the psychiatrist, and a third thing, the purse as a symbol, which they were discussing from related but separate viewpoints. They began to discuss her other important objects, her mother, husband, and employer.

The therapist said, "It sounds like you need someone to talk with so you can sort things out." This statement reflects the therapist's intuitive awareness that she needed someone to relate to who was not so close that she would be tempted to return to symbiotic fusion, thereby losing her sense of reality, and not so distant that she would need to desperately seek other objects with which to fuse. There were three distinct entities—the patient's self ("you"), the therapist ("someone to talk with"), and a third element ("things" to be sorted out). Patients uniformly describe a shift back into an appreciation of everyday reality as being accompanied by their psychological ability to experience themselves as separate and yet related to another person. "There are you and I and other things which are neither you nor I."

The next session the patient said, "I was getting all mixed up the last time I saw you. Everything seemed unreal and whirling around for a few minutes. It's kind of embarrassing, but I'm all right now."

"How has it been since you were last here?"

"Fine. I get to feeling a bit strange right when I fall asleep, but I think, 'We will be able to sort things out at the next session.' That thought helps. On the nights when my husband and I get along, I put my hand up against his shoulder and that helps too."

The patient had confirmed that her sense of reality was dependent upon her relatedness to other people.

Searles (1967b) described a different patient this way:

Non-differentiation . . . appears in this complaint of one man to his therapist, "I don't know, when I talk to you, whether I'm having a hallucination, or a fantasy about a memory, or a memory about a fantasy." He was unable to distinguish at all clearly and reliably between inner and outer worlds. A symbiotic mode of relatedness may hold sway over such a patient to the degree that he cannot maintain himself at a sufficient distance from persons and things around him to be able to perceive them at all objectively; one cannot truly perceive that in which one is immersed. [p. 123]

Searles here considered self–object merger to result in a loss of sense of reality. As in F.Y.'s case, the issue was one of experiencing the self as separate in relationship to other people and things.

A man described a similar experience when he came to the Menninger Hospital Emergency Unit.

L.T., a 27-year-old man, his golden-brown hair and beard intertwined in matted braids, complained, "I've been living in a dream."

"How long has this been going on," asked the resident psychiatrist, unbuttoning his tweed jacket.

"Four years. One day my dreams took over and started controlling me; and my thoughts became all mixed up with other people's. I was possessed."

This man lost his ability to see himself with distinct boundaries; his sense of everyday reality had dissolved.

The fact that one's sense of reality is dependent on relationships does not suggest that psychosis is entirely a social phenomenon. It does not mean that we can cure schizophrenia by curing a mad society. Many individuals with various psychoses have brain problems which interfere with their relatedness to others. They have abnormal perceptual-motor and cognitive processes (Hartocollis 1968, Holzman and Levy 1977, Johnstone et al. 1976, 1978, Bellak 1979, Hamilton and Allsbrook 1986) often associated with structural brain abnormalities (Johnstone et al. 1976, Weinberger et al. 1979). As reviewed by Fischman (1983), we can interfere experimentally with the sense of everyday reality by giving people various drugs. Psychosis can also be caused by an extreme alteration in the environment, as in the stimulus deprivation experiments mentioned on page 18. The relatedness needed for a secure sense of reality can be broken from either side, from the individual or from the surround.

PSYCHOSIS AND CONVICTION

Feelings of unreality—sometimes divided into estrangement and depersonalization (Federn 1952, Rinsley 1982)—are not the only abnormalities in the sense of reality.[2] Psychotic conviction can be equally dysfunctional.

Here is an example of this excess certainty in a private reality.

P.C. told his caseworker in Portland what he had experienced prior to his first hospitalization 2 years earlier. He had been working in an office, "trying to be a good servant." It seemed futile, and he despaired. He "submitted" himself to God and told him of his desperation and how lost he felt. "Dear Lord," he said, "I want to be your servant." Suddenly a great cloud of light surrounded him. He felt certain God had heard his prayer. He left the office and rushed out into the street to announce the good news, but he could not find the words. He felt the Holy Ghost speaking through his mouth. He shouted out that God sees all things and knows all things and knows everything everyone is searching for. That night he felt more convinced of his experience when he heard God speak his name. He concluded that he had been given a prophecy, that he had been chosen by the Lord to

[2]Estrangement is the sense that the world is unreal. Depersonalization is the sense that one's self is unreal. Usually, but not always, people who have trouble with one have trouble with the other. Perhaps there is a relationship between estrangement and depersonalization, because to have trouble with one without having trouble with the other requires better self–object differentiation than such patients usually have.

be Commander of the Holy Forces. There would be great bloodshed. All men would yield before him.

P.C. at first felt frightened and alone. Suddenly, he not only thought he might be close to his Lord—he perceived him as a cloud of light surrounding him. His description seemed to have some relation to Christianity until he felt a personal duty from his God to subjugate all men through holy war. His religious experience was idiosyncratic.

How do we understand this psychotic conviction in object relations terms? The patient was experiencing loss of the good self-representation and the good object-representation. He said he was trying to be a good servant, but he felt it was futile and he was all alone. He could not tolerate his aloneness. In his fantasy, he attempted to become the all-good servant of an omnipotent God. He suddenly felt surrounded by God, with whom he had a special relationship.

We could hypothesize that he projected his all-good internal image of God outside of himself. He then developed a special relationship with his own internal object representation. This preoccupation came to exclude all other relationships, so that there was no third point of reference which he could use to determine whether he was relating to an internal or an external object.

He remained isolated in his shabby downtown hotel room, writing religious tracts, which he never disseminated. He only came out of his room to eat, to preach on busy street corners, or to make infrequent trips to the community mental health center. Whenever anyone suggested an alternative viewpoint, he summarily and angrily rejected it. He did not take in information from outside.

Unlike the previous examples of a loss of sense of reality, this patient did maintain a self–object distinction in his internal world, but he did not distinguish between internal objects and external objects. Federn (1952) and Rinsley (1982) called this a shrinking of ego boundaries,[3] so that the internal images fall outside the boundaries of the self. P.C. clung so tenaciously to his omnipotent internal object that he deprived himself of an emotionally significant relationship with external objects. He did not pay attention to the third element, that which was neither self nor primary object. There were only P.C. and God, and nothing else mattered; so he remained locked within his psychotic conviction.

---

[3]As mentioned in Chapters 3 and 4, Federn used the term ego to refer both to self and to integrative ego functions.

People are not born considering the opinions of others, but have to learn it. To do so, they must gain enough security in their primary self and object relatedness that they can temporarily let go of it, certain that they can call it up again when needed. They must be secure enough to doubt. People suffering from psychotic conviction are not firm enough in their attachments and ideas to look outside themselves and to doubt. Both the excessive sense of conviction and the loss of sense of reality, then, can be seen to have in common an underlying need to fuse with or cling to an omnipotent internal object.

OUT-OF-BODY EXPERIENCES

As I have emphasized throughout this book, it is not only psychotic individuals who have unusual experiences of reality. Gabbard and Twemlow (1984) described 339 people who had out-of-body experiences. Most of their subjects were psychologically sound individuals who were not using drugs or alcohol; only 10 percent had had near-death experiences. Many were meditating at the time of their out-of-body feeling.

With a heightened clarity and vividness of the real world, each of these subjects felt his self separate from his body. Sometimes he could actually see his body at a distance from him. An example of an out-of-body experience (similar to those described by Gabbard and Twemlow) involved a man who related how, when he was meditating, he felt himself floating out of and hovering over his body. Everything in the room appeared exactly as it had been. A feeling of peace and clarity came over him. He felt intact and in harmony with the world around him. A moment later a twinge of anxiety and longing to return to his body arose in him. No sooner thought than done—he returned to his self–body unity.

Referring to Schilder's (1935) work on body image and body scheme and Federn's (1952) concept of body ego as elucidated by Rinsley (1962), Gabbard and Twemlow explained out-of-body experiences. They suggested that these subjects had let go of the investment of ego (cathexis) in their body image and so felt outside of themselves, while retaining self–object boundaries and a sense of reality. These authors used the word ego in ways many psychoanalytic writers would use self. To loosely translate their findings to the terminology used in this book, we could say that in a relaxed state of mind, the ego as observer disassociates the major self-representation from the current bodily perceptions and sensations. The self-image as having a shape and distinct boundaries is retained; but this image is freed from the image of oneself as being at one with a body with physical mass viewed from a third viewpoint. In other words, the perceptual bodily self is experienced outside the self–object boundary and so is experienced as an external object. When the observing ego realizes that this thing, this body out there, pertains to the self, it can reintegrate these two self-images as both being inside the self–object boundary.

People who have out-of-body experiences feel a sense of reality because they retain intact self–object boundaries. These boundaries are unconventional, however, in that they do not include the perceived body-self, which is normally experienced as inside the self–object boundary. Although these individuals are not psychotic, they have a sense of conviction which contradicts what outside observers may perceive, because they attribute a self-image—their perceived body-image—to the external object-world.

People who have out-of-body experiences usually have firm self–object boundaries and are secure enough in that capacity that they can temporarily alter their boundaries without permanently losing them. This capacity to differentiate and reintegrate the self along various lines appears to be a sign of health, not illness. Gabbard and Twemlow found their subjects, on the average, to be mentally healthier than a randomly selected population.

REALITY IN CULTURE

Modell, in his book *Object Love and Reality* (1968), described how societies develop a concept of reality in steps that parallel childhood acquisition of this concept. He began by observing that "the concept of 'reality' and the concept of 'an environment' are not 'givens' but are themselves the result of a considerable cultural achievement" (p. 10).

In animistic cultures, living qualities are attributed to inanimate objects. Waterfalls and trees and stones have spirits. They have subjective emotions and wishes, and they can initiate actions. From an object relations viewpoint, such ideas rely upon the believer's blurring self–other boundaries, thereby experiencing his emotions in the inanimate object.

The boundaries between objects are also blurred in animistic societies. In the magical practices of such cultures, the symbols manipulated do not represent the object; rather, they are the object.

Sand poured on the ground during a rain dance does not symbolize a rain shower. It causes the downpour, because the action of one thing is thought to be the same as the action of the other thing. They are treated as if they were the same thing.

This kind of magical and animistic thinking is similar to that of young children. Modell (1968) cited Piaget's studies as detailing how in children "the capacity to differentiate self from object, to distinguish an inside from an outside, to perceive separate objects in physical space, proceeds along a rigidly determined, innate timetable" (p. 9). It is this development which allows the eventual shift from a magical world to the world of everyday reality.

A part of this development is the creation of transitional object relationships (Winnicott 1953). Modell said a transitional object, such as a blanket or teddy bear, is "not a part of the self—it is 'something' in the environment. However, it is endowed with qualities that are created by the subject by the oscillation of introjection and projection" (p. 37). The child can project his internal image of a need-satisfying object onto his blanket and then wrap himself in it and reintroject it. A transitional object is neither self nor object, yet it is both.

Modell found similarities between a child's use of transitional objects and Paleolithic man's use of art. In their cave drawings, these early people seemed to be creating a need-satisfying object—the wished-for prey of their hunt. They projected their internal image onto a wall, by the process of painting, and then, as the evidence indicates, they interacted with these paintings sometimes by throwing spears at them, as if the paintings were the object itself. Even this transitional relatedness belies an increased sense of separateness. Mere thinking or hallucinating will not do. Some manipulation of things is required. Along with this increased sense of separateness comes a diminished sense of omnipotence. If we are not the object, we cannot automatically control it. Reality testing has begun.

Modell and others have pointed out that reality testing is the capacity to distinguish the inner world from the outer environment. In Western culture, it was the Greeks who first accepted the distinction between subject and object. Modell described how this distinction is the basis of all scientific thought. Simon, in his study *Mind and Madness in Ancient Greece* (1978), made a similar observation. Our phrase "scientific objectivity" is no mere coincidental phrasing. It implies the ability to define ourselves sufficiently so that we can remove ourselves from an object or event in order to see it aside from our emotions and drives. When we are objective, we see things as external objects, not as self.

Modell also described how, once the distinction could be made between self and object, the Western world was faced with further refining of the distinction between imagination and perception. This is the same sequence in which children develop their thinking. Numerous philosophers have pondered over how we can classify imaginary objects, such as unicorns, in relation to perceived objects, such as tables. In object relations terms, this is the distinction between internal and external objects. How do we differentiate between categories of concrete objects, such as all people, and other abstractions, such as temperature, or something which is even more abstract, like beauty or purity? These are some of the questions which could be raised in classical philosophy after the subject–object distinction was accepted.

RELATIVITY AND REALITY

We can go on from Modell's thesis to speculate about personal and cultural development of a sense of relativity. Children must acquire a fairly rigid sense of concrete reality before they can develop the ability for abstraction required for relative thinking in adolescence (Piaget 1969). Culturally, the concept of Newtonian masses and momenta as distinct entities had to be well established before Einstein could elucidate his theory in which masses and energies are interchangeable according to certain principles.

Not all people are ever able to appreciate relativity in the physical or even the psychological sense. Grappling with the new relativity has thrown our culture into a quandary. Many people have given in to the temptation to discount all knowledge and values in an anti-intellectual and amoral declaration—"Nothing matters, anyway, because it's all relative." Such extreme and amorphous conceptions of relativity belie an underlying grasping for certainty, if only the certainty that everything is uncertain. Even mature scientists who attempt to accept the incompleteness of knowledge without discounting it altogether cannot forgo reaching for the definite. Clark (1971) stated in his book on Einstein, "We shall know a little more than we do now. But the real nature of things, that we shall never know, never" (p. 504). While this statement demonstrates a mature and well-integrated acceptance of our limitations, it still postulates a definite knowledge that we cannot know. The wording assumes a concrete, "real nature of things," although it claims we cannot know that nature.

Perhaps it is our object-seeking nature which makes it impossible for us to conceive of a world without definite outside objects, even if we cannot truly know them. We can consider phenomena from varying viewpoints and tell ourselves that the world is in flux, that we can "never step in the same river twice," but we cannot maintain a view of the world without something outside ourselves. We must have something in relation to which we define ourselves, just as we cannot grow psychologically without a mother or mothering figure to whom we relate and from whom we differentiate. Even the most abstruse philosophy postulates something outside ourselves. Belief systems that claim that individuality is an illusion and that the goal of humankind is to return to the universal one cannot discuss these issues without conceptualizing a self in relation to an object and then attempting to "define away" the distinction by calling it illusion or by taking a broader and broader definition of the self, as in solipsism. These philosophies, to present their argument, must refer to the inside–outside distinction they are saying does not exist.

Being able to suspend a sense of differentiation and to consider ourselves from shifting viewpoints is useful and sometimes enlightening. Our psychological and biological nature, as infants developing from mothers and fathers, however, limits the variations of our conceptualizations. Psychological relativity, like the relativity of physics, is limited according to certain principles. We must always think of things in terms of self, object, and a third element, which is neither self nor primary object.

A RETURN TO THE CONCRETE

Regardless of our sophistication, the ability to rely on a conventional sense of reality is indispensable to daily functioning. A previously psychotic patient explained this in terms of self, object, and the physical world.

> T.H. believed he had lived in outer space for several years. He had been in the "fourth dimension," because, he said, the extreme abuse and neglect he had experienced as a child did not allow him to do otherwise. He was recovering now.
>
> Over coffee, his college friend posed the challenge of solipsism. "Things only seem the way they seem because you think that's the way it is. They are illusions." Then, he combined this solipsism with a Christian belief, saying, "So if you have enough faith, you can do anything."

The next day, T.H. reported this conversation to his therapist. "Do you know what I told him? 'I can't prove we aren't illusions, but it is not very practical to think we are. What would happen, if we stood 5 feet apart and closed our eyes and imagined as hard as we could; "You are an illusion, you are an illusion"; then, if we ran toward each other, what would happen?' " He chuckled, quite pleased with himself. " 'We would bump our noses, wouldn't we?' "

As this patient so graphically pointed out, no matter how powerful imagination can be, in order to function at the most basic level, we must retain our ability to conceptualize self as distinct from object and of tangible physical properties beyond the control of either self or object.

In this chapter, I discussed some aspects of the sense of reality in object relations terms. The experience of day-to-day events requires a capacity to distinguish self from object and yet to remain in relationship to the object. Additionally, to maintain a stable experiential world there must be a third element, which is not under the control of either self or object. The nature of our object relatedness defines and limits the variability of our experience. Because we psychologically differentiate from a fused, symbiotic oneness to develop a self in relation to an object, both of which can be contrasted to that which is neither self nor primary love object, we must continue to think in terms of such contrasts. To do otherwise is to return to psychological merger and the self–other boundary confusion of psychosis.

CHAPTER 19

THE EVOLUTION OF OBJECT RELATIONS THEORY

Like other people, psychoanalysts develop loyalties and are subject to the vagaries of group dynamics. The study of object relations has shown that adults continue to internalize, identify with, and struggle with the important people in their lives. These personal relationships influence scientific thought, as they do other realms of human commerce.

This chapter consists of semihistorical lore about how object relations theory evolved. The ideas derive from scholarly discussions of psychoanalytic development, accounts of prominent thinkers' lives, histories of various movements in psychiatry—but mostly from informal discussions with colleagues. Much of it is not verifiable. Some of it is.

SIGMUND FREUD

Freud (1905a) introduced the ideas of drives, aims, and objects into psychoanalysis. In his early work, his fascination remained with exploring the newly discovered sexual and aggressive drives in the unconscious. Eventually, his interest moved beyond the forces of love and hate to issues of how the human mind is organized. He then focused on a structural theory of id, ego, and superego (Freud 1923). Many of his followers, who are referred to as orthodox or classical analysts, as well as the later ego psychologists, also moved from an emphasis on id content (love and hate) to structural theory (id, ego, superego). They de-emphasized Freud's object relations theory, as well as his ventures into speculations on complex human relations as outlined in such monographs as "Totem and Taboo" (Freud 1913a) and "Civilization and Its Discontents" (Freud 1930).

Freud had already laid the groundwork for a theory of object relations in three papers, "Mourning and Melancholia" (1917), "Group Psychology and the Analysis of the Ego" (1921), and "Inhibitions, Symptoms, and Anxiety" (1926). In these papers, Freud explored the ways in which people internalize and identify with the people around them. "Mourning and Melancholia" described how they take into themselves and identify with their loved ones, especially those who have been lost or are about to be lost. "Group Psychology and the Analysis of the Ego" described how people project aspects of their self onto a leader and then reidentify with that aspect in the leader. This analysis of group function influenced Klein's (1946) eventual description of projective identification. In "Inhibitions, Symptoms, and Anxiety," Freud verged on recognition of the importance of attachment to the mother and fear of losing her over and above sexual and aggressive drives as the major determinants of human behavior.

THE MELANIE KLEIN–ANNA FREUD DEBATE

During Freud's lifetime, important psychoanalysts, such as Jung and Adler, had differences with him. After his death, the most pressing controversies within psychoanalysis became symbolized and dominated by a rivalry between two women, Anna Freud and Melanie Klein. These two women came to represent, respectively, ego psychology and object relations theory. The rivalry was intense.

Melanie Klein was born in Vienna. During her unhappy marriage, she was analyzed by Sandor Ferenzi (Grosskurth 1986). He encouraged Klein in her study of psychoanalysis and particularly in her application of analytic technique to the treatment of children. Subsequently, she moved to Berlin, where Karl Abraham became her mentor, her protector, and her analyst (King 1983). In 1926, she settled in London, where she soon became a prominent member of the British Psycho-Analytical Society.

Already in the late 1920s, her rivalry with Anna Freud over their different contributions to the understanding and treatment of children had begun. The controversy took place at a respectable distance. Various critical papers were presented at international conferences, but Freud remained in Vienna, Klein, in London.

Within the British Psycho-Analytical Society, work did not go smoothly. During the 1930s, Klein's daughter, Mellita Schmideberg, joined her mother's critics and "gradually she became her archopponent, challenging her ideas and attacking her in Scientific Meetings" (King 1983, p. 253). When Hitler invaded Austria in 1939, Princess Marie Bonaparte assisted Anna Freud, her father, and 36 other analysts to find refuge in London. Thus, larger social forces threw the two opponents together as members of the same institute.

Anna Freud, the youngest daughter of her famous father, never married. Her father had analyzed her; she became a psychoanalyst in her own right. She extended her father's work by applying his technique to the analysis of children. After her move to London, she gradually took a prominent place in the British Psycho-Analytical Society, alongside Melanie Klein.

During the war years, discussions between the associates of these two women became "acrimonious" and ". . . the atmosphere in Scientific Meetings became increasingly unpleasant . . ." (King 1983, p. 254). Arguments ostensibly concerned the role of hate and aggression in early development, the influence of innate determinants on psychic life, the timing of infantile sexual conflicts, and the technique of interpreting transference to children. Susan Isaacs, Joan Riviere, and John Rickman favored Klein's ideas. Edward Glover, Marjorie Brierley, and Barbara Low, among others, tended toward agreement with Anna Freud. Ella Sharpe and D. W. Winnicott were both criticized for the influence Klein played on their thinking, though they could not be described as Kleinians.

An American analyst trained in London recently described the controversy. "Those two women couldn't sit in the same room together. If Anna Freud walked into a meeting and Melanie Klein was speaking, she would turn around and walk out. They hated each other."

Many members had intense feelings about the controversy. One renowned member, Edward Glover, resigned from the Society over these and other related issues.

In 1945, Society members followed Strachey's lead in considering psychoanalysis an empirical science with room for controversy and growth. The differences had become so polarized that a strict structure was required to contain the controversy. Sylvia Payne, the new president, succeeded in helping the Society develop two parallel courses of study. Course A had teachers from all groups, and Melanie Klein's ideas were well represented. Course B taught technique after Anna Freud's fashion. Students could have their first supervisor from their own group, but had to have their second supervisor from a middle group. Both groups remained under the auspices of the same training committee, which was composed of members of both camps, by "ladies' agreement" (King 1983, p. 256).

How much did the personal wishes of Anna Freud and Melanie Klein to be the mother of child analysis play a role in the controversies? How much did substantive scientific issues play a role? Did the daily bombings in London contribute to the disquiet in this erudite society? What part did Sigmund Freud's illness and death play in this struggle? How much did other controversies, such as criticism of Jones's and Glover's leadership, become displaced onto the Anna Freud–Melanie Klein rivalry? Was this struggle a fight–flight basic assumption during a time of psychoanalytic uncertainty? These and other factors may have contributed to the rivalry.

With this armistice in the British Psycho-Analytical Society, the Klein–Freud controversy did not end. Ego psychology and object relations theory were not to achieve a new, partial reintegration until the influx of South American object relations theorists into the United States during the 1960s. This migration partially derived from the suppression of free speech by fascistic, military rulers in South America.

FAIRBAIRN, BION, AND WINNICOTT

In Scotland, Fairbairn (1954) developed a theory of object relations which complemented the ideas of Melanie Klein. He worked in relative isolation in Edinburgh. His ideas received their greatest exposure through the work of his student and analysand, Harry Guntrip (1969), who was also later analyzed by D. W. Winnicott. He eventually published an account of both these analyses (Guntrip 1975).

Fairbairn shifted from Freud's early emphasis on drives impelling people to act and focused increasingly on the need to seek objects and attach meaningfully to other people. He developed the idea of a divided ego, which consisted of a libidinal ego, an antilibidinal ego, and a central ego. To him the word ego included elements many authors now call self. The idea of separate egos led to the concept of good and bad object relations units (Rinsley 1982).

During the same time period, Wilfred Bion developed his own theory of object relations. He used his psychoanalytic background during World War II to develop a theory of group functioning which helped reestablish morale (Grotstein 1981b). Following the war, he continued his psychoanalytic training, with Melanie Klein as his analyst. Shifting his emphasis from groups to individuals, he used the concept of projective identification to elaborate metaphors of the container and the contained (Bion, 1962). He spent many productive years associated with the Tavistock Clinic and the British Psycho-Analytical Society in London before he settled in Los Angeles. A few years later, as some analysts report, that psychoanalytic institute went through struggles similar to those in the British Society. This time, Bion's ideas may have played a part in the controversy.

Unlike Fairbairn and Bion, D. W. Winnicott did not have a penchant for theoretical revision. This psychoanalyst-pediatrician used his sensitive attunement to mother–child relationships in developing his concepts of good enough mothering, the holding environment, and transitional objects (Winnicott 1953). These ideas were compatible with both Klein's and Anna Freud's thinking and were well accepted by American ego psychologists as well as British object relations theorists. His hint of mysticism combined with the common sense of a practical pediatrician captured the imagination of numerous readers. His work eventually served as one of the bridges between ego psychology and object relations theory. It played a great part in Tolpin's (1971) bringing together elements of object relations theory, ego psychology, and self psychology in a description of how a cohesive self develops.

NORTH AMERICAN EGO PSYCHOLOGY

While these developments were taking place in Britain, psychoanalysis flourished in the United States. Anna Freud's work was well received. Heinz Hartmann, Ernst Kris, Rudolf Loewenstein, and David Rapaport elaborated a complex ego psychology, which extended Anna Freud's work, as she described it in *The Ego and Its Mechanisms of Defense* (A. Freud 1936). The more strict ego psychologists are now the old guard in America. In the 1950s, they were the revolutionaries who opened the way for a shift from interpreting incestuous impulses in the unconscious to exploring how the ego develops—both as self and integrator. They devised techniques to facilitate ego growth. They promoted the application of psychoanalysis to children, adolescents, and, to some degree, to psychotics. They shifted the emphasis on technique from strict observation of neutrality to paying increasing heed to the relationship between therapist and patient.

Hartmann (1950) advanced the field when he distinguished between the ego as self and the ego as organizer-organization. Hartmann (1939) and Rapaport (1967) elaborated a concept of the inner world. Edith Jacobson (1964) delineated the processes of introjecting and identifying with love objects. Eric Erikson (1950) focused on the development of a sense of identity, or selfhood, from childhood and forward throughout life.

Mahler and colleagues (1975) in the landmark developmental studies in New York, drew upon the work of Hartmann, Jacobson, and others to understand her direct observations. She also relied heavily upon the work of Winnicott. An ego psychologist by allegiance, she did not emphasize the similarity of her conclusions to Klein's ideas about child development. The similarity remains striking, with the exceptions that Klein's stages are condensed into the first few months of life, and Klein does not acknowledge an autistic phase. Mahler minimized the similarity of her observations to those of Klein and emphasized compatibility of her observations with those of Piaget (1937) and Spitz (1965).

THE INTERPERSONAL SCHOOL OF PSYCHIATRY

Simultaneous with the development of ego psychology in the United States, Harry Stack Sullivan and Frieda Fromm-Reichmann became influential. Sullivan (1953) elaborated the idea of an interpersonal field, translated from physics. He realized that none of us can observe or change human behavior without being involved in the interpersonal field of the subject. This idea freed many psychotherapists from the notion of strict, therapeutic neutrality, which is a hypothetical construct and a practical impossibility. With psychotic patients, in particular, all illusions of neutrality fall away. The therapist must take himself into account as a real person in relation to the patient. Both patient and therapist are moving entities in the interpersonal field.

Fromm-Reichmann was deeply influenced by Sullivan's work with schizophrenic patients. She came to live in a white two-bedroom cottage built for her on the grounds of Chestnut Lodge Hospital in Maryland. Patients who walked from the hospital to her office in her home experienced her warmth, strength, and concern. Her personal and practical approach to understanding severely disturbed patients influenced countless therapists who knew her and more who read her most important work, *Principles of Intensive Psychotherapy* (1950). Equally influential may have been a patient's account of how Fromm-Reichmann helped her overcome a psychotic illness, related in *I Never Promised You a Rose Garden* (Green 1964).

Ego psychology and the interpersonal school of psychiatry coexisted in the United States. These two influential schools provided fertile ground for the eventual introduction of object relations theory.

SOUTH AMERICAN OBJECT RELATIONS THEORY

In the 1950s and 1960s, South America began a cultural renaissance, which most North Americans did not recognize until the late 1960s and early 1970s. During that time, Jorge Luis Borges, Pablo Neruda, and Gabriel Garciá Marquez, among a host of excellent writers, artists, and composers, rose to world-wide prominence. In addition, a new and creative school of psychoanalysis flourished.

Angel Garma, an Argentinian, had been analyzed by Klein and was among those who introduced her ideas to Latin America (Morales 1985). Racker (1957), who studied countertransference, Grinberg (1965), who made major contributions to the understanding of projective identification, and Salvador Minuchin (1974), who eventually became a prominent family therapist in the United States, all derived from the analytic community of Argentina. In Chile, Matte-Blanco (1981) combined Bion's ideas with the principles of mathematical logic. It was also in Chile that Otto Kernberg and his second analyst, Ramon Ganzarain, had their roots. There were many other less well known, but also influential, psychoanalysts interested in object relations theory in countries throughout Central and South America.

Unlike their North American counterparts, many South American analysts overtly tied their teaching to liberal political thought. The suppression of freedom of thought and speech, which are the very cornerstones of psychoanalytic technique and scientific discourse, contributed to the migration of many psychoanalysts to the United

States. Some of these psychoanalysts found their lives in danger and could never return to their homeland.

KERNBERG

Otto Kernberg moved from Chile to Topeka, Kansas, where he joined the faculty of the Menninger Foundation. He set to work bringing together American ego psychology and the British school of object relations. He relied on Jacobson's (1964) understanding of how children internalize, differentiate, and integrate their experiences. He combined these insights with Klein's (1946) concepts of splitting and projective identification to develop a new understanding of borderline personality disorder (Kernberg 1975). Later, his predictions of the stages of development were found to coincide nearly exactly with those of another ego psychologist – Mahler. Like Klein, Kernberg had condensed the steps into the first year or so of life. When Mahler's data became well established, he gave data precedence over theory and shifted his time frame to match Mahler's (Kernberg 1980).

Kernberg was careful to trace his work back to that of the ego psychologists at each point, especially to the work of Hartmann and Jacobson. He also wrote a paper which delineated the many differences between his ideas and Klein's (Kernberg 1969). Like other ego psychologists, he rejected the following aspects of Klein's theories: (1) the concept of an inborn death instinct; (2) the concept of an innate knowledge of sexual intercourse; (3) the overemphasis on innate as opposed to environmentally determined development; (4) the condensation of psychic development into the earliest months; (5) the lack of distinction between normal and pathological development; and (6) the imprecise and odd terminology.

Kernberg acknowledged general agreement with Klein's work in the following areas: (1) the emphasis on early object relations in normal and pathological development; (2) the concepts of splitting and projective identification; (3) the highlighting of aggression as important in early development; (4) the recognition of early precursors of identity and values; and (5) the recognition of the continuity between pregenital and early genital conflicts.

Regarding technique, he included among Klein's positive contributions the application of analysis to children, the interpretation of splitting and projective identification, and the understanding of envy as leading to negative therapeutic reactions.

He titled his paper "A Contribution to the Ego-Psychological Critique of the Kleinian School" (1969) and allied himself with ego psychologists. Writing this critique allowed him to reintroduce many of Klein's more useful ideas without alienating his colleagues. Kernberg (1980) also used Bion's ideas and general systems theories to develop a theory of psychiatric administration. This work on the manner in which the personality of the leader affects the organization—and how regressive pressures within the organization affect the leader—helped move object relations into compatibility with wider and more modern scientific thought.

It was apparently Kernberg's purpose to continue the shift of psychoanalysis from the attempt at pure observation of intrapsychic phenomena in the psychoanalytic situation to the including of interpersonal studies. His capacity to unite contrasting viewpoints creatively was the uniqueness of his contribution. It resulted in at least partial rapprochement of the British–Latin American school of object relations theory with the British–North American school of ego psychology.[1]

OTHER INTEGRATIONS

Kernberg was not the only psychoanalyst to make integrative efforts in recent years. Harold Searles is renowned for candid accounts of his countertransference in work with schizophrenic patients at Chestnut Lodge Hospital. He came under the influence of Sullivan's and Fromm-Reichmann's ideas. A wide-ranging thinker and practical clinician, he took what was useful from the ego psychologists and the object relations school (Searles 1961), particularly aspects of Bion's and Rosenfeld's contributions (Searles 1963; Kernberg 1969).

In other integrative efforts, Rinsley (1982) discussed Federn's and Fairbairn's contributions. Adler (1985) combined elements of ego psychology with Kohut's self psychology. Grotstein (1987) brought together ego psychology, Bion's object relations theory, and Kohut's studies on narcissism, combining them with useful speculations on brain functioning. McGlashan (1982) at Chestnut Lodge studied

---

[1]The argument that Kernberg failed in his integrative effort is clearly stated by Milton Klein and Tribich (1981). They assert, "Kernberg's contention that his reformulation is compatible and homeomorphic with both object relations theory and Freudian theory is incorrect" (p. 27). Unlike Klein and Tribich, I believe that Kernberg's effort to bring together significant portions of Freud's ideas, ego psychology, and object relations theory was largely successful.

pseudodepression in schizophrenia using contributions from neurophysiology, the interpersonal school of psychiatry, and object relations theory. Gunderson (1982) applied empirical research to refine psychoanalytic diagnostic criteria for borderline disorders.

These and other integrative efforts have formed but part of a creative reaction against factious polemics and the unproductive alternative of atheoretical eclecticism. An integrative school of psychology and psychiatry has developed a ground swell.

THE KERNBERG–KOHUT DEBATE

The dialectic of ideas has not stopped with these new syntheses. Further efforts to differentiate and integrate psychological theories continue.

Once Kernberg's ideas became known, they were set off against those of Kohut. Mental health professionals compared and contrasted these ideas. Kernberg and Kohut actively criticized each other's work.

Kohut studied narcissistic personality disorders in Chicago, as Kernberg had studied borderline disorders in Topkea and later in New York. He learned that patients preoccupied with ideas of self-aggrandizement suffer from feelings of self-depletion. They continually attempt to rectify these feelings through exaggerated claims of self-importance. In analysis, they often need to see the analyst in glowing terms. He called this tendency the idealizing transference (Kohut 1971). He also found that such patients need to maintain this idealizing transference for long periods. In his view, the analyst should not tamper with this admiration by confronting hostility, but should empathize with the patient's need for a special relationship.

Unlike Kohut, Kernberg (1975) considered idealization of the analyst as a thin disguise for underlying envy and devaluation. He emphasized systematic confrontation of the negative transference. If the analyst accepted the idealization, it would only confirm the patient's unspoken conviction of the therapist's corruption and untrustworthiness.

In informal discussions among therapists, controversy over empathy versus confrontation became polarized. For example, a small group of psychiatrists from Topeka attended a conference in Chicago. After the meetings, they gathered over dinner with two Chicago psychiatrists and a clinical psychologist. Over a large, round table the conversation quickened. Therapists traded examples of empathizing for months with narcissistic patients and having it turn out well or ill.

Successful and unsuccessful confrontations were mentioned. Those who favored confrontation were in danger of being considered to have created the anger they perceived in their patients, because of their own confrontational personality style. Those who favored prolonged empathy were suspected of having so poorly come to terms with their own aggression that they had to deny it in their patients.[2] These arguments were similar to other conversations at the winter meeting of the American Psychoanalytic Association at the Waldorf-Astoria Hotel in New York. For the present and near future, there seems little prospect for resolution. Additional clinical observation and child developmental research will be needed to allow further advances in this area of controversy.

It is not only personalities, geography, and loyalties that contribute to the Kohut–Kernberg debate. Major theoretical differences underlie the controversies over technique. Kohut (1971) denied that aggression plays an important role in early development. He suggested that children primarily need empathic parental responses. Through a process of transmuting internalization,[3] they make this empathy a part of themselves in the form of healthy self-esteem and a capacity to self-soothe, both of which allow development of a cohesive sense of self. He argued that narcissistic disturbances derive from a failure of parental empathy; they constitute a kind of emotional deficiency disease. According to this formulation, devaluing and rage, common among narcissistic individuals, stem from empathic failure in parents and later in the therapist.

Kernberg (1975) has emphasized that the child's own unmodulated aggression plays a major role in development of narcissistic disturbances. A constitutional or environmentally acquired excess of aggression can lead to an inability to introject and integrate benign object relations. Hostility is projected onto the parents so they are experienced as less involved and less giving than they may truly be. Because of this projection, the child cannot perceive any good objects to internalize. Feeling depleted of good internal objects, narcissistic individuals envy those whom they consider more fortunate than they and devalue them. Their idealizations are defensive attempts to hide or mitigate this destructive devaluing. Their underlying rage and envy show through when idealization breaks down. Grandiosity is a similar defense against feelings that the self is depleted.

---

[2]Adler (1986) has discussed the interaction of theory, technique, and the personality of the therapist in relation to the Kernberg–Kohut debate.

[3]It is this emphasis on internalization of aspects of relationships in the development of a self which makes Kohut's ideas a theory of object relations.

This controversy over possible psychological etiologies of narcissistic disorders is related to a centuries-old wrangling over the nature of aggression in humans. Are human beings inherently loving? Is hostility merely an increasingly forceful attempt to fulfill legitimate needs? Is viciousness an effort to protect loved ones? Is human destructiveness in the form of war and the threat of nuclear annihilation evidence of an aggressive drive, perhaps even a self-directed death instinct? Perhaps hatred and war derive from the flawed nature of mankind, or original sin, or industrialized society, or economic inequities caused by capitalist social organization or totalitarian suppression. These basic questions about human motivation undoubtedly contribute to the controversy over the role of aggression in personality development. Further integrative efforts are needed before there can be progress in this area.

FAMILY THERAPY AND OBJECT RELATIONS THEORY

Another area of controversy and nascent integration lies in the rapprochement of family therapy and object relations theory (Slipp 1984). These two fields of study have both loosely allied themselves with general systems theory (Minuchin 1974, Kernberg 1980, Minuchin and Fishman 1981). They are concerned with internal–external boundaries and the transfer of supplies across those boundaries. As mentioned on page 263, splitting and boundary blurring can be seen in families, as well as in individuals.

Although efforts to discuss systematically the interrelationship of family studies and psychoanalytic object relations approaches to human problems have barely begun, certain speculations can be made. In object relations terms, family therapy attempts to alleviate symptoms in individuals by shifting boundaries in the external object world. Who is responsible for given functions in the family is clarified and changed. Who gets what information from whom is explored and altered. The exchange of information, that is, communication, is a boundary phenomenon in that ideas, fantasies, and emotions are passed from one person to another. The external shifts in the family system, which result from exploring and altering boundaries, affect the internal object relations of each family member, perhaps through processes of projection and introjection. Individual therapy shifts internal object relations by discussing and altering the transference and personal relationship with the therapist. Family therapy shifts internal relationships by discussing and altering the family structure.

Both fields of inquiry place themselves within general systems theory and have overlapping techniques and theories. Yet integration of object relations theory and family therapy remains rudimentary. This is a task for the future.

Several factors in addition to substantive scientific issues impede progress in this area. Professional organizations, like all groups, must define themselves in contrast to other groups. Economic competition for patients and social striving for prestige also play a formidable role in fueling disagreements. It is likely that these factors, in addition to scientific and clinical issues, will continue to interfere with the rapprochement of interpersonal and intrapsychic approaches to understanding human beings.

HYPNOTISM AND OBJECT RELATIONS THEORY

Hypnotism and object relations theory is another area ripe for integrative efforts.

Psychoanalysis initially developed out of a hypnotic technique. Charcot's and Janet's ideas about hypnotism and suggestion influenced Freud's early work (Jones 1953, Ellenberger 1970). Freud turned from hypnosis to discover the method of free association (Breuer and Freud 1895). He and other psychoanalysts eschewed the use of hypnosis, calling it a technique designed to bypass resistances and consequently to leave them unchanged.

Hypnotism has remained to provide a persuasive demonstration of a dynamic internal world, and it has continued to be profitably studied outside of established psychoanalytic organizations. Erickson (1935) showed how he could cure a neurosis by treating a second metaphoric illness. A patient who had a neurotic conflict was hypnotized, and a second conflict, which symbolized the first one, was suggested. Once the new illness was established, it was treated. As treatment progressed, symptoms resolved in both the metaphoric and the original disorder. Perhaps these symbolic representations and metaphoric communications could be understood in terms of internal self- and object-representations and of influencing them by parallel processes.

The current interest in using hypnosis to explore multiple personalities has obvious analogies with object relations theory, which have been explored incompletely. These rare cases show distinct, partially integrated personalities which do not have conscious awareness of one another's existence. These somewhat distinct personalities may serve various functions for the whole person. One personality may be the "executive," similar to the observing ego. Another may be the "childish self," and another the "disciplinarian." Each personality has some partial integration of good and bad self and some differentiation from objects. Can this disorder be understood as excessive differentiation of self from self, instead of self from object? Can it be considered a failure to integrate self with self? Do all people have multiple part-selves with relatively different and separate ongoing experience, as Hilgard (1977) and Beahrs (1982) have suggested? What causes this interesting failure to integrate in the more complex multiple personalities, and what leads to establishment of multiple personality as opposed to borderline personality? These and other questions at the interface of hypnotic investigations and object relations theory have not yet been intensively addressed.

Baker (1981) is one who has made overt use of object relations theory in another arena of hypnotic work. He described how an understanding of this theory can help the hypnotist use suggestion to guide a psychotic patient in shifting back and forth between the internal and external world, between self-awareness and object-awareness in progressive steps. As a part of this process the hypnotist suggests that a patient establish a good symbiotic relationship with him and then gradually suggests steps toward differentiation. These exercises can assist the patient in overcoming self- and object-fragmentation or merger and lead toward more a coherent experience. Baker's work holds promise for the application of hypnotherapy to treatment disorders previously thought to be unaffected, or even worsened, by hypnosis. He has begun an integration of hypnotic theory and practice with object relations theory.

This chapter has described the development of object relations theory from Freud through contemporary theorists and clinicians. Debates between ego psychologists and object relations theorists began in Britain and carried over to the Americas. With the influx of South American analysts into North America, a new possibility for integrating object relations theory and ego psychology developed.

At this juncture, new areas of investigation are ripe for comparison and integration with object relations theory. Advances must be accompanied by terminologic clarification and unification. Additions to and revisions of object relations theory will augment therapists' ability to understand and help their patients in relation to themselves and others.

It is as true of psychoanalysis today as it was in 1919 when Freud said, "We have never prided ourselves on the completeness and finality of our knowledge and capacity. We are just as ready now as we were earlier to admit the imperfections of our understanding, to learn new things, and to alter our methods in any way that can improve them" (p. 159).

REFERENCES

Adams, F. (1929). *Genuine Works of Hippocrates*, vols. 1 and 2. New York: William Wood.

Adler, G. (1977). Hospital management of borderline patients and its relation to psychotherapy. In *Borderline Personality Disorders: The Concept, the Syndrome, the Patient*, ed. P. Hartocollis, pp. 307–323. New York: International Universities Press.

—— (1984). The treatment of narcissistic and borderline personality disorder. Paper presented at the Oregon Psychiatric Association Meeting, Kah-Nee-Ta, April 1984.

—— (1985). *Borderline Psychopathology and Its Treatment*. New York: Jason Aronson.

—— (1986). Psychotherapy of the narcissistic personality disorder patient: two contrasting approaches. *American Journal of Psychiatry* 143:430–436.

American Psychiatric Association (1980). *Diagnostic and Statistical Manual of Mental Disorders*, Third Edition. Washington, D.C.: American Psychiatric Press.

Appelbaum, A. H. (1979). Personal communication.

Baker, E. L. (1981). An hypnotherapeutic approach to enhance object relatedness in psychotic patients. *International Journal of Clinical and Experimental Hypnosis* 29:136–147.

Bateson, G., Jackson, D. D., Haley, J., and Weakland, J. (1956). Toward a theory of schizophrenia. *Behavioral Science* 1:251–264.

Beahrs, J. O. (1982). *Unity and Multiplicity: Multilevel Consciousness of Self in Hypnosis, Psychiatric Disorder, and Mental Health.* New York: Brunner/Mazel.

Bell, S. J. (1970). The development of the concept of object as related to mother–infant attachment. *Child Development* 41:291–311.

Bellak, L. (1979). Schizophrenic syndrome related to minimal brain dysfunction: a possible neurologic subgroup. *Schizophrenia Bulletin* 5:480–489.

Bertalanffy, L. von (1950). An outline of general systems theory. *British Journal for the Philosophy of Science* 1:134–163.

Bettelheim, B. (1977). *The Uses of Enchantment: The Meaning and Importance of Fairy Tales.* New York: Knopf.

Bion, W. R. (1956). Development of schizophrenic thought. In *Second Thoughts: Selected Papers on Psychoanalysis.* New York: Jason Aronson, 1967.

_____ (1957). Differentiation of the psychotic from the non-psychotic personalities. *International Journal of Psycho-Analysis* 38:266–275.

_____ (1959). Attacks on linking. *International Journal of Psycho-Analysis* 40:308–315.

_____ (1961). *Experiences in Groups.* London: Tavistock.

_____ (1962). *Learning from Experience.* London: Heinemann.

Blanck, G., and Blanck, R. (1974). *Ego Psychology: Theory and Practice.* New York: Columbia University Press.

_____ (1979). *Ego Psychology II: Psychoanalytic Developmental Psychology.* New York: Columbia University Press.

Boesky, D. (1983). The problem of mental representation in self and object theory. *Psychoanalytic Quarterly* 52:564–583.

Boverman, H. (1983). Personal communication.

Bowen, M. (1960). A family concept of schizophrenia. In *The Etiology of Schizophrenia*, ed. D. D. Jackson, pp. 346–372. New York: Basic Books.

Bower, T. G. R. (1965). The determinants of perceptual unity in infancy. *Psychonomic Science* 3:323–324.

Bowlby, J. (1969). *Attachment and Loss*, vol. 1: *Attachment.* New York: Basic Books.

_____ (1973). *Attachment and Loss*, vol. 2: *Separation: Anxiety and Anger.* New York: Basic Books.

Brazelton, T. B. (1969). *Infants and Mothers: Differences in Development.* New York: Delacorte.

_____ (1975). Early infant–mother reciprocity. *Ciba Symposium.*

Brende, J. O. (1983). A psychodynamic view of character pathology in Vietnam combat veterans. *Bulletin of the Menninger Clinic* 47:193–216.

Brenner, C. (1973). *An Elementary Textbook of Psychoanalysis,* Revised Edition. New York: International Universities Press.

Breuer, J., and Freud, S. (1895). Studies on hysteria. *Standard Edition* 2:1–335.

Brody, S., and Axelrad, S. (1970). *Anxiety and Ego Formation in Infancy.* New York: International Universities Press.

Brown, G. W., Monck, E. M., Carstairs, G. M., and Wing, J. K. (1962). Influence of family life on the course of schizophrenic illness. *British Journal of Preventive and Social Medicine* 16:55–68.

Bruhl, O. (1959). Japanese mythology. In *New Larousse Encyclopedia of Mythology,* trans. R. Aldington and D. Ames, pp. 403–422. New York: Hamlyn.

Bulfinch, T. (1855). *Bulfinch's Mythology.* New York: Avenel Books, 1978.

Burnham, D. L. (1966). The special-problem patient: victim or agent of splitting? *Psychiatry* 29:105–122.

Burnham, D., Gladstone, A., and Gibson, R. (1969). *Schizophrenia and the Need–Fear Dilemma.* New York: International Universities Press.

Cameron, N. (1961). Introjection, reprojection, and hallucination in the interaction between schizophrenic patient and therapist. *International Journal of Psycho-Analysis* 42:86–96.

Cantwell, D. (1986). Panel discussion. Oregon Psychiatric Association, Portland, January 1986.

Carnegie, D. (1926). *How to Develop Self-Confidence and Influence People by Public Speaking.* New York: Simon & Schuster, 1956.

Carnegie, D. (1936). *How to Win Friends and Influence People.* New York: Simon & Schuster, 1981.

Chodorow, N. (1974). Family structure and feminine personality. In *Woman, Culture, and Society,* ed. M. Z. Rosaldo and L. Lamphere, pp. 43–66. Palo Alto, CA: Stanford University Press.

Chopra, H. D., and Beatson, J. A. (1986). Psychotic symptoms in borderline personality disorder. *American Journal of Psychiatry,* 143:1605–1607.

Clark, R. W. (1971). *Einstein: The Life and Times.* New York: Avon Books.

Cobliner, W. G. (1965). The Geneva school of genetic psychology: parallels and counterparts. Appendix. In *The First Year of Life,* ed.

R. A. Spitz, pp. 301–356. New York: International Universities Press.

Colson, D. B., Allen, J. G., Coyne, L., Deering, D., Jehl, N., Kearns, W., and Spohn, H. (1985). Patterns of staff perception of difficult patients in a long-term psychiatric hospital. *Hospital and Community Psychiatry* 36:168–172.

Cutler, D. L., and Tatum, E. (1983). Networks and the chronic patient. In *Effective Aftercare for the 1980's*. New Directions for Mental Health Services, No. 19. San Francisco: Jossey-Bass.

Deutsch, H. (1934). Some forms of emotional disturbance and their relationship to schizophrenia. *Psychoanalytic Quarterly* 11:301–321, 1942.

Doctorow, E. L. (1984). Willi. In *Lives of the Poets*, pp. 25–35. New York: Random House.

Doehrman, M. J. G. (1976). Parallel processes in supervision and psychotherapy. *Bulletin of the Menninger Clinic* 40:9–104.

Drinka, G. F. (1984). *The Birth of Neurosis: Myth, Malady and the Victorians*. New York: Simon & Schuster.

Eisenberg, L., and Kanner, L. (1956). Early infantile autism, 1943–1955. *American Journal of Orthopsychiatry* 26:256–266.

Eissler, K. R. (1953). The effect of the structure of the ego on psychoanalytic technique. *Journal of the American Psychoanalytic Association* 1:104–143.

Ekstein, R. (1983). *Children of Time and Space, of Action and Impulse*. New York: Jason Aronson.

Ellenberger, H. F. (1970). *The Discovery of the Unconscious: The History and Evolution of Dynamic Psychiatry*. New York: Basic Books.

Engen, T., and Lipsitt, L. P. (1965). Decrement and recovery of responses to olfactory stimuli in the human neonate. *Journal of Comparative and Physiological Psychology* 59:312–316.

Erickson, M. H. (1935). A study of experimental neurosis hypnotically induced in a case of ejaculatio praecox. *British Journal of Medical Psychology* 15:34–50.

Erikson, E. H. (1950). *Childhood and Society*. New York: W. W. Norton.

Fairbairn, W. R. D. (1940). Schizoid factors in the personality. In *Psychoanalytic Studies of the Personality*, pp. 3–27. London: Routledge & Kegan Paul.

_____ (1941). A revised psychopathology of the psychoses and the psychoneuroses. In *An Object Relations Theory of Personality*, pp. 28–58. New York: Basic Books.

_____ (1943). The war neuroses—their nature and significance. In *An Object Relations Theory of Personality*, pp. 256–288. New York: Basic Books.

_____ (1954). *An Object Relations Theory of the Personality*. New York: Basic Books.

Falloon, I. R. H., Boyd, J. L., McGill, C. W., Razani, J., Moss, H. B., and Gilderman, A. M. (1982). Family management in the prevention of exacerbations of schizophrenia: a controlled study. *New England Journal of Medicine* 306:1437–1440.

Federn, P. (1952). *Ego Psychology and the Psychoses*. New York: Basic Books.

Fenichel, O. (1945). *The Psychoanalytic Theory of Neurosis*. New York: W. W. Norton.

Fischman, L. G. (1983). Dreams, hallucinogenic drug states, and schizophrenia: a psychological and biological comparison. *Schizophrenia Bulletin* 9:73–94.

Fisher, H. F., Tennen, H., Tasman, A., Borton, M., Kubeck, M., and Stone, M. (1985). Comparison of three systems for diagnosing borderline personality disorder. *American Journal of Psychiatry* 142:855–858.

Fraiberg, S. R. (1969). Libidinal object constancy and mental representation. *Psychoanalytic Study of the Child* 24:9–47.

Frank, J. (1974). The restoration of morale. *American Journal of Psychiatry* 131:271–274.

Frazer, J. G. (1890). *The Golden Bough*. New York: Macmillan, 1922.

Freud, A. (1936). *The Ego and Its Mechanisms of Defense*. New York: International Universities Press, 1946.

_____ (1965). *Normality and Pathology in Childhood*. New York: International Universities Press.

Freud, S. (1900). The interpretation of dreams. *Standard Edition* 4, 5:1–626.

_____ (1905a). Three essays on the theory of sexuality. *Standard Edition* 7:121–245.

_____ (1905b). Fragment of an analysis of a case of hysteria. *Standard Edition* 7:3–122.

_____ (1909). Notes upon a case of obsessional neurosis. *Standard Edition* 10:153–318.

_____ (1910). The future prospects of psycho-analytic therapy. *Standard Edition* 1:139–151.

_____ (1911). Formulations on the two principles of mental functioning. *Standard Edition* 12:213–266.

_____ (1912a). Recommendations to physicians practicing psychoanalysis. *Standard Edition* 12:109–120.

_____ (1912b). The dynamics of transference. *Standard Edition* 12:97–108.

_____ (1913a). Totem and taboo. *Standard Edition* 13:1–162.

_____ (1913b). The occurrence in dreams of material from fairy tales. *Standard Edition* 12:281–287.

_____ (1914a). On narcissism: an introduction. *Standard Edition* 14:69–102.

_____ (1914b). Remembering, repeating and working through: further recommendations on the technique of psycho-analysis. *Standard Edition* 12:145–156.

_____ (1915). Observations on transference-love: further recommendations on the technique of psycho-analysis. *Standard Edition* 12:157–171.

_____ (1917). Mourning and melancholia. *Standard Edition* 14:243–258.

_____ (1919). Lines of advance in psycho-analytic therapy. *Standard Edition* 17:157–168.

_____ (1921). Group psychology and the analysis of the ego. *Standard Edition* 18:69–143.

_____ (1923). The ego and the id. *Standard Edition* 19:3–66.

_____ (1926). Inhibitions, symptoms, and anxiety. *Standard Edition* 20:87–172.

_____ (1930). Civilization and its discontents. *Standard Edition* 21:57–145.

_____ (1940). An outline of psycho-analysis. *Standard Edition* 23:141–207.

Freud, S., and Oppenheim, D. E. (1911). Dreams in folklore. *Standard Edition* 12:180–203.

Frick, R. B. (1982). The ego and the vestibulocerebellar system: some theoretical perspectives. *Psychoanalytic Quarterly* 51:93–122.

Frick, R., and Bogart, L. (1982). Transference and countertransference in group therapy with Vietnam veterans. *Bulletin of the Menninger Clinic* 49:151–160.

Friedman, L. (1978). Trends in the psychoanalytic theory of treatment. *Psychoanalytic Quarterly* 47:524–567.

Fromm-Reichmann, F. (1950). *Principles of Intensive Psychotherapy.* Chicago: University of Chicago Press.

Frosch, J. (1964). The psychotic character: clinical psychiatric considerations. *Psychiatric Quarterly* 38:81–96.

_____ (1970). Psychoanalytic considerations of the psychotic character. *Journal of the American Psychoanalytic Association* 18:24–50.

Gabbard, G. O. (1979). Stage fright. *International Journal of Psycho-Analysis* 60:383–392.

_____ (1986). The treatment of the "special" patient in a psychoanalytic hospital. *International Review of Psycho-Analysis* 13:333–347.

Gabbard, G. O., and Twemlow, S. W. (1984). *With the Eyes of the Mind: An Empirical Analysis of Out-of-Body States.* New York: Praeger.

Giovacchini, P. L. (1975). Various aspects of the analytic process. In *Tactics and Techniques in Psychoanalytic Therapy,* vol. 2, ed. P. L. Giovacchini, pp. 5–94. New York: Jason Aronson.

_____ (1979). *Treatment of Primitive Mental States.* New York: Jason Aronson.

Gitelson, M. (1962). The curative factors with psycho-analysis. *International Journal of Psycho-Analysis* 43:194–205.

Goldstein, K. (1954). The concept of transference in treatment of organic and functional nervous disease. *Acta Psychotherapeutica* 2:334–353.

Goldstein, M. J., Rodnick, E. H., Evans, J. P., May, P. R. A., and Steinberg, M. R. (1978). Drug and family therapy in the aftercare of acute schizophrenics. *Archives of General Psychiatry* 35:1169–1177.

Green, H. (1964). *I Never Promised You a Rose Garden.* New York: Holt, Rinehart & Winston.

Greenacre, P. (1957). The childhood of the artist: libidinal phase development and giftedness. *Psychoanalytic Study of the Child* 12:27–72.

Greenberg, J. R., and Mitchell, S. A. (1983). *Object Relations in Psychoanalytic Theory.* Cambridge, MA: Harvard University Press.

Greene, M. A. (1984). The self psychology of Heinz Kohut: a synopsis and critique. *Bulletin of the Menninger Clinic* 48:37–53.

Greenson, R. R. (1965). The working alliance and the transference neurosis. *Psychoanalytic Quarterly* 34:155–181.

_____ (1971). The "real" relationship between the patient and the psychoanalyst. In *The Unconscious Today: Essays in Honor of Max Schur,* ed. M. Kanzer, pp. 213–232. New York: International Universities Press.

Grimm, J. K. L., and Grimm, W. K. (1812). Little Red-Cap. In *The Complete Grimms' Fairy Tales,* pp. 139–143. New York: Pantheon, 1972.

Grinberg, L. (1965). Contribución al estudio de las modalidades de la identificación proyectiva. *Revista de Psicoanalisis* 22:263–278.

_____ (1979). Countertransference and projective counteridentification. *Contemporary Psychoanalysis* 15:226–247.

Grinker, R. R., Werble, B., and Drye, R. C. (1968). *The Borderline Syndrome: A Behavioral Study of Ego-Functions.* New York: Jason Aronson.

Grolnick, S. A., Barkin, L., Muensterberger, W., eds. (1978). *Between Reality and Fantasy: Transitional Objects and Phenomena.* New York: Jason Aronson.

Grosskurth, P. (1986). *Melanie Klein: Her World and Her Work.* New York: Knopf.

Grotstein, J. S. (1981a). *Splitting and Projective Identification.* New York: Jason Aronson.

_____ (1981b). Wilfred R. Bion: the man, the psychoanalyst, the mystic. In *Do I Dare Disturb the Universe? A Memorial to Wilfred R. Bion,* ed. J. S. Grotstein, pp. 1–35. Beverly Hills, CA: Caesura.

_____ (1987). The borderline as a disorder of self-regulation. In *The Borderline Patient: Emerging Concepts in Diagnosis, Etiology, Psychodynamics, and Treatment,* ed. J. S. Grotstein, J. Lang, and M. Solomon. Hillsdale, NJ: Analytic Press.

Gunderson, J. G. (1982). Empirical studies of the borderline diagnosis. In *Psychiatry, 1982: Annual Review,* ed. L. Grinspoon, pp. 425–437. Washington, DC: American Psychiatric Press.

Gunderson, J. G., Kerr, J., and Englund, D. W. (1980). The families of borderlines. *Archives of General Psychiatry* 37:27–33.

Guntrip, H. J. S. (1962). The clinical-diagnostic framework: the manic-depressive problem in light of the schizoid process. In *Schizoid Phenomena, Object-Relations and the Self,* ed. H. J. S. Guntrip, pp. 130–164. New York: International Universities Press, 1969.

_____ (1969). *Schizoid Phenomena, Object-Relations and the Self.* New York: International Universities Press.

_____ (1975). My experiences of analysis with Fairbairn and Winnicott. *International Review of Psycho-Analysis* 2:145–156.

Hamilton, N. G. (1980). The trickster: the use of folklore in psychoanalytic psychotherapy. *Bulletin of the Menninger Clinic* 44:364–380.

_____ (1981). Empathic understanding. *Psychoanalytic Inquiry* 1:417–422.

_____ (1986). Positive projective identification. *International Journal of Psycho-Analysis* 67:489–496.

Hamilton, N. G., and Allsbrook, L. (1986). Thirty cases of "schizophrenia" reexamined. *Bulletin of the Menninger Clinic* 50:323–340.

Hamilton, N. G., Green, H. J., Mech, A. W., Brand, A. A., Wong, N., and Coyne, L. (1984). Borderline personality: DSM–III versus a previous usage. *Bulletin of the Menninger Clinic* 48:540–543.

Hamilton, N. G., Ponzoha, C. A., Cutler, D. L., and Wiegel, R. M. (1987). Negative symptoms of schizophrenia and social networks. Paper presented at American Psychiatric Association Annual Meeting, Chicago, May 12, 1987.

Hamilton, N. G., Rogers, B. J., Morgan, F. D., Ponzoha, C. A., and Schwartz, L. D. (1986). Countertransference in a psychiatric outpatient clinic. Paper presented at Grand Rounds, Oregon Health Sciences University, Portland, April 1986.

Hartmann, H. (1939). *Ego Psychology and the Problem of Adaptation.* New York: International Universities Press, 1958.

_____ (1950). Comments on the psychoanalytic theory of the ego. In *Essays on Ego Psychology,* pp. 113–141. New York: International Universities Press.

_____ (1952). The mutual influences of the ego and the id. *Psychoanalytic Study of the Child* 7:9–30.

_____ (1959). Psychoanalysis as a scientific theory. In *Essays on Ego Psychology,* pp. 318–350. New York: International Universities Press, 1964.

_____ (1964). *Ego Psychology and the Problem of Adaptation.* New York: International Universities Press.

Hartocollis, P. (1968). The syndrome of minimal brain dysfunction in young adult patients. *Bulletin of the Menninger Clinic* 32:102–114.

Heuscher, J. E. (1974). *A Psychiatric Study of Myths and Fairytales,* Second Edition. Springfield, IL: Charles C Thomas.

_____ (1980). The role of humor and folklore themes in psychotherapy. *American Journal of Psychiatry* 137:1546–1549.

Hilgard, E. R. (1977). *Divided Consciousness.* New York: Wiley.

Hoch, P. H., and Polatin, P. (1949). Pseudoneurotic forms of schizophrenia. *Psychiatric Quarterly* 23:248–274.

Holzman, P. S., and Levy, D. L. (1977). Smooth pursuit eye movements and functional psychoses: a review. *Schizophrenia Bulletin* 3:15–27.

Horner, A. J. (1984). *Object Relations and the Developing Ego in Therapy.* New York: Jason Aronson.

Horowitz, L. (1985). Divergent views on the treatment of borderline patients. *Bulletin of the Menninger Clinic* 49:525–545.

Isaacs, S. (1943). The nature and function of phantasy. In *Developments in Psychoanalysis,* ed. M. Klein, P. Heimann, S. Isaacs, and J. Riviere, pp. 67–121. London: Hogarth, 1952.

Jackson, J. H. (1884). Evolution and dissolution of the nervous system: lecture 1. *British Medical Journal* 1:591–593.

Jacobson, E. (1964). *The Self and the Object World.* New York: International Universities Press.

Jensen, K. (1932). Differential reaction to taste and temperature stimuli in newborn infants. *Genetic Psychology Monograph* 12: 361–479.

Johnstone, E. C., Crow, T. J., Frith, C. D., Husband, J., and Kreel, L. (1976). Cerebral ventricular size and cognitive impairment in chronic schizophrenia. *Lancet* 2:924–926.

Johnstone, E. C., Crow, T. J., Frith, C. D., Stevens, M., Kreel, L., and Husband, J. (1978). The dementia of dementia praecox. *Acta Psychiatrica Scandinavica* 57:305–324.

Jones, E. (1953). *The Life and Work of Sigmund Freud.* New York: Basic Books.

Jung, C. G. (1912). *Symbols of Transformation: An Analysis of the Prelude to a Case of Schizophrenia.* In *The Collected Works of C. G. Jung,* vol. 5, trans. R. F. C. Hull, pp. 255–272. New York: Pantheon, 1954.

_____ (1945). Medicine and psychotherapy. In *The Collected Works of C. G. Jung,* vol. 16, trans. R. F. C. Hull, pp. 84–93. New York: Pantheon, 1954.

Kaplan, L. S. (1978). *Oneness and Separateness: From Infancy to Individual.* New York: Simon & Schuster.

Katz, H., Frank, A., Hamm, D., and Gunderson, J. G. (1983). Psychotherapy of schizophrenia: what happens to treatment dropouts. Paper presented at the American Psychiatric Association Meeting, New York, April 1983.

Kernberg, O. F. (1965). Notes on countertransference. *Journal of the American Psychoanalytic Association* 13:38–56.

_____ (1967). Borderline personality organization. *Journal of the American Psychoanalytic Association* 15:641–685.

_____ (1969). A contribution to the ego-psychological critique of the Kleinian school. *International Journal of Psycho-Analysis.* 50:317–333.

_____ (1970). A psychoanalytic classification of character pathology. *Journal of the American Psychoanalytic Association* 18:800–820.

_____ (1974a). Further contributions to the treatment of narcissistic personalities. *International Journal of Psycho-Analysis* 55:215–240.

_____ (1974b). Contrasting viewpoints regarding the nature and psychoanalytic treatment of narcissistic personalities: a preliminary communication. *Journal of the American Psychoanalytic Association* 22:255–267.

_____ (1975). *Borderline Conditions and Pathological Narcissism.* New York: Jason Aronson.

_____ (1976). *Object Relations Theory and Clinical Psycho-Analysis.* New York: Jason Aronson.

_____ (1977). Structural change and its impediments. In *Borderline Personality Disorders: The Concept, the Syndrome, the Patient*, ed. P. Hartocollis, pp. 275–306. New York: International Universities Press.

_____ (1980). *Internal World and External Reality.* New York: Basic Books.

_____ (1981). The therapeutic community: a reevaluation. *National Organization of Private Psychiatric Hospitals Journal* 12:46–55.

_____ (1982). Self, ego, affects, and drives. *Journal of the American Psychoanalytic Association* 30:893–917.

_____ (1984). *Severe Personality Disorders: Psychotherapeutic Strategies.* New Haven: Yale University Press.

_____ (1986). Identification and its vicissitudes as observed in psychosis. *International Journal of Psycho-Analysis* 64:147–159.

Kernberg, O. F., Goldstein, E. G., Carr, A. C., Hunt, H. F., Bauer, S. F., and Blumenthal, R. (1981). Diagnosing borderline personality: a pilot study using multiple diagnostic methods. *Journal of Nervous and Mental Disease* 169:225–234.

King, P. H. M. (1983). The life and work of Melanie Klein in the British Psycho-Analytical Society. *International Journal of Psycho-Analysis* 64:251–260.

Klaus, M. H., Jerauld, R., Kreger, N., McAlpine, W., Steffa, M., and Kennell, J. H. (1972). Maternal attachment: the importance of the first postpartum days. *New England Journal of Medicine* 286:460–463.

Klein, M. (1932). *The Psycho-Analysis of Children.* London: Hogarth.

_____ (1940). Mourning and its relation to manic-depressive states. In *Contributions to Psycho-Analysis, 1921–1945*, pp. 311–338. London: Hogarth.

_____ (1946). Notes on some schizoid mechanisms. *International Journal of Psycho-Analysis* 27:99–110.

_____ (1957a). *Envy and Gratitude.* London: Tavistock.

_____ (1957b). On identification. In *New Directions in Psycho-Analysis*, ed. M. Klein, pp. 309–345. New York: Basic Books.

_____ (1959). Our adult world and its roots in infancy. In *Envy and Gratitude and Other Works, 1946–1963*. New York: The Free Press, 1975.

Klein, M., and Riviere, J. (1964). *Love, Hate, and Reparation.* New York: W. W. Norton.

Klein, M., and Tribich, D. (1981). Kernberg's object relations theory: a critical evaluation. *International Journal of Psycho-Analysis* 62:27–43.

Knight, R. P. (1953). Borderline states. *Bulletin of the Menninger Clinic* 17:1–12.

Kohut, H. (1971). *The Analysis of the Self*. New York: International Universities Press.

_____ (1977). *The Restoration of the Self*. New York: International Universities Press.

Kohut, H., and Wolf, E. S. (1978). The disorders of the self and their treatment: an outline. *International Journal of Psycho-Analysis* 59:413–425.

Kolb, J. E., and Gunderson, J. G. (1980). Diagnosing borderline patients with a semistructured interview. *Archives of General Psychiatry* 37:37–41.

Kraepelin, E. (1919). *Dementia Praecox and Paraphrenia*, trans. R. M. Barclay. Edinburgh: E. and S. Livingstone.

Kroll, J., Pyle, R., Zander, J., Martin, K., Lari, S., and Sines, L. (1981). Borderline personality disorder: Construct validity of the concept. *Archives of General Psychiatry* 38:1021–1026.

Kulick, E. (1985). On countertransference boredom. *Bulletin of the Menninger Clinic* 49:95–112.

Lao Tzu (1955). *The Way of Life*, trans. R. B. Blakney. New York: New American Library.

Lasch, C. (1978). *The Culture of Narcissism: American Life in an Age of Diminishing Expectation*. New York: W. W. Norton.

Lester, E. P. (1983). Separation-individuation and cognition. *Journal of the American Psychoanalytic Association* 31:127–156.

Levi-Strauss, C. (1963). The sorcerer and his magic. In *Structural Anthropology*, vol. 1, trans. C. Jacobson and B. G. Schoepf, pp. 167–205. New York: Basic Books.

Lidz, T. (1964). *The Family and Human Adaptation*. London: Hogarth.

Lipsitt, L. P., and Levy, N. (1959). Electrotactual threshold in the neonate. *Child Development* 30:547–554.

Lipton, S. D. (1977). The advantages of Freud's technique as shown in his analysis of the Rat Man. *International Journal of Psycho-Analysis* 58:255–273.

Luomala, K. (1949). Maui-of-a-Thousand-Tricks: his oceanic and European biographers. *Bernice P. Bishop Museum Bulletin*, No. 198.

Mahler, M. S. (1952). On child psychosis and schizophrenia: autistic and symbiotic infantile psychoses. *Psychoanalytic Study of the Child* 7:286–305.

_____ (1965). On the significance of the normal separation-individuation phase. In *Drives, Affects and Behavior*, vol. 2, ed. M.

Schur, pp. 161–169. New York: International Universities Press.

———— (1971). A study of the separation–individuation process and its possible application to borderline phenomena in the psychoanalytic situation. *Psychoanalytic Study of the Child* 26:403–424.

Mahler, M. S., and Gosliner, B. J. (1955). On symbiotic child psychosis: genetic, dynamic and restitutive aspects. *Psychoanalytic Study of the Child* 10:195–212.

Mahler, M. S., Pine, F., and Bergman, A. (1975). *The Psychological Birth of the Human Infant*. New York: Basic Books.

Masson-Oursel, P., and Morin, L. (1959). Indian mythology. In *New Larousse Encyclopedia of Mythology*, trans. R. Aldington and D. Ames, pp. 325–378. New York: Hamlyn.

Masterson, J. F. (1976). *Psychotherapy of the Borderline Adult: A Developmental Approach*. New York: Brunner/Mazel.

Masterson, J. F., and Rinsley, D. B. (1975). The borderline syndrome: the role of the mother in the genesis and psychic structure of the borderline personality. *International Journal of Psycho-Analysis* 56:163–177.

Matte-Blanco, I. (1981). Reflecting with Bion. In *Do I Dare Disturb the Universe? A Memorial to Wilfred R. Bion*, ed. J. S. Grotstein, pp. 491–535. Beverly Hills, CA: Caesura.

Maugham, W. S. (1944). *The Razor's Edge*. New York: Doubleday.

Mayer, W. (1950). Remarks on abortive cases of schizophrenia. *Journal of Nervous and Mental Disease* 112:539–542.

McGlashan, T. H. (1982). Aphanasis: the syndrome of pseudo-depression in schizophrenia. *Schizophrenia Bulletin* 8:118–134.

———— (1983). The borderline syndrome: testing three diagnostic systems. *Archives of General Psychiatry* 40:1311–1318.

McIntosh, D. (1986). The ego and self in the thought of Sigmund Freud. *International Journal of Psycho-Analysis* 67:429–448.

Menninger, K. A. (1942). *Love against Hate*. New York: Harcourt, Brace.

Menninger, K. A., Mayman, M., and Pruyser, P. (1963). *The Vital Balance*. New York: Viking.

Meissner, W. W. (1980). A note on projective identification. *Journal of the American Psychoanalytic Association* 28:43–67.

———— (1981). *Internalization in Psychoanalysis*. New York: International Universities Press.

Minuchin, S. (1974). *Families and Family Therapy*. Cambridge, MA: Harvard University Press.

Minuchin, S., and Fishman, H. C. (1981). *Family Therapy Techniques*. Cambridge, MA: Harvard University Press.

Mirsky, A. F., Silberman, E. K., Latz, A., and Nagler, S. (1985). Adult outcomes of high-risk children. *Schizophrenia Bulletin* 11:150–154.

Modell, A. H. (1968). *Object Love and Reality: An Introduction to a Psychoanalytic Theory of Object Relations*. New York: International Universities Press.

Morales, M. (1985). Personal communication.

Newberry, T. B. (1985). Levels of countertransference toward Vietnam veterans with posttraumatic stress disorder. *Bulletin of the Menninger Clinic* 49:151–160.

Novotny, P. C. (1980). Personal communication.

Ogden, T. H. (1979). On projective identification. *International Journal of Psycho-Analysis* 60:357–373.

———— (1982). *Projective Identification and Psychotherapeutic Technique*. New York: Jason Aronson.

Ornstein, P. H. (1974). On narcissism: beyond the introduction: highlights of Heinz Kohut's contributions to the psychoanalytic treatment of narcissistic personality disorders. *Annual of Psychoanalysis* 2:127–149.

Oster, H. S. (1975). The perception of color in ten-week-old infants. Paper presented at the Society for Research in Child Development, Denver, 1975.

Ovid. In *Metamorphoses*, trans. R. Humphries. Bloomington: Indiana University Press, 1955.

Peale, N. V. (1952). *The Power of Positive Thinking*. New York: Prentice-Hall.

Peterson, D. R. (1954). The diagnosis of subclinical schizophrenia. *Journal of Consultation Psychology* 18:198–200.

Piaget, J. (1936). *The Origins of Intelligence in Children*. New York: International Universities Press, 1954.

———— (1937). *The Construction of Reality in the Child*. New York: Basic Books, 1954.

———— (1969). The intellectual development of the adolescent. In *Adolescence: Psychosocial Perspectives*, ed. G. Caplan and S. Lebovici, pp. 22–26. New York: Basic Books.

Pine, F. (1984). The interpretive moment: Variations on classical themes. *Bulletin of the Menninger Clinic* 48:54–71.

Poggi, R. G., and Ganzarain, R. (1983). Countertransference hate. *Bulletin of the Menninger Clinic* 47:15–35.

Pollock, G. H. (1985). Abandoning and abusing caretakers. In *Parental Influence in Health and Disease*, ed. J. E. Anthony and G. H. Pollock, pp. 349–400. Boston: Little, Brown.

Pruyser, P. W. (1975). What splits in "splitting?" *Bulletin of the*

Menninger Clinic 39:1–46.

Pruyser, P. W., and Luke, J. T. (1982). The epic of Gilgamesh. *American Imago* 39:73–93.

Racker, H. (1957). The meanings and uses of countertransference. *Psychoanalytic Quarterly* 26:303–357.

Rank, O. (1914). The myth of the birth of the hero: a psychological interpretation of mythology. Nervous and Mental Disease Monograph Series, no. 18, trans. F. Robbins and S. E. Jelliffe. New York: Journal of Nervous and Mental Disease Publishing Company.

Rapaport, D. (1967). A theoretical analysis of the superego concept. In *Collected Papers*, ed. M. M. Gill, pp. 685–709. New York: Basic Books.

Rinsley, D. B. (1962). A contribution to the theory of ego and self. *Psychiatric Quarterly* 36:96–120.

_____ (1968). Economic aspects of object relations. *International Journal of Psycho-Analysis* 49:38–48.

_____ (1972). A contribution to the nosology and dynamics of adolescent schizophrenia. *Psychiatric Quarterly* 46:159–186.

_____ (1977). Personal communication.

_____ (1978). Borderline psychopathology: a review of aetiology, dynamics and treatment. *International Review of Psycho-Analysis* 5:45–54.

_____ (1982). *Borderline and Other Self Disorders*. New York: Jason Aronson.

_____ (1987). Personal communication.

Rioch, M. J. (1970). The work of Wilfred Bion on groups. *Psychiatry* 33:56–66.

Ritvo, S., and Solnit, A. J. (1958). Influences of early mother–child interaction on identification processes. *Psychoanalytic Study of the Child* 13:64–86.

Rodman, R. F. (1967). Interrupting psychotherapy with patients who exceed the limits. *British Journal of Medical Psychology* 40:359–370.

Rose, D. S. (1986). "Worse than death": psychodynamics of rape victims and the need for psychotherapy. *American Journal of Psychiatry* 143:817–824.

Rosenfeld, H. (1983). Primitive object relations and mechanisms. *International Journal of Psycho-Analysis* 64:261–267.

Rutter, M. (1971). Pathogenesis of infantile autism. In *Abstracts: Fifth World Congress of Psychiatry, Mexico*. Mexico: Prensa Médica Mexicana.

Sachs, D. M., and Shapiro, S. H. (1976). On parallel processes in therapy and teaching. *Psychoanalytic Quarterly* 45:394–415.

Sandler, J., and Rosenblatt, B. (1962). The concept of the representational world. *Psychoanalytic Study of the Child* 17:128–145.

Schafer, R. (1948). *The Clinical Application of Psychological Tests.* New York: International Universities Press.

_____ (1968). *Aspects of Internalization.* New York: International Universities Press.

_____ (1978). *Language and Insight.* New Haven: Yale University Press.

Schilder, P. (1935). *The Image and Appearance of the Human Body.* London: Routledge & Kegan Paul.

Scott, E. M. (1984). Some suggestions based on the association of personality disorders and alcoholism. Paper presented at the Oregon Psychiatric Association, Kah-Nee-Ta, April 1984.

Searles, H. (1955). The informational value of the supervisor's emotional experiences. *Psychiatry* 18:135–146.

_____ (1959). Integration and differentiation in schizophrenia: an over-all view. *British Journal of Medical Psychology* 32:261–281.

_____ (1961). Phases of patient–therapist interaction in the psychotherapy of schizophrenia. In *Collected Papers on Schizophrenia and Related Subjects,* pp. 521–559. New York: International Universities Press, 1965.

_____ (1963). Transference psychosis in the psychotherapy of chronic schizophrenia. In *Collected Papers on Schizophrenia and Related Subjects,* pp. 654–716. New York: International Universities Press, 1965.

_____ (1967a). The "dedicated physician" in psychotherapy and psychoanalysis. In *Cross Currents in Psychiatry and Psychoanalysis,* ed. R. W. Gibson, pp. 128–143. Philadelphia: JB Lippincott.

_____ (1967b). The schizophrenic individual's experience of his world. *Psychiatry* 30:119–131.

Segal, H. (1964). *Introduction to the Work of Melanie Klein.* New York: Basic Books.

Shapiro, E. R., Shapiro, R. L., Zinner, J., and Berkowitz, D. A. (1977). The borderline ego and the working alliance: indications for family and individual treatment in adolescence. *International Journal of Psycho-Analysis* 58:77–87.

Sheehy, M., Goldsmith, L., and Charles, E. (1980). A comparative study of borderline patients in a psychiatric outpatient clinic. *American Journal of Psychiatry* 137:1374–1379.

Simon, B. (1978). *Mind and Madness in Ancient Greece.* Ithaca, NY: Cornell University Press.

Slipp, S. (1984). *Object Relations: A Dynamic Bridge between Individual and Family Treatment.* New York: Jason Aronson.

Slochower, H. (1970). *Mythopoesis: Mythic Patterns in the Literary Classics.* Detroit: Wayne State University Press.

Soloff, P. H., and Ulrich, R. R. (1981). Diagnostic interview for borderline patients: a replication study. *Archives of General Psychiatry* 38:686–692.

Solomon, P., and Kleeman, S. T. (1975). Sensory deprivation. In *Comprehensive Textbook of Psychiatry/II,* vol. 1, ed. A. M. Freedman, H. I. Kaplan, and B. J. Sadock, pp. 455–459. Baltimore, MD: Williams & Wilkins.

Spillius, E. B. (1983). Some developments from the work of Melanie Klein. *International Journal of Psycho-Analysis* 64:321–332.

Spitz, R. A. (1946). The smiling response: a contribution to the ontogenesis of social relations. *Genetic Psychology Monographs* 34:57–125.

———— (1965). *The First Year of Life: A Psychoanalytic Study of Normal and Deviant Development of Object Relations.* New York: International Universities Press.

Spitzer, R. L., Endicott, J., and Gibbon, M. (1979). Crossing the border into borderline personality and borderline schizophrenia. *Archives of General Psychiatry* 36:17–24.

Stanton, A., and Schwartz, M. (1954). *The Mental Hospital: A Study of Institutional Participation in Psychiatric Illness and Treatment.* New York: Basic Books.

Stern, A. (1938). Psychoanalytic investigation of and therapy in the borderline group of neuroses. *Psychoanalytic Quarterly* 7:457–489.

———— (1945). Psychoanalytic therapy in the borderline neuroses. *Psychoanalytic Quarterly* 14:190–198.

Sullivan, H. S. (1953). *The Interpersonal Theory of Psychiatry.* New York: W. W. Norton.

Tolpin, M. (1971). On the beginnings of a cohesive self: an application of the concept of transmuting internalization to the study of the transitional object and signal anxiety. *Psychoanalytic Study of the Child* 26:316–352.

Torrey, E. F. (1983). *Surviving Schizophrenia: A Family Manual.* New York: Harper and Row.

Tuchman, B. W. (1978). *A Distant Mirror: The Calamitous Fourteenth Century.* New York: Alfred A. Knopf.

Tyson, P. (1982). A developmental line of gender identity, gender role, and choice of love object. *Journal of the American Psychoanalytic Association* 30:61–86.

Vaughn, C. E., and Leff, J. (1976). The measurement of expressed emotion in the families of psychiatric patients. *British Journal of Social and Clinical Psychiatry* 15:157–165.

Weinberger, D. R., Torrey, E. F., Neophytides, A. N., and Wyatt, R. J. (1979). Structural abnormalities in the cerebral cortex of chronic schizophrenic patients. *Archives of General Psychiatry* 36:935–939.

Wertheimer, M. (1961). Psychomotor coordination of auditory and visual space at birth. *Science* 134:19–62.

Will, O. A., Jr. (1975). Schizophrenia: psychological treatment. In *Comprehensive Textbook of Psychiatry/II*, vol. 2, ed. A. M. Freedman, H. I. Kaplan, and B. J. Sadock, pp. 939–954. Baltimore: Williams & Wilkins.

Winnicott, D. W. (1935). The manic defense. In *Collected Papers*, pp. 129–144. London: Tavistock, 1958.

_____ (1949). Hate in the countertransference. *International Journal of Psycho-Analysis* 30:69–74.

_____ (1953). Transitional objects and transitional phenomena: a study of the first not-me possession. *International Journal of Psycho-Analysis* 34:89–97.

_____ (1960). The theory of the parent–infant relationship. In *The Maturational Process and the Facilitating Environment*, pp. 37–55. New York: International Universities Press.

Wong, N. (1980). Borderline and narcissistic disorders: a selective overview. *Bulletin of the Menninger Clinic* 44:101–126.

Wynne, L. C., and Singer, M. T. (1963). Thought disorder and family relations of schizophrenics: a research strategy. *Archives of General Psychiatry* 9:191–198.

Zetzel, E. R. (1965). The theory of therapy in relation to a developmental model of the psychic apparatus. *International Journal of Psycho-Analysis* 46:39–52.

_____ (1966). 1965: Additional notes upon a case of obsessional neurosis: Freud 1909. *International Journal of Psycho-Analysis* 47:123–129.

Zilboorg, G. (1941). Ambulatory schizophrenia. *Psychiatry* 4:149–155.

INDEX